Acknowledgments My first thanks go to Steve Martin of www.rippletraining.com and Mitch Kelldorf of www.h5productions.com for allowing me to share the love of flight and the love of video through their footage. And directly to Steve, thank you for your support, trust, and encouragement from day one, my friend.

Many thanks to Noah Kadner and Christopher Phrommayon as well as Steve Bayes, Peter Steinauer, Kenny Meehan, and Toby Sidler of the Final Cut Pro team for the opportunity and support. This was a huge project to entrust with me and I am grateful.

Also at Apple, my thanks to Eugene Evon, Cindy Waller, Judy Lawrence, John Signa, Shane Ross, Raj Saklikar and Camille von Eberstein. These are my hard-working colleagues and friends that strive to put the "Apple" in Apple Certified Training. Their tireless commitment to make the highest caliber Apple Certified Training for OS X, iOS, and Pro Apps is humbling and appreciated.

A big thank you to Lisa McClain of Peachpit Press. Her unwavering commitment to me and the project created this book. And with the editorial tasks, thanks to Darren Meiss for taking on an adventure.

Lastly, to my 24-7 incredible editor and friend Bob Lindstrom, Bob is the best there is. Bob, thanks.

Contents At a Glance

Lesson 1	Getting Started	1
Lesson 2	Importing Media	13
Lesson 3	Organizing Clips	45
Lesson 4	Making the First Edit	105
Lesson 5	Revising the Edit	211
Lesson 6	Enhancing the Edit	271
Lesson 7	Finishing the Edit	333
Lesson 8	Sharing a Project	389
Lesson 9	Managing Libraries	409
Lesson 10	Advancing Your Workflow	429
Appendix A	Keyboard Shortcuts	465
Appendix B	Editing Native Formats	477
	Glossary	481
	Index	483

Table of Contents

Lesson 1	Getting Started	1
	Learned from a Legacy	2
	Upgrading Existing Events and Projects	3
Reference 1.1	Using This Book	4
Exercise 1.1.1	Downloading the Source Media Files	5
Exercise 1.1.2	Preparing the Source Media Files	5
Reference 1.2	Introducing the Job and the Workflow	9
	Lesson Review	11

Lesson 2	Importing Media	13
Reference 2.1	Understanding Clips, Events, and Libraries	14
Exercise 2.1.1	Creating a Library	16
Exercise 2.1.2	Preparing to Import Camera Source Files	18
Reference 2.2	Using the Media Import Window	19
Exercise 2.2.1	Creating a Camera Archive	22
Reference 2.3	Importing Source Media from a Camera	24
Exercise 2.3.1	Navigating Within a Filmstrip Preview	26
Exercise 2.3.2	Importing Clips from a Camera Card	28
Reference 2.4	Choosing Media Import Options	31
Exercise 2.4.1	Applying Media Import Options	34
Reference 2.5	Import Files from a Volume	36
Exercise 2.5.1	Importing Existing Files from a Volume	38
Exercise 2.5.2	Dragging from the Finder or Other Apps	40
	Lesson Review	42

Lesson 3	Organizing Clips 45
Reference 3.1	Introducing the Libraries, Browser, and Viewer Panes 46
Reference 3.2	Using Keywords. 48
Exercise 3.2.1	Keywording a Clip 50
Exercise 3.2.2	Keywording a Range. 61
Exercise 3.2.3	Adding Notes to a Clip. 65
Reference 3.3	Assigning Ratings 69
Exercise 3.3.1	Applying Ratings. 70
Exercise 3.3.2	Customizing a Favorite. 80
Reference 3.4	Search, Sort, and Filter. 81
Exercise 3.4.1	Filtering an Event 86
Exercise 3.4.2	Working with Smart Collections 91
Exercise 3.4.3	Detecting People and Shot Composition. 93
Reference 3.5	Roles 96
Exercise 3.5.1	Assigning Roles. 97
	Lesson Review 103
Lesson 4	Making the First Edit 105
Reference 4.1	Understanding a Project 106
Exercise 4.1.1	Creating a Project 106
Reference 4.2	Defining the Primary Storyline. 109
Exercise 4.2.1	Appending the Primary Storyline. 111
Exercise 4.2.2	Rearranging Clips in the Primary Storyline 119
Reference 4.3	Modifying Clips in the Primary Storyline. 121
Exercise 4.3.1	Performing Insert Edits 122
Exercise 4.3.2	Rippling the Primary Storyline. 126
Reference 4.4	Timing the Primary Storyline. 131
Exercise 4.4.1	Inserting a Gap Clip 133
Exercise 4.4.2	Blading and Deleting 136
Exercise 4.4.3	Joining a Through Edit. 139
Exercise 4.4.4	Refining Some Sound Bite Edits. 140
Reference 4.5	Editing Above the Primary Storyline. 143
Exercise 4.5.1	Adding and Trimming Connected B-roll 144
Exercise 4.5.2	Understanding Connected Clip Sync and Trimming Behaviors. 152
Reference 4.6	Creating a Connected Storyline 156
Exercise 4.6.1	Converting Connected Clips into a Connected Storyline . . . 157
Exercise 4.6.2	Appending Clips to a New Connected Storyline 161

Apple Pro Training Series

Final Cut Pro X 10.1

Brendan Boykin

Apple
Certified

Apple Pro Training Series: Final Cut Pro X 10.1
Brendan Boykin
Copyright © 2014 by Brendan Boykin

Published by Peachpit Press
www.peachpit.com
To report errors, please send a note to errata@peachpit.com.
Peachpit Press is a division of Pearson Education.

Apple Series Editor: Lisa McClain
Editor: Bob Lindstrom
Production Editor: Maureen Forys
Apple Project Manager: Raj Saklikar
Apple Reviewers: Noah Kadner, Christopher Phrommayon
Technical Reviewers: Noah Kadner, Christopher Phrommayon
Copy Editor: Darren Meiss
Proofreader: Darren Meiss
Compositor: Jeff Wilson, Happenstance Type-O-Rama
Indexer: Jack Lewis
Cover Illustration: Paul Mavrides
Cover Production: Cody Gates, Happenstance Type-O-Rama

ISBN 13: 978-0-321-94956-1
ISBN 10: 0-321-94956-0
9 8 7 6 5 4 3 2 1
Printed and bound in the United States of America

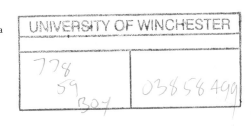

Reference 4.7   Editing Below the Primary Storyline 179
Exercise 4.7.1   Connecting a Music Clip 180
Reference 4.8   Finessing the Rough Cut 181
Exercise 4.8.1   Adjusting the Edits 183
Exercise 4.8.2   Adjusting Clip Volume Levels 187
Exercise 4.8.3   Connecting Two Additional B-Roll Clips 189
Exercise 4.8.4   Refining Edits Using Cross Dissolves and Fade Handles 192
Reference 4.9   Sharing Your Progress 197
Exercise 4.9.1   Sharing an iOS-Compatible File 198
                 Lesson Review 206

Lesson 5   Revising the Edit 211
Reference 5.1   Versioning a Project 212
Exercise 5.1.1   Snapshotting a Project 213
Reference 5.2   Lifting from a Storyline 216
Exercise 5.2.1   Lifting Clips Out of a Storyline 217
Reference 5.3   Replacing a Clip 217
Exercise 5.3.1   Replacing the Primary Storyline 219
Exercise 5.3.2   Creating Time at 0:00 221
Reference 5.4   Working with Markers 228
Exercise 5.4.1   Creating Markers 230
Reference 5.5   Using the Position Tool 235
Exercise 5.5.1   Realigning Sound Bites and B-roll to Music 235
Reference 5.6   Working with Auditions 243
Exercise 5.6.1   Repositioning Storylines and Deleting Within 244
Exercise 5.6.2   Importing the Aerials 246
Exercise 5.6.3   Working with an Audition Clip 247
Reference 5.7   Trimming the Tops and Tails 251
Exercise 5.7.1   Trimming the Aerials 253
                 Lesson Review 267

Lesson 6   Enhancing the Edit 271
Reference 6.1   Retiming Clips 272
Exercise 6.1.1   Setting a Constant Speed Change 273
Exercise 6.1.2   Editing with Blade Speed 278
Reference 6.2   Working with Video Effects 285
Exercise 6.2.1   Experimenting with Video Effects 287
Exercise 6.2.2   Creating a Depth of Field Effect 293

Reference 6.3   Working with Video Transitions. 300
Exercise 6.3.1   Experimenting with Transitions 300
Reference 6.4   Compositing Using Spatial Parameters 312
Exercise 6.4.1   Creating a Two-Up Split Screen 314
Exercise 6.4.2   Exploring the Video Animation Editor 321
Reference 6.5   Compounding Clips 325
Exercise 6.5.1   Collapsing a Composite into a Compound. 326
Lesson Review 328

Lesson 7   Finishing the Edit 333
Reference 7.1   Using Titles 334
Exercise 7.1.1   Adding and Modifying a Lower Third 335
Reference 7.2   Working with Audio. 342
Exercise 7.2.1   Adding Sound to a Clip 343
Exercise 7.2.2   Adjusting Volume Levels over Time 358
Reference 7.3   Understanding Audio Enhancements 372
Reference 7.4   Correcting the Image 373
Exercise 7.4.1   Neutralizing a Clip 374
Exercise 7.4.2   Matching Color 384
Lesson Review 386

Lesson 8   Sharing a Project 389
Reference 8.1   Creating a Viewable File 390
Exercise 8.1.1   Sharing to an Online Host. 391
Exercise 8.1.2   Sharing to a Bundle. 397
Exercise 8.1.3   Sharing a Master File 399
Reference 8.2   Creating an Exchangeable File 404
Reference 8.3   Utilizing Compressor 404
Lesson Review 407

Lesson 9   Managing Libraries 409
Reference 9.1   Storing the Imported Media 410
Exercise 9.1.1   Importing as "Leave Files in Place". 412
Exercise 9.1.2   Importing as Managed Clips. 415
Exercise 9.1.3   Moving and Copying Clips Within a Library. 419
Exercise 9.1.4   Making a Library Portable. 421
Lesson Review 426

Lesson 10   Advancing Your Workflow 429

Sub-workflow 10.1   Using Manual Settings for a New Project. 430

Sub-workflow 10.2   Synchronizing Dual System Recordings. 435

Sub-workflow 10.3   Using Chroma Key. 439

Sub-workflow 10.4   Working with Multicam 449

Lesson Review 464

Appendix A   Keyboard Shortcuts 465

Assigning Keyboard Shortcuts. 466

Reviewing the Default Command Set. 468

Appendix B   Editing Native Formats

Native Video Formats 478

Native Still-Image Formats 478

Native Audio Formats 479

Glossary. 481

Index 483

Getting Started

Editing is storytelling. It's choosing from a sometimes vast array of video and audio clips, and assembling them into a coherent experience that can educate, excite, motivate, or move viewers. Built on that fundamental truth of video editing, Final Cut Pro X enables a rich workflow that permits you to approach editing as a storyteller, rather than an equipment technician. The goal of this book is to guide you through that creative workflow, structuring and refining a complete storytelling project from start to finish. Along the way, you'll learn features and acquire skills to realize high-quality editorial results using Final Cut Pro.

GOALS

▶ Upgrade earlier versions of events and projects

▶ Download and prepare lesson media files

▶ Understand basic Final Cut Pro workflow

For the new editor, Final Cut Pro will help you tell your story without the technical frustrations you may have experienced with other video editing systems. For the seasoned editor, Final Cut Pro can reinvigorate your editing creativity with unique features such as the innovative Magnetic Timeline that encourages you to experiment with your story and make complex editorial changes while eliminating the necessity to micromanage individual clips and their relationships.

Welcome to Final Cut Pro X

Learned from a Legacy

Just as offline digital editing once revolutionized traditional splice-and-tape techniques, Final Cut Pro aims to take digital editing to the next level. As cutting-edge programming, Final Cut Pro uses the power of 64-bit architecture and every cycle of the CPUs and multiple GPUs to realize breathtaking performance. When combined with a Mac Pro, Final Cut Pro dramatically accelerates a professional editing workflow.

As an editing suite, Final Cut Pro is the foundation of an experience that naturally carries you from one creative choice to the next, rather than becoming mired in technical tasks. In addition to its powerful editing capabilities, Final Cut Pro incorporates flexible metadata tools that help you organize the increasing quantity of media an editor must organize in today's digital world. And when editing is completed, you're able to distribute your final projects to whichever format or platform your client or audience requires. The result is a forward-looking application that removes conventional stumbling blocks so that all editors can create and share their stories using the highest-quality software and hardware available.

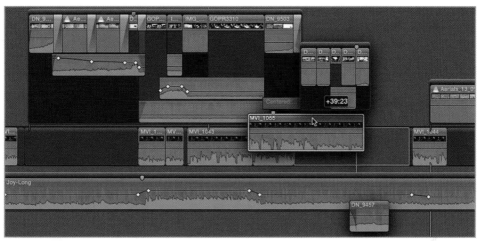

All clips synchronized with a primary storyline clip follow along without clip collisions in the Magnetic Timeline.

Upgrading Existing Events and Projects

If you used versions of Final Cut Pro X prior to 10.1, you have probably created a few events and projects. As a result, the first time you open Final Cut Pro X 10.1, a dialog asks if you want to upgrade those events and projects.

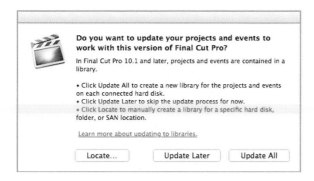

NOTE ► The conventional wisdom among editors is not to update or upgrade any software or hardware while you are in the middle of a job. When you do decide to update, first make a backup copy of your files, the application, and third-party plug-ins.

You may click Update Later if you choose not to upgrade your events and projects at this time, thereby leaving them accessible to previous versions of Final Cut Pro X. You may upgrade at a later time using File > Update Projects and Events.

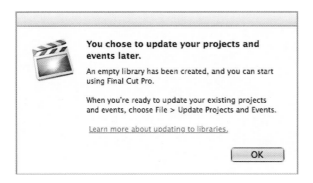

NOTE ▶ If you have been using Event Manager X from Intelligent Assistance, refer to their website for migration instructions.

If you are ready to upgrade, you may convert all of your events and projects to the new library system by clicking Update All. A new library is created for each volume, and all events and projects on each volume are combined into one library. During the update process, you'll be asked if you want to delete the earlier versions. If you did not back up the files or if you are not upgrading to Final Cut Pro X 10.1 on all of your edit systems, you may want to keep the files. You can freely reorganize the updated events and projects, and create additional libraries.

NOTE ▶ If you are on an XSAN or wish to update individual event and project combinations, choose the Locate option. Doing so creates a library per folder (SAN location) containing a Final Cut Events folder and a Final Cut Projects folder.

No matter whether you choose to update existing projects or not, you can still proceed with this book's lessons and create new libraries, events, and projects without affecting your existing work in any way.

Reference 1.1
Using This Book

This book is available in multiple formats. The electronic versions may include enhanced content such as:

▶ Glossary: Pause the mouse pointer over words that appear styled to review a term's definition.

▶ Keyboard shortcuts: Click/tap keyboard shortcuts to jump to Appendix A's keyboard shortcut pages. Appendix A includes an abridged list of the 300+ commands you may assign to keyboard shortcuts.

NOTE ▸ Due to technical differences between various ebook formats and platforms, some of the digital features described will not be available in all formats.

Performing the Exercises

The exercises in this book build on each other from Lesson 1 to Lesson 9. You are advised to complete each exercise, starting with Exercise 1.1.1 in this lesson, before attempting the next exercise; and to move through each lesson before proceeding to the next.

Exercise 1.1.1
Downloading the Source Media Files

The source media files you'll use throughout the book are available for download from Peachpit Press. The source media files are organized into zip-compressed files that automatically unzip after download unless you have changed your browser's preferences.

To download these files, you must have your guide's access code — provided on a card in the back of the printed editions of this book or on the "Where Are the Lesson Files?" page in electronic editions of this book. When you have the code:

1   Go to www.peachpit.com/redeem and enter your access code.

2   Click Redeem Code, and sign in or create a Peachpit.com account.

3   Locate the downloadable files on your Account page under the "Lesson & Update Files" tab.

4   Click the lesson file links to download them to your Downloads folder.

   After downloading the zip files from the website, you are ready to proceed with the following exercise.

Exercise 1.1.2
Preparing the Source Media Files

After downloading the zip files, you will place the files into a folder that you may create in any location you have permission to access. Examples of an accessible location to which you may read/write files are: the desktop, home folder, or Documents folder. If you have an external volume you'd like to use, ensure that you have read/write permission and that the volume is formatted as Mac OS Extended (HFS+).

1   In the Dock, click the Finder icon to open a Finder window.

The Finder is an application used to navigate your Mac computer's filesystem.

2   Navigate to the location where you want to create a media folder for the downloaded media.

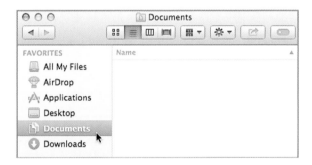

If you aren't sure where to create the media folder, a great location to use for training purposes is your Documents folder, which is labeled with your username. The preceding image shows the Documents folder.

NOTE ▶ Ideally, you would save this media folder to an external volume.

3   After choosing a storage location, choose File > New Folder.

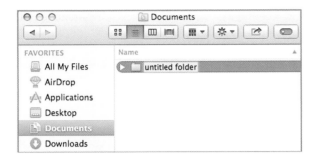

A new, untitled folder is created with its name highlighted, ready to be renamed.

4   Type *FCPX Media*, and press Return.

The FCPX Media folder appears, and you are ready to add the downloaded files to it.

5   In the Dock, to the left of the Trash, find the Downloads folder.

To easily drag the files out of the Downloads folder, you'll open the folder into its own Finder window.

NOTE ▸ If you have removed the Downloads folder from the Dock, you may find the Downloads folder in your home folder.

6   Click the Downloads icon, and then at the top of the stack that appears, click the "Open in Finder" shortcut.

A second Finder window, Downloads, appears on the desktop.

7   For convenience, arrange the two windows side-by-side on the desktop.

8   From the Downloads folder, drag the following files/folders to the FCPX Media folder: GoPro SD Card 1.dmg, LV1, LV2, and LV3.

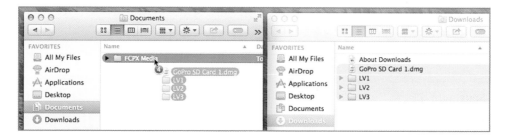

After moving the files to the FCPX Media folder, you will manage these media files exclusively within Final Cut Pro.

NOTE ▶ If any of the files/folders end with the extension .zip, double-click the file to unpack its contents.

9   Throughout this book, the exercises will reference the FCPX Media folder and its contents. You'll need to remember where you saved the folder when accessing its contents within Final Cut Pro. From the Dock or the Applications folder, open Final Cut Pro.

Reference 1.2
Introducing the Job and the Workflow

All books need a story, and in this book two production companies, H5 Productions and Ripple Training, recorded **sound bites** and **B-roll** for a video about aerial cinematography. As an editor, you've agreed to cut a 1:30- to 2-minute vignette for them about H5's owner and helicopter pilot, Mitch Kelldorf, and his passion for flight and film.

In the first four lessons of this book, you will edit a first version "rough cut" using the same, real-world workflow that thousands of Final Cut Pro editors follow. At the end of Lesson 4, you will export your rough cut to "show to the client."

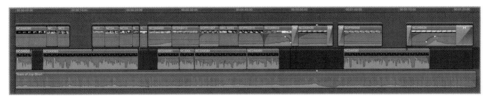

The rough cut

Starting in Lesson 5, you'll implement the client's suggested changes and insert additional material. You'll finesse the rough cut with additional edits, and then move into the sweetening tasks of adding titles, effects, and speed changes. Finally, you'll turn your attention to refining the audio mix before you examine the share options for exporting the project.

The finished edit

Lesson 10 describes "sub-workflows" you can use to replace or supplement your editing workflow. Among these are techniques for synchronizing clips recorded in a dual-system setup, used often in HD-DSLR setups; and editing clips recorded in a multicamera scenario.

Learning the Workflow

When you look at the Final Cut Pro editing workflow from the 30,000-foot level, you see three phases: import, edit, and share.

During the import phase—sometimes referred to as ingest or transfer—you process source media files into clips. Then, those clips are stored and organized in preparation for the edit phase.

Organizing clips within an event

The edit phase—where you'll spend most of your time with Final Cut Pro—is when the magic begins. This phase comprises several sub-workflows, including trimming clips down to the best material, adding graphics, and mixing the audio.

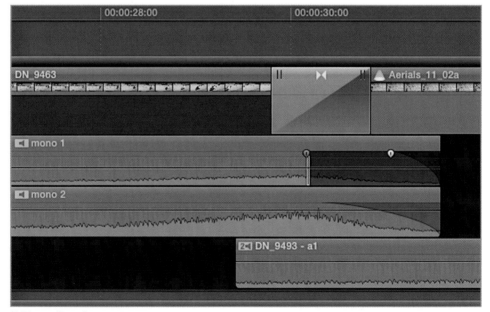

Editing split-audio components

The share phase is when you prepare your finished editing project for distribution to various online hosts or clients, for playback on a variety of devices, and for final archiving.

The export presets in the Share pop-up menu

That's the high-level Final Cut Pro workflow within which you will build your stories. As you continue through this book, you'll learn the many tools and techniques, the buttons and keyboard shortcuts, you'll use again and again during your editing workflow. So as you begin this editing odyssey, start by committing one keyboard shortcut to memory: Command-Z. If you click a button or press a key and don't get the expected result, just press Command-Z. Then, try the edit again. Don't be afraid to experiment. Final Cut Pro is built to encourage exploration of all your editing options and all your creativity.

Lesson Review

1. Describe the three post-production workflow phases in Final Cut Pro.

2. When Final Cut Pro asks if you want to update your projects and events to Final Cut Pro X 10.1, what options are available?

3. Should you update any post-production software during an editing job in progress?

Answers

1. Import: The ingest process of storing your story's source media files and organizing the clips that represent those source files. Edit: The creative process of assembling, trimming, and effecting clips to tell a story. Share: the export process of distributing your completed story to various platforms.

2. The options presented are to upgrade all projects and events into one library per volume, to allow you to selectively upgrade now, or to return to the upgrade process later.

3. A common practice in the post-production industry is to not update software, and in some cases hardware, while working on an editing job.

Lesson **2**

Importing Media

The Final Cut Pro post-production "preflight," or pre-edit, is performed during the import phase of your workflow. Devoting some time to *media management* and clip organization when beginning the editorial process pays off heavily during the later phases of an edit. As part of the import process you learn in this lesson, you will utilize two methods of storing media while converting those media files into the clips you'll use for your project. Before you start the import process, however, you need to be aware of the media management structure used in Final Cut Pro.

GOALS

► Define the clip, event, and library containers

► Understand the differences between managed and external media files

► Create a camera archive

► Import files using Media Import and the Finder

Reference 2.1
Understanding Clips, Events, and Libraries

Your Mac uses nested folders as containers in which you store, manipulate, organize, and share information. Similarly, Final Cut Pro uses specialized clip, event, and library containers to store and organize your media.

The Clip Container

After acquiring source media files, such as those you downloaded in the previous lesson, you will import them into Final Cut Pro for editing. The import process creates a clip inside Final Cut Pro that represents each source media file. Each clip varies in its contents: Some combine audio and video content, others contain only video or audio. Think of each clip simply as a media container. To edit a video file, you must import the file into Final Cut Pro. Final Cut Pro places the file's contents into a clip container.

The Event Container

Clips are organized into larger containers called events. Events may contain a wide variety of clips, but are best utilized to organize clips that have one or more common elements. A common element could be interviews, shots for a movie scene, or stock footage. The event container can include a varied cornucopia of clips or a narrowly defined selection of clips. It's up to you to define the specifics of event containers.

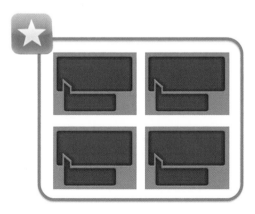

▶ **What Should Go into an Event?**

Events may store whichever clips you choose. Some editors like to create one event, throw all available clips into that event, and later go "gold digging" to find the nuggets. Other editors prefer to create multiple events, each one storing clips grouped by acquisition date, camera card, scene of the movie, or a subtopic within a documentary edit. Your events could represent a combination of those options because only you define the contents of your events.

Before you decide what goes into your events, remember that an event is a storage container. It not only organizes your clips within Final Cut Pro (which you'll learn more about in Lesson 3), but it's also used in conjunction with the larger library container to define where your source media files are stored.

The Library Container

A library is the largest content container in Final Cut Pro. Libraries allow you to bundle your events and thousands of clips for powerful yet simple management of your projects. Libraries facilitate the easy handoff of a project or multiple projects to another editor or production colleague. You need at least one library open to edit your project; and you may simultaneously open as many as you want.

Some special rules apply to clips, events, and libraries that you'll learn throughout this book. Let's start importing clips, and see how Final Cut Pro quickly guides you through the process.

Exercise 2.1.1
Creating a Library

Because all clips you'll edit are contained inside an event, and an event is contained inside a library, you'll need to create a library before you can import media. A library can be saved on any accessible local or network volume.

1   In Final Cut Pro, choose File > New > Library.

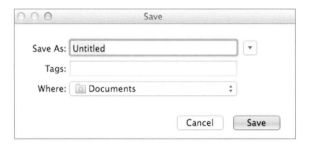

A Save dialog appears asking where to store your library. A library container can be saved to any available storage device. Preferably, you'll have access to a high-speed local or network volume.

2   Navigate to the same location in which you saved the FCPX Media folder.

NOTE ▸ In Lesson 1, you downloaded and moved the media to a new folder named *FCPX Media* that you created at one of the suggested locations: an external volume, the Documents folder, or the desktop.

3   In the Save As field, enter *Lifted*, and click Save.

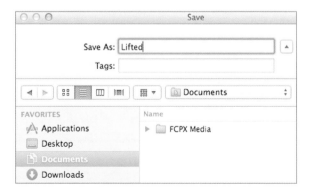

In the Libraries pane to the left, you will see a new library, Lifted, which automatically contains an event named for today's date. You also have one library that was created when you first opened Final Cut Pro. Let's close that library and any others you may have to protect their contents.

4   Control-click the unwanted library, and from the shortcut menu, choose Close Library.

5   Repeat for any additional libraries you may have listed.

Closing existing libraries protects their contents while you are working with the materials used in this book. You will also realize improved hardware performance when you have a minimum number of libraries open. And don't worry, you'll later learn how to open existing libraries.

Inside the Lifted library, you'll find a single event that has the current date as its name. Because you will import media from one of this project's GoPro cameras into that event, let's rename the event to something more descriptive.

6   Click the text label of the event. When the text label switches to a text entry field, enter *GoPro*, and press Return.

The event is renamed. You've created a new library and prepared an event to receive the source media files as clips.

Exercise 2.1.2
Preparing to Import Camera Source Files

For this exercise, you will mount a cloned (simulated) SD card you downloaded in Lesson 1. This clone simulates accessing a physical camera SD card.

> **NOTE ▶** This exercise assumes that you have a new installation of OS X. By default, Image Capture, an additional application with OS X, will be the first to recognize a camera or camera card mounted on your Mac.

1   Press Command-H to hide Final Cut Pro and get quick access to your desktop.

2   Locate the FCPX Media folder you created in Lesson 1.

3   Inside the FCPX Media folder, double-click the GoPro SD Card 1.dmg file.

In a moment, an SD card icon will appear on your desktop. This software card simulates connecting a physical camera card to your computer.

When your Mac senses the simulated camera card, Image Capture may open to access the card. If Image Capture does not open, you may skip to step 5.

4   Allow Image Capture to open, and then choose Image Capture > Quit Image Capture to close the application.

5　To return to Final Cut Pro, click its Dock icon

Final Cut Pro has remained in the background, awaiting your return. Depending on your system configuration, the Media Import window may already have opened for you.

6　If Media Import did not open automatically, click the Media Import button.

Before you import anything, let's examine the Media Import interface.

Reference 2.2
Using the Media Import Window

The Media Import window presents a unified interface for ingesting source media files into Final Cut Pro. The Media Import window specifies where source media files reside and how their clip representations are cataloged within a library's event(s). You can edit these clips into a project as the beginning of the post-production workflow.

Final Cut Pro is designed to get you editing quickly and easily by minimizing technical barricades. The Media Import window has three panes: sidebar, Browser, and Viewer.

▶   **Sidebar:** To the left, the sidebar lists available devices (cameras, volumes, and favorites) as sources for importing.

▶   **Browser:** Displays the source media files available for import from the device selected in the sidebar.

▶   **Viewer:** Previews the source media file selected in the lower Browser.

The sidebar is the first pane you will see when you open the Media Import window. It includes a list of Final Cut Pro–compatible devices.

Once you select a device in the sidebar, the device's media files appear in the Browser pane, which has two available views: filmstrip or list.

NOTE ▶ The available view options are dependent on the selected device type.

Source media files that appear in the Browser are ready for importing. You needn't worry about configuring additional settings. If Final Cut Pro can access the file to preview it, you can import it.

Once you've selected which media files to import, an Import Options dialog appears. The media management features of Final Cut Pro will ensure that you know where the clips you're about to import for editing will be stored. You have access to some incredibly powerful, user-configurable options in just a few clicks.

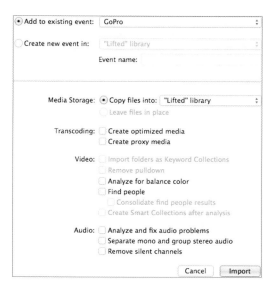

After setting the import options, Final Cut Pro ingests the source media files as clips that appear in the main window's Browser, ready for editing. When you combine the 64-bit architecture of Final Cut Pro and OS X with Mac hardware, you have virtually instantaneous editing access to the clips, even at 4K resolution, while the import is still underway. Forget same-day editing. This is same-hour editing.

▶ **Codecs? Frame Rate? Aspect? What?**

These are some of the specifications that describe media files, much as "US Letter" is a specification that describes paper trimmed to 8.5 x 11 inches. These three terms define the mathematical compression and the dimensions, the frames per second recorded, and the pixel size settings for video images, respectively.

Exercise 2.2.1
Creating a Camera Archive

Before you start importing, you must perform one very important process: Back up your source media. The Create Archive command allows you to clone your source media device within the application that Final Cut Pro will manage and catalog. Although some editing workflows allow you to back up your source media files outside the application, the purpose of Create Archive is to ensure that you have a backup of your original source media files, just in case. We've all deleted a file at some point that we wished we could get back.

1   From the Cameras section of the list, select the GoPro1 camera card.

The contents of the card appear in the Browser area. Before you start previewing the media files, you should begin the backup process.

2   At the bottom of the leftmost sidebar, click the Create Archive button.

A dialog asks you to name the new archive and choose a save location. Be sure to choose a meaningful name for the archive. It could be the name of the client, scene, project name, project number, or any combination of metadata that will later help you distinguish this archive from every other archive.

3   For this exercise, type *Heli Shots-GoPro* to describe the files as the helicopter shots from the GoPro SD Card 1.

4   If necessary, click the disclosure triangle to display the rest of the Finder window.

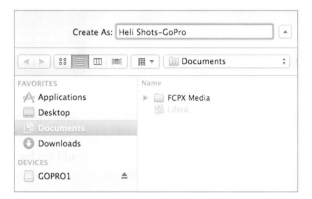

You have the option to add the camera archive to the Favorites section of the left sidebar for convenient access. For now, leave this option deselected.

5   Navigate to your Documents folder, and click the New Folder button.

6   Enter *Lifted Archives* as the new folder name. Click Create in the New Folder dialog,
and then in the Media Import dialog, click Create.

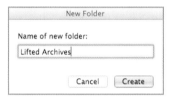

A timer appears next to the GoPro1 card in the sidebar. You may proceed with the
importing process before the archive has completed.

▶ **Why Should I Create Camera Archives?**

Final Cut Pro imports source files from a variety of camera formats. For the most efficient import process, the Media Import window uses the source camera metadata. The metadata is stored among several files of the camera card/magazine, or is embedded in the media files. Some of the external files are hidden when viewing the source files in the Finder, so if you drag the source files from the card to your computer, you will not be copying all the associated metadata. As a result, in some cases, the source files will not be recognized by the Media Import window at all. Best practice is to clone your camera card/magazine using the Create Archive function. Creating an archive, rather than dragging files from the camera, preserves the camera metadata and volume structure, and allows Final Cut Pro to recognize the source format.

▶ **Where Should I Store Camera Archives?**

The events that contain your clips should be stored on a media volume physically separate from your Macintosh HD volume. Ideally, the media volume is a RAID (redundant array of independent disks) volume, often referred to as a protected volume. A RAID is a group of disks bound together by hardware or software that configures those disks as a single volume that may also utilize redundancy to create a backup within the RAID. If the media volume is your only secondary volume, storing the camera archives on the media volume maintains everything on one volume, which helps you to keep your editing project consolidated. However, keeping all the parts of your editing project on one unprotected (non-RAID) volume creates a single point of failure. A best practice is to store your camera archives on a protected volume separate from your libraries.

Reference 2.3
Importing Source Media from a Camera

The Media Import window accesses a camera's source media files. You saw that when creating an archive or clone of the camera card/magazine as a backup. However, creating an archive is not importing files to your project. The archive is merely a backup of the original content. Now it's time to import the media files as clips into an event, which will contain the clips you'll use in Final Cut Pro.

You'll begin by learning how to navigate the filmstrip representations of each media file. The mouse or trackpad is not the only way, or even the fastest way, to navigate Final Cut Pro. The navigation techniques you learn here will apply throughout the rest of the application and your editing workflow, and will aid you in using Final Cut Pro more efficiently.

▶ **Command Editor**

Final Cut Pro has over 300 customizable keyboard commands you can assign using the Command Editor window (Final Cut Pro > Commands > Customize).

More information on using the Command Editor is available in the "Assigning Keyboard Shortcuts" section of Appendix A.

In the following exercises, you'll learn about some of the import methods in Final Cut Pro. First, you'll import camera media files from a GoPro used to shoot extra helicopter B-roll. Then you will import a batch of clips, including the interview of the pilot and the bulk of the B-roll files.

All of these methods use the Import Options dialog, which includes media management options and optional analysis tools for identifying the shot composition and/or technical errors within the clips.

Exercise 2.3.1
Navigating Within a Filmstrip Preview

As an independent editor, you may spend hours poring over source media files. Using keyboard commands to move through those materials may save only seconds at a time, but those seconds can compound into hours over the life of a complex editing project.

1   With the simulated SD card still mounted, select it from the Cameras section at the top of the sidebar.

At the lower-left of the Browser pane, two buttons control how the source files are displayed: Filmstrip and List. Let's start with the filmstrip view to get your first taste of skimming.

2   Click the Filmstrip View button, if necessary.

The source media files from the cloned SD card are displayed as thumbnails. They allow you to quickly skim a file's contents.

3   Move your pointer across a file's thumbnail to skim the media.

A preview of the file's contents appears in both the thumbnail and in the Viewer pane above the thumbnails. The preview also plays the audio track if one is included in the file. You may also play the file in real time.

4   With the pointer placed over a thumbnail, press the Spacebar.

The Spacebar initiates real-time file preview. Pressing Spacebar again pauses the preview.

5   Press the Spacebar again to pause playback.

You've already seen how you can skim a clip to quickly preview its content. For a longer duration clip, real-time playback may be too slow and skimming may be too fast. Using the keyboard shortcuts enables precise playback control. The keyboard shortcuts for playback are referred to as the J K L keys.

6   Skim to the start of **GOPR0005**, and then press L to start playback.

The clip plays forward at normal speed.

7   Press K to pause, and then press J to play the clip in reverse.

8   Press J again.

The playhead moves in reverse at twice normal speed. You can press J up to four times, increasing the search rate each time. The same is true for forward playback by pressing L.

9   Press L a couple times. The clip plays forward, moving faster with each press. Press K to pause.

You will later learn additional navigation controls. Now that you can navigate the previews, let's continue importing camera files. You are going to import a couple of files in their entirety.

Expanding the Filmstrip View

Although the Filmstrip view defaults to thumbnails, you may expand those thumbnails into an expanded filmstrip preview. This allows you finer control over the skimmer when reviewing longer duration clips.

1   In the Media Import window, drag the Zoom slider to the right.

The time notation on the right indicates the length of playback time each filmstrip frame represents.

2   For example, drag the slider until the time is set to 1s.

Each frame in the filmstrip now represents one second of source media.

3   Drag the slider to the left, or press Shift-Z until All appears, which indicates that each media file is represented by one thumbnail.

Exercise 2.3.2
Importing Clips from a Camera Card

Now that you know how to preview clips, you can scan the camera card for the media files you'll import. You may find yourself using both mouse and keyboard navigation while you learn the Final Cut Pro interface.

1   With the SD card still selected, notice the Import All button below the thumbnails.

If you wanted to import all the source media files into an event as clips, you would click this button. The Import Options dialog would then allow you set some import preferences. But we'll look at that method later. For now, let's practice importing just a few clips at a time.

2   Select the thumbnail for **GOPR3310**.

The thumbnail is highlighted by a yellow border to indicate that the file is selected. You could import this clip immediately by clicking the Import Selected button. But wait, you have more clips to select.

3   Click the **GOPR0009** thumbnail.

GOPR0009 is selected and **GOPR3310** is deselected. As with OS X, you need to hold down the Shift or Command modifier keys when clicking to select multiple items.

4   While holding down the Command key, click **GOPR3310** again to select both clips.

Importing Ranges from Within a Camera File

The preceding method is great when you want to import entire files, but at times you'll want to import only parts of a media file. Fortunately, Final Cut Pro allows you to ingest sections of camera files without importing the entire file. These portions are known as range selections, or ranges. There are multiple ways to set a single range within a thumbnail preview:

▶ Cue the skimmer or playhead to the desired frame, and then press I to mark a start point. Then cue after the final desired frame and press O to mark an end point.

▶ Position the mouse pointer over the desired start point, and then drag to the desired end point. The duration info displays as you drag.

Within **GOPR0003**, let's import two segments for the edit. Although you could import this source file as one clip and trim it later, you will take this opportunity to break the file into two clips by creating two ranges. To create multiple ranges within a clip, begin by setting the first range using one of the two previously described methods.

> **NOTE** ▶ Depending on the camera/video file format, range selection within a clip may not be available.

1   In **GOPR0003**, mark a start point at the beginning of the file, and an end point about 10 seconds later.

This range covers the helicopter on the pad with rotors turning. Now you will set a second range within the file.

2   Cue the skimmer or playhead to just before the helicopter lifts off, and then press Command-Shift-I.

3   While still in **GOPR0003**, skim to just after the helicopter has exited the frame and press Command-Shift-O to mark the end point.

Now you need to select the ranges you will import. You do this by holding down Command and clicking the desired thumbnails and ranges.

4   Command-click the five whole files and the two ranges in **GOPR0003** to select them for import.

5   With the five files and two ranges selected, click the Import Selected button.

The Media Import Options dialog appears. Next you will define the media management for these selected files.

Reference 2.4
Choosing Media Import Options

The Media Import Options dialog guides you through three important areas of Final Cut Pro media management:

▶   The virtual storage location of clips within the interface

▶   The physical storage location of those clips on accessible volumes

▶   The available transcoding and analysis automations

Choosing Virtual Storage

The top third of the Media Import window defines the clip organization within Final Cut Pro. Because a source media file must be accessible as an event clip to be available for editing, the options dialog enables you to add clips to an existing event or create a new event for the clips. Let's first look at the "Add to existing event" option.

When you select "Add to existing event," the pop-up menu lists the events available in the open libraries. You may place a clip in any event inside any library. All you are defining here is where the clip will be organized within Final Cut Pro.

When you select "Create new event," a name field enables, as does a pop-up menu for choosing a library in which to store the event. The naming convention you use for events is completely up to you. The event's name may be as simple as the client's name, the current editing project, or a barcode number assigned to the raw media.

This section of the Media Import Options dialog defines which event in the library will contain the imported clips.

However, the event's name is overshadowed in importance by the pop-up menu just above it. This pop-up menu contains a list of all available libraries. Again, this section of the Media Import dialog controls where the clip appears within Final Cut Pro.

Choosing Physical Storage

Earlier, you learned that an event is a storage container for clips. And this is completely true. The deeper question is, are the source media files for those clips really stored inside the event? This is a decision you make when you choose to use either **managed media** or **external media**.

Managed media is the simplest approach to using Final Cut Pro for a single user, a mobile editor, or for archiving. With managed media, you give full control of media management to Final Cut Pro. Once you hand that control over to the application, you no longer access your media in the Finder. Final Cut Pro will manage how and where the media is stored. You simply choose which library the media is assigned to. And because you created the library earlier, you've already defined where the managed media will be stored.

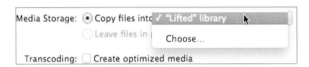

However, external media is the best practice for media management within Final Cut Pro, especially in environments where the source media files are shared among multiple users. External media management requires that you identify a storage location outside the Final Cut Pro libraries. Doing so allows other editors easy access to the same source media files without interrupting your workflows. This option also keeps the libraries small, enabling faster load times, less memory consumption, and easy sharing when passing a library to another user who has access to the same storage location.

NOTE ▶ A caution when using external media: Because external source media files are managed in the Finder, moving a file to another volume will render an associated clip offline in Final Cut Pro.

When you import media as external, you select any accessible location on any volume to store the source media files. The location is easily selected from the "Copy files into" pop-up menu.

When importing source media files from a volume rather than a camera card, the second media storage option "Leave files in place" is available. Also known as "Edit in place," this option does exactly what it says. No source media files are copied or moved during import.

Using Transcode and Analysis Options

More Media Import options are available in the Transcoding area. Selecting one or both of the transcode options creates an additional source media file for the clip.

▸ **Create optimized media:** Generates an Apple ProRes 422 version of the source file, a benefit for compositing, multiple effects, and reducing processing loads.

▸ **Create proxy media:** Generates an Apple ProRes 422 (Proxy) version of the source file with embedded audio, a compressed yet easy-to-process codec that allows you to store more source files on a volume.

Selecting analysis options can automate clip sorting within the event, analyze clips to identify a specific technical aspect of a clip, and perform a nondestructive repair of a detected audio error.

NOTE ▸ You may apply transcoding and analysis options to one or more clips during the edit phase of your workflow.

▸ **Import folders as Keyword Collections:** Replicates an existing folder structure at the Finder level within the event using keywords. Results of this analysis are covered in Lesson 3.

▸ **Remove pulldown:** Applies to source media files recorded in a special frame-cadence format.

▸ **Analyze for balance color:** Creates a one-click neutralizing correction averaged across the clip's duration; covered further in Lessons 4 and 7.

▸ **Find people:** Analyzes the clip for shot composition and facial detection (Lesson 3).

▸ **Consolidate find people results:** Averages the Find People results based on two-minute sections of a clip.

▶ **Create Smart Collections after analysis:** Aggregates the results of the Find People analysis into a dynamic collection (Lesson 3).

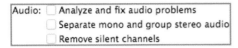

▶ **Analyze and fix audio problems:** Nondestructively repairs serious audio issues such as ground-loop hum or background rumble.

▶ **Separate mono and group stereo audio:** Defines how source audio channels are configured.

The clip-sorting options use existing or newly created metadata. You will learn more about metadata in Lesson 3.

Exercise 2.4.1
Applying Media Import Options

Now that you've familiar with the Media Import options, let's continue importing the camera clips.

1   After clicking the Import Selected button in Exercise 2.3.2, the Media Import Options dialog appears.

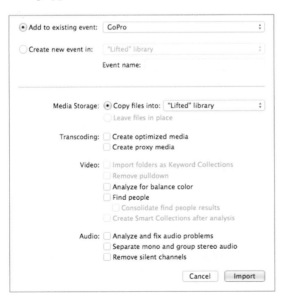

These options control the storage location, assigned event and library containers, some metadata assignments, and the analysis options.

You created the library and an event for this editing project in Exercise 2.1.1. Now, you will add clips and source media files to them.

2   If necessary, from the "Add to existing event" pop-up menu, choose the GoPro event in the Lifted library.

You've instructed the import process to create clips in the GoPro event that represent those source media files. Now you will tell Final Cut Pro where to store the source media.

3   If necessary, in the Media Storage category, from the "Copy files into" pop-up menu, choose the Lifted library.

These source media files will become managed media files within the Lifted library. The source media files will be copied from the SD card to the GoPro event stored in the library. Because these will be managed media files, your only concern is whether you placed the library on a volume with enough free space to store all of the managed media.

4   Deselect any other transcode or analysis options. Click Import.

The media files for this part of the course do not need to be analyzed by any of these automation tools. Like the transcode options previously discussed, you may analyze any clip at any time. Doing the analysis during import is optional.

As you start the import, notice that:

▶   The Media Import window closes automatically when the import process is underway.

▶   The clips appear in the Browser with a small stopwatch.

▶   You can start skimming and editing the newly imported clips.

▶   A few extra items appear in the Event Library, which we'll discuss in Lesson 3.

Reference 2.5
Import Files from a Volume

If you are collaborating with someone else on a project, at some point you will need to import files handed to you on a volume or emailed/FTP'd to you (rather than accessing an original camera card containing media). Or you may receive a breaking news clip shared through the cloud. Like any other file for import, the received file must be in a format that Final Cut Pro can read and play.

> **NOTE ▶** See Appendix B of this book and the Supported Formats section of the Apple Final Cut Pro Tech Specs webpage for definitive information on natively supported file formats.

The import from a volume process starts much like importing content from the SD card:

- ▶ Mount the volume.
- ▶ In Final Cut Pro, click the Media Import button.
- ▶ Select your source device in Media Import's left sidebar.
- ▶ Navigate to the desired file(s) in the Browser.
- ▶ Select the files, and then click the Import All/Import Selected button.
- ▶ When the Import Options dialog appears, the process is the same with an additional media storage option available.

A difference between volume and camera import will be visible in the Browser pane: Importing from a volume displays files in list view only.

Leaving Files in Place

When you imported content from the SD card, the "Copy files into" option was your only choice. Final Cut Pro required that you copy the media files from the SD card into an attached volume. This requirement is a good thing. If the files were not copied, the resulting clips would go **offline** when you ejected the camera card. The offline state would have occurred because the clip within Final Cut Pro would still be referencing the source media files on the now-removed SD card.

When you import source media files from a volume, Final Cut Pro gives you the option to copy or not to copy those source files. You would copy the source media files if they were stored, for example, on a borrowed volume you had to return before you were finished editing. Copying is also a preferred choice when you import media from a shared storage volume to a portable volume to make your project portable. When you elect to copy source media files, you have the option to copy into managed media files or external media files (as discussed in Reference 2.4).

The second option, "Leave files in place," does not copy the source files, but simply references them at their current locations. This external media option is very useful in a shared storage environment of multiple users. It allows an editor to use the same source media files as other editors within the same workgroup without creating redundant copies on the server.

Beyond the slight difference in media management options, importing from a volume is as easy as importing from a camera.

▶ **Using Symlinks**

When you're using external media, the source media files are not copied into the library. Instead, **symlinks** (simulated clips) are created inside the event that refer to the externally stored source media files. That external location may be anywhere on any accessible volume. Using external media files is the best practice for any editor, whether working alone or in a multiuser environment.

Exercise 2.5.1
Importing Existing Files from a Volume

In this exercise, you will import files that were processed and organized outside of Final Cut Pro. These are the source B-roll and sound bites media files you will need for the vignette.

1 Click the Media Import button, or press Command-I.

The Media Import window opens. You will be importing from the downloaded files.

2 Navigate to the location where you placed the downloaded media in Lesson 1.

This location is either an external volume, your Documents folder, or your desktop. The necessary media is in the FCPX Media Import folder. Selecting your home folder in the sidebar is one possible starting point.

3 Take a look inside the FCPX Media folder for the LV1/LV Import folder. Specifically, look inside the LV Import folder to display its contents.

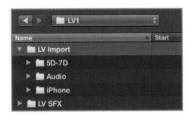

The media files have been sorted by folder. You can take advantage of this organizational structure in Final Cut Pro.

4 With the LV Import folder selected, click Import Selected.

The Import Options dialog opens. You will select a few options this time.

5   At the top, select "Create new event in," and from the pop-up menu, choose the Lifted library. Type *Primary Media* as the event name.

Remember, you can set up the event and library to organize your media however you wish. Unlike the previous import, this time during import you will reference external media that is left in place. Because you have constant access to the volume where the media files reside, you do not need to copy the source media.

6   In the Media Storage category, select "Leave files in place."

Another difference from the previous import is that you will import a folder of media files. Final Cut Pro can harness the metadata of the Finder folder structure using keywords. Similar to OS X tags, keywords are metadata tokens applied to a clip. Keywords may be used to quickly sort and find distinct or related (or unrelated) clips. This feature is very handy when your library contains a few hundred or a few thousand clips.

7   From the Video category, select "Import folders as Keyword Collections."

NOTE ▶ The command applies keywords only when a folder is selected for import. Importing selected files within the folder will not apply keywords.

8   Click Import.

The Media Import window closes, and the new event appears in your Lifted library.

9   Click the disclosure triangle next to the Primary Media event to display its contents.

The folders you selected were converted into keywords. The "Import folders as Keyword Collections" import option carries the Finder folder "structure" into the event.

NOTE ► You will learn how to create and manage keywords, along with other metadata tricks, in Lesson 3.

Exercise 2.5.2
Dragging from the Finder or Other Apps

Final Cut Pro events accept files you drag directly from the Finder or other applications. But you do need to know how media import options are handled in these cases. When you're dragging files directly to Final Cut Pro, the import options control such things as managed and external media status, transcoding, and analysis options.

1   Choose Final Cut Pro > Preferences or press Command-, (comma).

2   In the Preferences window, click the Import icon.

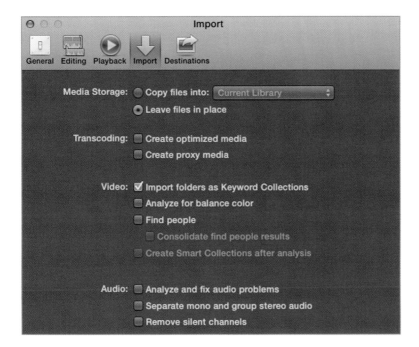

This should look familiar. Because dragging an item to an event in a library is understood as an import operation, these import options manage the details. Notice that the top section of the standard Media Import window is missing. The library and event are defined by which item you drag to in the Libraries pane.

The pointer identifies which of the media storage options is active and allows you to override those options.

▶ When an item is dragged to an event—or a Keyword Collection in an event—and the "Copy files into media storage" option is selected, the pointer displays a plus sign inside a circle.

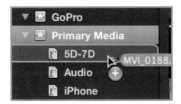

▶ When an item is dragged to an event or Keyword Collection and the "Leave in place" Media Storage option is selected, the pointer displays a hooked arrow.

▶ If the pointer indicates a copy, you can override it and perform a "Leave in place" import by holding down Command-Option before releasing the mouse button.

▶ If the pointer indicates a "Leave in place" import, you may override it and perform a copy import by holding down Option before releasing the mouse button.

You've now imported the source media files into Final Cut Pro. You should feel good knowing that you can create a library and some events for getting media into Final Cut Pro. Although you could start editing right away with these imported files, the resulting clips could be numerous and unorganized. In Lesson 3, you will organize these imported clips for faster recall of particular clips.

Lesson Review

1. Which of these three is the largest media container: clip, event, or library?
2. Describe possible organizational criteria for sorting clips and projects into events.
3. Name and describe the built-in command for backing up camera media files.
4. Where should you store camera archives?
5. What two views are available in the Media Import window, and when are the two views available?
6. What setting on the Zoom slider in filmstrip view allows you to see each clip as a single thumbnail?
7. What keyboard shortcuts or modified-skimming keys let you mark multiple range selections within a clip?
8. In the Media Import Options dialog, which of these two sections sets media files as managed or external?

⦿ Create new event in:	"Lifted" library	⬍
Event name:		

A

Media Storage: ● Copy files into: "Lifted" library ⇕

○ Leave files in place

B

9. Fill in the blank: With the "Create optimized media" option selected, Final Cut Pro X transcodes imported media to the _____ codec.

10. When dragging items from the iPhoto application to an event, where do you set the option to copy (or not copy) the photo into the Final Cut Events folder?

11. You are about to import source media files grouped into various folders. Which Media Import option must be selected to replicate the folder structure within an event?

Answers

1. The library is the largest of the media containers.

2. The criteria is whatever you choose: a scene of a film, a segment of a news-magazine show, a webisode, stock footage, raw media from an SD card, all versions of the projects, and so on. An event is a flexible storage container that can be as all-encompassing or as granularly compartmentalized as your raw media and projects.

3. The Create Archive command creates a clone of your source media device, preserving the folder structure and metadata along with the source media files.

4. Camera archives may be stored anywhere; however, to reduce the chance of a single-point failure taking down an entire editing job, camera archives should be stored on a volume physically separate from the media storage volume you use for editing.

5. Filmstrip and list view. The two views are available when importing from a recognized camera card file structure; otherwise, only the list view is available in the browser of the Media Import window.

6. All. The setting defines the time length represented by each thumbnail of the clip.

7. The keyboard shortcuts are Command-Shift-I and Command-Shift-O. Holding down Command while skimming a clip also marks ranges.

8. B. "Copy files into" creates managed media while "Leave files in place" creates externally referenced media.

9. Apple ProRes 422

10. Final Cut Pro > Preferences

11. Import Folders as Keyword Collections

Organizing Clips

With the 64-bit architecture of Final Cut Pro X and OS X, you could start editing before the import process is complete. Whether you chose managed media or external media, Final Cut Pro will start you off by referencing the source files at their current storage locations. If you chose to copy, Final Cut Pro will auto-switch to the copied version when it is imported. You've already noticed that Final Cut Pro has organized some clips in your Libraries pane. However, most editors need to perform a little more pre-edit organization. With a thousand or so clips, the long-form editor must be organized for maximum efficiency. When you divert time to digging for a clip, it breaks your editing rhythm and halts your storytelling momentum. If you are an SDE (same-day-edit) editor, perhaps working for a news organization, your video probably needed to be on the air "yesterday." Although Final Cut Pro allows you to start editing quickly without performing all the pre-edit options presented here, you will most likely be required to organize your clips for the next show and for archival use after the newscast.

GOALS

- ► Apply keywords to a clip and clip ranges
- ► Search and filter clips by keywords
- ► Batch rename clips
- ► Add notes and ratings to a clip
- ► Create Smart Collections
- ► Detect people and composition within clips
- ► Understand and assign roles

The metadata underpinning of Final Cut Pro is the key to efficient, creative editing. This chapter explores the possibilities of organizing your clips within the application. These additional pre-edit steps will make the application work for you and help in getting your story told.

Reference 3.1
Introducing the Libraries, Browser, and Viewer Panes

In Chapter 2, you imported media into events which were kept inside a library. You learned that a library can be stored anywhere on a connected volume. You also discovered that the source media files, represented by clips within an event, may be stored internally (managed) or externally for an event and library. Whether your media is managed or external, your focus should now shift to using the clips within the Final Cut Pro interface, and not so much at the Finder level outside the application. Final Cut Pro includes tools to manage clips, and even their storage locations, entirely within the app, which leaves you to concentrate on the actual editing. The entire editing workflow depends on being able to find the right clip at the right creative moment. To discover those clip gems, you'll utilize the top three panes of the interface: the Libraries, Browser, and the Viewer.

The Libraries pane is where you'll find open libraries and their associated events. After importing clips and applying a couple of enabled analysis tools, Final Cut Pro creates metadata about each clip along with collections of clips that share the same metadata. You may utilize this metadata to parse and group clips in your own way to fit your personal editing workflow.

These collection containers display their contents in the Browser, which is where you skim, select, and mark ranges of clip content. The Browser includes a powerful set of features to sort and organize clips within event collections. The Browser also may be used to create complex collections you can store in an event for later use.

In the Viewer, your story will come to life. All the metadata wrangling you will do is based on what you can see in the Viewer. The Viewer displays a clip's contents when you skim the clip in the Browser. When you press the J K L keys, the result is shown in the Viewer. Final Cut Pro allows you to change the layout so that the Viewer moves to a second display with a larger viewing area. And by incorporating features of OS X and Apple TV to your workflow, you may wirelessly push the Viewer's display to an even larger display.

You will utilize all three of these panes to enhance your clips with metadata. Remember, although these organizational steps aren't required for editing in Final Cut Pro, being able to find, track, and share your finished project based on metadata is leaps and bounds faster than the traditional approach of cramming as much clip info into the filename or into a few columns of additional information.

Reference 3.2
Using Keywords

Keywords are applied to clips to decrease your clip search times and to speed up the storytelling process. Your choice of keywords can be fairly generic to help you locate a wide range of content. In fact, a keyword so granular that it describes only one clip may be a wasted keyword. In that case, a simple clip name change may be preferable to applying a keyword.

You may apply a keyword to an entire clip or to a range within a clip. If a clip's contents started with a helicopter takeoff and ended with a helicopter landing, you might apply three keywords to the single clip:

▶   Helicopter: Applied to the entire clip

▶   Takeoff: Applied to the start of the clip

▶   Landing: Applied to the end of the clip

You may apply as many keywords as you wish to a clip. When applying a keyword, the keyword ranges may overlap. This gives you incredible sort and sift capabilities without media management nightmares. A keyword is not a subclip, not a nested clip, and best of all, does not involve duplicating a clip. Final Cut Pro links those to one source media file. And no matter how granular you do get with a keyword in segmenting the content of a clip, you always have access to the entire source media file during the edit.

When a keyword is manually applied, a blue stripe appears along the top of the clip's filmstrip.

The keyword also appears in the list view when the clip's details are displayed by clicking the clip's disclosure triangle.

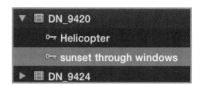

You may quickly create a selection based on the keyword by selecting the keyword shown under the clip in list view, or by clicking the blue stripe at the top of the clip's filmstrip.

An *analysis keyword* is a keyword added to a clip based on the analysis options chosen during import. In the Import Options dialog and the Import preferences pane, you can enable these analysis tools during import; however, you may specifically request an analysis later in your edit workflow.

Whether manually or automatically generated, the keywords organize your clips into Keyword Collections stored in the Libraries pane. Keyword Collections are virtual folders that display clips or ranges of clips that have the same keyword. In the next few exercises, you will see that keywording is a huge step toward harnessing the power of metadata to make an efficient edit.

Exercise 3.2.1
Keywording a Clip

In Lesson 2, you imported a folder of source media files from a volume. During that import, you assigned keywords to the clips based on their presence in that folder and subfolders. As a result, your Lifted library lit up with additional items when Final Cut Pro assigned keywords to those clips. Let's review some of those keywords and learn how you can create your own.

> **NOTE ▶** The Import Folders as Keyword Collections option during media import is also available when dragging folders from the Finder directly into an event. That option may be enabled in the Import preferences.

1   In the Libraries pane, select the Lifted library's Primary Media event.

Selecting the event instructs Final Cut Pro to display the clips associated with that event.

2   In the Browser, click the Filmstrip View button.

3   To ensure that you are seeing the same clip order pictured in this exercise, from the Action pop-up menu (the gear icon), choose Group Clips By > None and Sort By > Name.

4   Drag the Zoom slider to All.

Adjusting the Zoom slider to All displays one thumbnail per clip.

5   Look at the notation text in the lower part of the Browser.

This text describes the overall contents of the selected library item. Currently, of 28 clips, you perhaps have one clip selected. The total duration of any one or more selected clips is displayed. To see as many of the 28 clips as possible, let's make a slight change to the Browser's display options.

6   Click the Clip Appearance button, and from the pop-up menu, deselect Show Waveforms, if necessary.

7   Drag the Clip Height slider to the left to reduce the thumbnail height.

You may need to drag and then release the mouse button to see the results.

8   To see even more clips, drag the divider bar between the Browser and the Viewer to the right.

Another option is to collapse the Libraries pane from view.

9   In the Libraries pane, click the "Hide the Libraries" button.

You now have more room, but you need to see the Libraries pane for this exercise.

10   Click the "Show the Libraries" button to display the pane.

Adding a Keyword to One or More Clips

Your Primary Media event contains 28 clips, and the Keyword Collections listed within the event contain subgroupings of those event clips. Final Cut Pro created these collections based on the folders you imported in Lesson 2. These collections are helpful, but you should take some time to create additional collections for finer subgroupings.

1   In the Libraries pane, select the 5D-7D Keyword Collection to view its contents.

    The Browser updates to display the 23 clips associated with the 5D-7D keyword. You'll find a mixture of B-roll and interview clips here. To quickly find the interview clips (which you'll be using in Lesson 4), let's create a Keyword Collection that references them.

2   Within the 5D-7D Keyword Collection, click to select the first on-camera sound bite of Mitch, the owner and pilot of H5 Productions.

3   To select the remaining sound bite clips, use a combination of the Shift and/or Command keys to select all of Mitch's sound bites.

    The Browser recognizes your selection of 6 clips with a total running time of just over 2 minutes and 47 seconds. To group these clips into a separate Keyword Collection, you will assign a keyword in the Keyword Editor.

4   In the toolbar, click the Keyword Editor button.

    The Keyword Editor HUD (heads-up display) opens.

The Keyword Editor already contains two keyword tokens: 5D-7D and LV Import. This demonstrates part of the power of metadata within Final Cut Pro: You may attach as many keywords as you want to a clip. The end result is that a single clip may appear in several Keyword Collections without the need to actually duplicate the clip on the volume. To see that feature in action, you will apply an additional keyword to these sound bites.

5   In the Keyword Editor, type *Interview* and press Return.

Not only did the the Interview token appear in the Keyword Editor, but you also gained a collection in the Primary Media event.

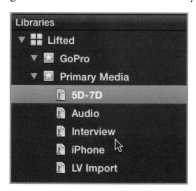

6   In the Libraries pane, select the newly created Interview Keyword Collection.

The Browser updates to display the six clips assigned to the Interview keyword. Later when you start the edit in Lesson 4, the Interview Keyword Collection will be your go-to source for these sound bites.

7   Take a moment to explore the other Keyword Collections in the Primary Media event. Look for the following:

▶   The number of clips within each Keyword Collection

▶   Which clips appear in each Keyword Collection

Removing a Keyword

Did you notice that the LV Import Keyword Collection contains all 28 clips? This Keyword Collection functions the same as selecting the event itself. Because this duplication is not necessary, let's remove the keyword LV Import from all 28 clips. Fortunately, you do not have to do this one clip at a time.

1   In the Primary Media event, Control-click the LV Import Keyword Collection and choose Delete Keyword Collection from the shortcut menu, or press Command-Delete.

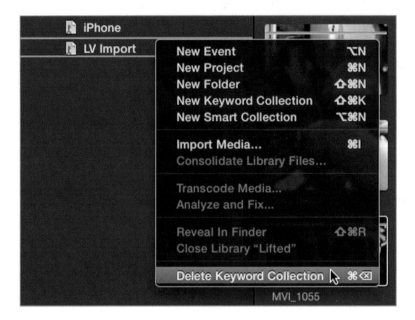

The Keyword Collection is removed; however, the clips remain in the event and the other collections. Just as you may freely add keywords to a clip, so can you freely delete keywords.

Adding Clips to a Keyword Collection

The end result of the following exercise is the same as adding the Interview keyword to sound bites as you did earlier. However, in this method you first create the Keyword Collection, and then drag the clips into it to assign the keyword.

1   In the Libraries pane, Control-click the Primary Media event, and choose New Keyword Collection.

An untitled Keyword Collection is created.

2   To name the collection, type *B-roll*, and press Return.

Of course, this Keyword Collection is currently empty. An easy way to add clips to this collection and assign the B-roll keyword is to drag clips into this collection.

3   In the event, select the 5D-7D Keyword Collection.

4   In the 5D-7D Keyword Collection, click the first B-roll clip, and then Shift-click the last B-roll clip.

You have selected every clip in the collection that does not contain Mitch's interview.

5   Drag the selected clips to the B-roll Keyword Collection in the Libraries pane. When the B-roll Keyword Collection is highlighted, release the mouse button.

6   Confirm that the clips received the B-roll keyword by selecting the B-roll Keyword Collection.

The 17 clips appear in both collections without any source media files being duplicated. So now you can search clips by keyword for B-roll or the 5D-7D camera type. Later, you will learn to search by multiple terms to create complex searches.

Adding Keywords Using Shortcuts

When using Final Cut Pro, you often have more than one way to achieve similar results. In this exercise you will use a combination of shortcuts in the Keyword Editor to apply more keywords to clips.

1   In the Keyword Editor HUD, click the Keyword Shortcuts disclosure triangle.

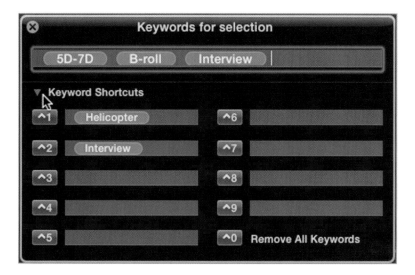

Your keyword shortcuts may be already populated. That's OK. You will clear them all before proceeding. You may clear the shortcuts at any time without affecting existing keywords or collections. However, modifying keywords in the uppermost field will change previous clip assignments.

2   Delete each keyword field's contents to clear all the existing shortcuts. Click the token in the shortcut field, and press Delete.

NOTE ► Do not click the Control-0 (^0) button or press the shortcut because doing so will erase the keywords assigned to the currently selected clip.

3   Starting with Control-1 (^1), enter the following keywords:

► Control-1 *B-roll*

► Control-2 *Hangar*

► Control-3 *Pre-Flight*

► Control-4 *Takeoff*

► Control-5 *In Flight*

► Control-6 *Landing*

► Control-7 *Flight Controls*

Your Keyword Shortcuts section now looks like this:

Using these new shortcuts, you may quickly apply their associated keywords to one or more clips at once.

4   In the 5D-7D collection, select **DN_9390**, **DN_9446**, and **DN_9452**.

These are B-roll clips, but they are also pre-flight clips. Use the shortcuts (Control-3 or the shortcut button in the Keyword Editor HUD) to quickly apply the Pre-Flight keyword.

5   Press Control-3 to also tag these B-roll clips with the Pre-Flight keyword.

The clips' assigned keywords now include Pre-Flight. As this is the first time you've applied the Pre-Flight keyword, a Pre-Flight Keyword Collection appears in the Libraries pane under the Primary Media event.

6   Using the following matrix, keyword the clips using the specified Keyword Collections:

NOTE ▶ A few clips are ignored for now and will not be keyworded at this time.

Keyword Collection: 5D-7D

Clip	Hangar	Pre-Flight	In Flight	Landing	Flight Controls
DN_9287*		X			
DN_9390	X	X			
DN_9415			X		
DN_9420			X		
DN_9424			X		
DN_9446		X			
DN_9452		X			
DN_9453		X			
DN_9454		X			X
DN_9455		X			
DN_9457		X			
DN_9463*		X			
DN_9465	X	X			
DN_9470	X	X			
DN_9488	X	X			
DN_9493			X		
DN_9503			X		

* Contains more than one action that would qualify for a keyword applied to a specific selection within the clip; you'll explore that scenario in the next exercise.

Keyword Collection: iPhone

Clip	Hangar	Pre-Flight	In Flight	Landing	Flight Controls
IMG_6476			X		X
IMG_6486			X		
IMG_6493			X		X

That takes care of most of the clips in the Lifted library...in the Primary Media event. Remember, you imported some GoPro clips in the GoPro event.

Batch Renaming of Camera Clips

You've updated the clips in the library so far using a phase of flight or aviation reference. You will continue to do so using the following table. However, before you resume keywording, the Final Cut Pro import process changed the name of the clips to a date/time stamp. The date/time stamp is when the camera created the file. Although this is handy during import to avoid filename duplication with existing clips, in a collaborative environment, a producer or client may be referencing the camera's assigned filename. Because the following table lists the camera filenames, you will need to see the original camera name per clip.

1   In the Libraries pane, select the GoPro event.

2   In the Browser, select one clip, and then press Command-A to select all the GoPro clips.

3   Choose Modify > Apply Custom Name > Original Name from Camera.

The clips' names revert back to the camera-assigned names. Now, you can finish keywording the B-roll for the GoPro clips.

NOTE ▶ You may need to click in a blank area of the Browser to force the clip names to update.

Event: GoPro

Clip	Runup	Hover	Takeoff	In Flight	Landing
GOPR0003 (1st)	X				
GOPR0003 (2nd)			X		
GOPR0005		X	X		
GOPR0006	X	X	X		
GOPR0009					X
GOPR1857				X	
GOPR3310			X		

Assigning too many keywords to a clip is super easy. You can assign as many as you want, but at a certain point time spent keywording isn't an efficient use of your time. Each editing job will vary as to what keywords and to what detail level with those keywords are needed. Final Cut Pro allows you to determine the right amount of needed keywords.

Exercise 3.2.2
Keywording a Range

In Exercise 3.2.1, you applied keywords to clips. Keywording is not limited to the clip's entire duration. Keywords may be applied to ranges within a clip. You may overlap as many keywords as required to further describe the ranges of a clip.

1   In the Libraries pane, select the B-roll Keyword Collection.

2   Select the **DN_9287** clip, and skim the clip to review its contents.

   NOTE ▶ You'll deal with the needed color correction in a later lesson.

   This clip could have two possible ranges: the helicopter sitting on the ramp, and the helicopter taking off. You will use keywords to identify the two ranges.

3   Skim the **DN_9287** clip again, and then mark a range from the start of the clip to just before the helicopter takeoff.

The range selection is about 18 seconds long. You'll keyword this as ramp footage. Because Ramp is not a previously used or shortcut-assigned keyword, you will use the Keyword Editor to manually assign it to the range.

4   In the Keyword Editor (Command-K), type *Ramp* and press Return.

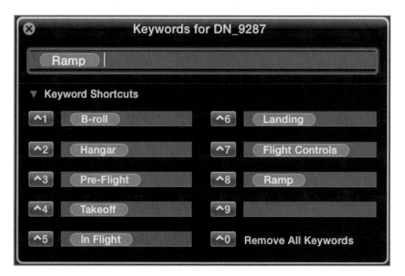

The keyword is assigned to the marked range, which is now filed in the newly created Ramp Keyword Collection in the Primary Media event.

5   In the Libraries pane, select the Ramp Keyword Collection, and skim the **DN_9287** clip.

Notice that the takeoff portion of the clip is not visible. In the Browser, you see only the on-the-ramp portion of the clip, or what is called a *subclip* that matches the selected Keyword Collection.

6   Select the B-roll Keyword Collection to see the entire duration of the **DN_9287** clip.

7   In the same clip, mark a new range selection from just before the helicopter takes off to the end of the clip.

Earlier, you created keyboard shortcuts for several keywords, including Control-4 for Takeoff.

8   Press Control-4 to assign the Takeoff keyword to the range.

9   In the Libraries pane, select the Takeoff Keyword Collection, and then skim the **DN_9287** clip.

Did you notice that the keywords 5D-7D, B-roll, and Pre-Flight were assigned to this entire clip in the previous exercises? When you are working with a clip range, the keywords applied to other ranges or the entire duration of the clip do not appear in the Keyword Editor. But you do have a way to display all of a clip's keywords all the time.

Viewing Keywords in List View

In list view, all the keywords applied to a clip are visible when you are viewing the event or a collection that is not limiting the clip to a range.

1   In the Browser, click the List View button. If necessary, click the disclosure triangle for clip **DN_9287**.

Name	Start	End	Duration
▼ DN_9287	00:00:19:07	00:00:31:01	00:00:11:18
5D-7D, B-roll, Interview, Pr...	00:00:00:00	00:00:31:01	00:00:31:01
Takeoff	00:00:19:07	00:00:31:01	00:00:11:18

Notice that some of the keywords are on the same line, which indicates that those keywords occupy the same content of the clip. You may verify that by referencing the start and end points to the right.

Carefully review the values for the start and end points for the applied keywords. Although you may see all the applied keywords at once in the list, you are not necessarily viewing all the clip's source media.

2   Select the Ramp Keyword Collection, select the "5D-7D, B-roll, Pre-Flight" keyword line listed under the clip, and then skim the filmstrip to verify that you do not see the takeoff.

3   Check the start and end points for the same line of keywords compared to the **DN_9287** line's start and end points.

The ranges are different. Right now, you are restricted to seeing the range defined by the Ramp keyword, which is why the clip's start and end points and the Ramp keyword's points are the same.

4   In the Libraries pane, select the B-roll Keyword Collection, and in the Browser, skim the **DN_9287** clip again.

You are now skimming the full duration of the source material represented by the clip. Take a glance at the clip's start and end points, and note that they now mirror the B-roll keyword's start and end points.

Although this exercise may feel like Final Cut Pro minutiae, it demonstrates an important concept to understand before performing the next exercise: When you start editing, you have no subclip limits, but when looking at a clip in the Browser, the applied keywords, metadata, and the active Keyword Collection do restrict you to only the subclipped content.

Let's back up and review how to apply two keywords, Ramp and Takeoff, to another clip. The same range situation applies to clip **DN_9463**: The helicopter is on the ramp and then takes off.

5   Create two ranges within **DN_9463**, applying the same two keywords to the appropriate ranges.

▶ **Tight or Loose?**

When creating what is commonly referred to as subclips in Final Cut Pro, you do not need to worry about setting precise start or end points. When you use the subclip in the edit, you will have access to all the source material represented by the original clip. There are no "subclip limits" within the duration of the original clip.

Exercise 3.2.3
Adding Notes to a Clip

Keywords are great, but as mentioned earlier, they should be used in a purposefully generic way to create Keyword Collections that reference more than one clip. The unique details describing a clip's contents may be added to a clip's metadata using the Notes field. The Notes field is accessible in the list view of the Browser, and in another pane called the Info inspector.

1   In the Libraries pane, select the B-roll Keyword Collection, if necessary.

You are looking at the clips tagged with the B-roll keyword in Lesson 2.

It would be useful if some of the B-roll clips had descriptive text associated with them. This text will be searchable, allowing you to filter your event down from hundreds, if not thousands, of clips to the single clip you need for your edit.

2   Switch the Browser to list view, if necessary, and then locate **DN_9390**.

3   Skim the clip to review its content.

This clip starts in black with the hangar door closed. The door starts opening as Mitch, the pilot, walks over to the helicopter to preflight the camera. That's a lot of descriptive information to add to the clip, but Final Cut Pro will allow you to do so. Let's append a shorter description to the clip's Notes field.

4   In the list view, scroll right in the list to locate the Notes column.

Because you will be using this column repeatedly, you may want to reposition the column closer to the Name column.

5   Drag the Notes column header to a location closer to the Name column, and then release the mouse button.

Now you can visually pair the clip and its ranges to their respective notes. Not only can you apply notes to an entire clip in Final Cut Pro, you can also apply notes to a clip's keyword ranges.

6   At the intersection of the Notes column and the **DN_9390** row, click to display a text pointer.

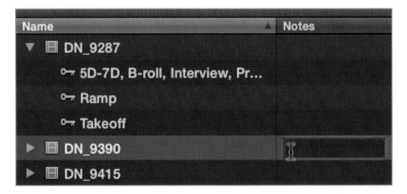

7   In the text field, type *Hangar door opens; Mitch enters L crossing R to preflight camera*, and then press Return.

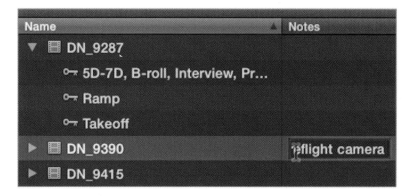

If you can't view all the entered text, one solution is to review the help tag.

8   Without clicking, locate the pointer over the text you entered in the Notes field.

A help tag appears, displaying the Note text.

Viewing the Info Inspector

As with many Apple applications, inspector or info panes display clip details. And these details include more than you probably want to know about the clip. They definitely include information you don't need to see while editing. In the present case, the Info inspector provides a bigger text field in which to review the note you applied.

1   In the Browser, verify that DN_9390 is selected.

2   Click the Inspector button (an icon of slider controls).

The inspector presents information in up to four subpanels, accessed via buttons at the top of the inspector.

3   Click the Info button to open the Info inspector.

Here you can see both basic and detailed information about the selected clip, including its name and format details such as frame size, frame rate, duration, and audio sampling rate. Below the Name field is the Notes field in which you can review the notes you previously entered. You can also use this field to modify or enter new information about the clip.

4   Change the Notes field to read, *Hangar door opens; Mitch L-R; camera preflight*. Click outside the field to update the notes metadata.

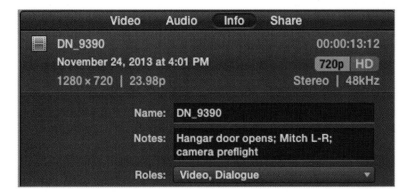

5   Now that you've learned two ways to enter notes metadata, use either method to enter clip metadata as follows:

▶   **DN_9420**: *Sunset through helicopter windows*

▶   **DN_9424**: *Flying into the sunset*

▶   **DN_9446**: *Getting in; tilt-up to engine start*

▶   **DN_9452**: *CU engine start*

▶   **DN_9453**: *Pan/tilt Mitch and instrument panel*

▶   **DN_9454**: *Flipping switches; pushing buttons*

▶   **DN_9455**: *High angle (HA) Mitch getting in helicopter*

▶   **DN_9457**: *HA helicopter starting; great start up SFX*

As you can see, your notes can be as generic or as detailed as you want or need them to be.

▶   **Assigning Notes to Clip Ranges**

You just finished applying notes to the entire clip. But don't forget that you can apply notes to clip ranges. One potential use for notes is to enter interview notes or even text transcriptions of the interview that occurs within that clip.

Reference 3.3
Assigning Ratings

Just when you thought that keywords and notes were all you needed, Final Cut Pro includes more metadata tools to further organize your clips. One of those tools is the ratings system.

Made up of three statuses—Favorites, Unrated, and Rejected—ratings may be used in conjunction with other metadata tools or as a stand-alone system. The concept is simple: Every clip starts out in an event as Unrated. As you review a clip in the Browser, you may rate the clip as a Favorite, Rejected, or Unrated. Also, as you did with keywords, you may rate a range within a clip.

Some editors use the ratings rather than keywords. And other editors blend the two features to easily create complex searches that reveal the exact clip needed for the edit. Documentary editors are often handed hours or days of interviews to sift, sort, and craft into the spine of a sound bite–driven story.

One approach to sifting interviews involves marking both useable sound bites along with extraneous material. This process of marking sound bites with potential storytelling power is known as "pulling selects." Traditionally, pulling selects involved finding an appropriate sound bite, and then immediately editing the select into a project or Timeline. Although Final Cut Pro allows this style of editing, let's explore other potential steps between finding the sound bite and making a project edit. Skimming, pitch correction, and ratings in Final Cut Pro can make this time-consuming process both fast and efficient.

Exercise 3.3.1
Applying Ratings

In Exercise 2.5, you imported the interview clips. Like any imported media, they include useable and non-useable editing content. In this exercise, you will use the ratings system to pare down those interview clips, creating a searchable group of sound bites.

1   In the Lifted library, select the Interview Keyword Collection listed under the Primary Media event.

The Browser displays the interview clips. Note that these interview clips were edited from a longer, continuous clip to limit their file sizes for the purposes of this book. Although the clips have been slightly pre-trimmed, they still include extraneous material for you to remove.

▶ **Breaking Down the Interview in the Field**

File-based camera technology allows you to instantly start and stop recording. Although the term "speed" is still used by cinematographers and videographers to indicate a camera appropriately recording a scene, digital cameras are recording scenes from the moment recording begins. And in some cases, when using pre-record settings, they start a few seconds before recording begins. Considering this instantaneous response, your editing workflow may benefit from the camera operator placing a quick stop/start cycle between interview answers. A quick double-punch of the camera's Record button automatically forces each interview question and answer into its own clip; this simple pre-edit process at acquisition may be a quick way to jump-start your edit.

NOTE ▶ As with any change to your workflow, test this method from start to end before committing it to a project.

2   If necessary, set the Browser to list view.

You need the clip's metadata to be accessible during this process.

3   If necessary, click the Name column header until the clip list is alphabetized in ascending order.

4   In the Browser, select **MVI_1042**.

The clip's filmstrip appears, ready for you to skim, mark, and rate the clip.

5   Play the clip from the beginning.

The clip opens with Mitch at the start of a sentence with a great statement, "Flying is something I've had a passion for since I was a little kid."

6   Cue the playhead to just before Mitch says, "Flying is."

You could skim back to this point, click with the pointer, or press the J K L keys to locate the playhead at that point. But once you are in the neighborhood, you'll need to use the frame-by-frame navigation controls to precisely locate the point.

7   To search frame by frame, press the Left and Right Arrow keys.

Tapping the Left Arrow key steps the playhead backward one frame at a time. Pressing the Right Arrow key moves the playhead forward one frame at a time. You may also hold down either of those keys to play the clip backward or forward at one-third speed.

You are about to set the start point of the select. This point does not have to be frame accurate at the moment; however, a little care now can go a long way later in the edit. Look for a frame where Mitch's eyes are open and his mouth is closed.

8   When the playhead is cued to the desired start point, press I.

Now let's find an end point. Mitch finishes the sentence with, "a little kid," but launches immediately into his next thought. Although marking the select does not require frame-accurate precision, take a few moments before executing the next step.

9   Cue the playhead to the point after Mitch says, "kid," and before he starts his next sentence.

One frame of pause is there. You want to cue the playhead on that "silent" frame. Final Cut Pro is an inclusive editor, which means that the frame your playhead is parked on is the frame that receives the edit point. The frames after the playhead are trimmed away.

10 When the playhead is accurately cued, press O to mark the end point of the range.

With the new range marked, you are ready to pull this select. The Favorite status of the rating system is great for this. And it requires only a simple key press.

11 Click the Favorite button (the green star) or press F to set the marked range as a favorite.

A green stripe appears along the top of the clip's filmstrip within the range to identify it as a favorite. You will also find new metadata added in the list view.

12 In the list view, click the disclosure triangle next to **MVI_1042** to display the clip's tags.

A new tag, Favorite, appears in the list below the keywords that were applied automatically by Final Cut Pro. Let's use the Notes field to add some topical words for later searching.

13 Click the text field at the intersection of the Favorite row and the Notes column, and then type *passion when kid*. Press Return.

You're done identifying that range, so let's move on to the next clip, **MVI_1043**.

NOTE ▶ Between Notes and Start, drag the column header divider to the right to open more space for the Notes column.

14 With clip **MVI_1043** selected in the list, locate the start of the phrase, "One thing that is interesting."

Mitch mutters an extended "uhhh" here. Leave that in for now.

15 With the playhead cued before Mitch says, "Uhhh. One thing," press I to mark the start point for the range.

16 To set the end point, cue to after Mitch says, "Frame of what we're shooting. So..."

This is another tricky point to set because Mitch quickly continues with the next sentence, but keep the "So" in the clip for now.

17 Press O to mark the end point, and then press F to rate this sound bite as a favorite.

18 In the Notes column for this favorite, type *imagery technical pilot framing*.

This clip has another possible sound bite at its end. Let's also mark that as a favorite.

19 Find and mark a start point before Mitch says, "As I'm technically".

20 Find and mark an end point after Mitch says, "experiencing. So...". Press F to mark this range as a favorite.

Before you mark the rest of the sound bites, you should understand some additional facts about ratings.

▶ **Favorites Aren't Always Favorites**

Some editors have observed that a favorite is not necessarily going to become a used sound bite, so applying a Favorite tag is too strong a descriptor. Other editors have suggested that the favorites rating process yields lots of favorites with no real ranking of strong versus weak sound bites. However, actual workflow analysis indicates that pulling selects using favorites results in roughly the same number of clips as a traditional approach to choosing selects. And while the traditional select method deletes clips no longer considered selects from the Timeline, a favorited clip may just as easily be removed from the Timeline, yet remain a favorite for easy recall if needed. The traditionally selected clip, not so much.

Unrating a Favorite

How do you clear a favorite? You unrate it. Remember, every clip is imported as unrated. While this default rating will come in handy when sorting and filtering later, let's experiment with a clip to see it in action.

1   In the Libraries pane, select the GoPro event.

2   In the Browser, select the **GOPR1857** clip, and press F to favorite this clip.

    The green favorite stripe appears at the top of the filmstrip.

    To remove this favorite rating, you simply unrate the clip by pressing U. But let's explore unrating a range in a bit more detail. You currently have the entire clip rated as a favorite, but the second half of the clip has unnecessary content depicting passengers holding an iPhone and iPad. Let's unrate that superfluous section.

3   Using the I and O keys, set a range that includes the iPhone and iPad users intruding on the shot.

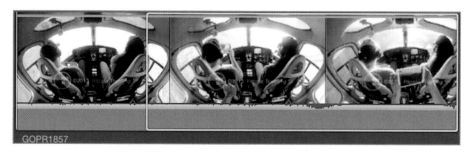

4   Press U to unrate that range's content.

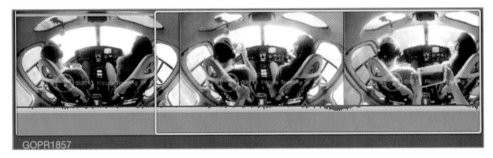

The green stripe is removed from the range.

Rejecting Clips

Maybe you want to be more assertive in marking a portion of a clip's contents as unusable. The Rejected rating is what you need, and it's appropriately assigned to the Delete key. But don't fear, you are not about to delete clips or source media files, just hide them from view.

> **NOTE** ▸ The Delete key may also be known as the Backspace key or the Big Delete key. In our context, "Delete key" does not refer to the small, forward delete key found on full-size or extended keyboards.

1   With **GOPR1857**'s unrated range selected, press Delete.

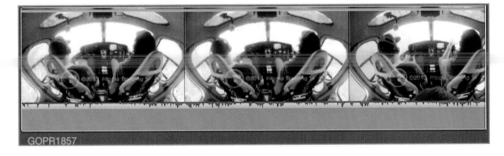

Although it doesn't look like much happened, the rejected range has been hidden from view.

2   Skim to the end of the clip, and you will find that the iPhone and iPad section is gone.

The Browser defaults to hiding rejected portions of clips. Let's reconfigure the Browser to display all ratings.

In the Browser, a filter pop-up menu is currently set to Hide Rejected.

3   In the filter pop-up menu, choose All Clips.

Now the range you rejected a moment ago reappears with a red stripe across the top of its filmstrip. Also, in the list view, notice that the **GOPR1857** clip has a listing for a rejected range.

4   In the Browser's list view, click the **GOPR1857** clip's listing.

What if you wanted to unrate that rejected portion because you've changed your mind? First you would need to select the previously marked range. The listed ratings will help you do so.

5   In the list view for GOPR1857, select the Rejected rating.

The filmstrip range is marked for the duration of the rejected rating.

6   Press U to unrate this range in the clip.

The Rejected rating in the list view is removed.

As you just saw in the last three steps, rejecting a clip or range of a clip does not delete the clip as you were able to unrate the rejected range. Pressing the Delete key simply assigns a rejected rating. With the Browser set to filter out rejected clips/ranges, your Browser is visually decluttered of distractions to help you focus on finding the story.

Exercise 3.3.2
Customizing a Favorite

In addition to adding metadata in the Notes field, you may rename the favorite text tag for each subclip you create. This change will not affect the clip's name. This is only a metadata change within Final Cut Pro.

1   In the list view of the Interview Keyword Collection, locate the Favorite tags for clip
    MVI_1043.

2   Click the text next to the first listed favorite.

    NOTE ▶ Clicking toward the first letter of the tag selects the field for editing.

3   In the text field, type *image in the frame*, and press Return.

4   Replace the second favorite text with *technically flying in awe*.

Just like that you've added more custom clip metadata that will pay off during your edit.

Adding More Metadata

Now it's time to customize the remaining interview metadata. The following table lists the start and end points for favorite ranges you should apply to each sound bite. You will also find notes to apply to each favorite. If you wish, you may also customize the Favorite tag for each subclip. Use the list or filmstrip views, or the inspector to complete this exercise.

Keyword Collection: 5D-7D

Clip	Start	End	Notes
MVI_1044	Start of clip	opener for me	new discovery
MVI_1045	Every time we maybe	see or capture	crest reveal don't know capture
MVI_1046	At the end of the day	adventure I went on	wow look what I saw
MVI_1055	The love of flight	uh, so (end of clip)	really the passion is

Reference 3.4
Search, Sort, and Filter

Whether you use keywords, ratings, notes, or a combination of the three to add information about clips, you are already well on your way to enjoying the metadata backbone of Final Cut Pro. For years, editors have tried to cram as much metadata as possible into a clip's filename, with sometimes befuddling results. With Final Cut Pro, we are now at the point where a clip's name may actually become irrelevant during the edit.

The search, sort, and filter features allow an editor to quickly find a clip based on camera metadata, Final Cut Pro metadata, and user-added metadata. Here are a few of examples of each metadata type:

Camera	Final Cut Pro	User
Frame rate	People detection	Ratings
Frame size	Shot detection	Notes
Recording date	Analysis keywords	Keywords

Sorting Clips

The Filter pop-up menu provides fast ways to sort your clips, including:

▶ All Clips: Displays all clips in the selected library, event, or collection

▶ Hide Rejected: Displays only clips rated as favorite or unrated

▶ No Ratings or Keywords: Displays clips that are unrated or do not have any keywords

▶ Favorites: Displays only clips rated as favorite

▶ Rejected: Displays only clips rated as rejected

The Filter pop-up menu defaults to Hide Rejected to help you hide the distraction of unusable content, while displaying the good to great content. Every editing project may require several approaches to finding the best B-roll and sound bites. Maybe an editor starts by removing the unusable content. Or, as you have already done in this lesson, you began by rating the sound bite selects as favorites. Either approach gets you down to the best part of the clips.

Searching Metadata

The search field in the Browser allows you to perform basic text searches.

The text entered in this field searches against the following metadata fields:

▶ Clip name

▶ Notes

▶ Reel

▶ Scene

▶ Take

▶ Markers

Applying Filters

But there is more to the search field. Clicking the magnifying glass opens a Filter HUD in which you can set additional search criteria, available by clicking the Add Rule (+) button. Here is a breakdown of the rule categories and criteria available in this HUD:

▶ Text: See the preceding section "Searching Metadata."

▶ Ratings: Displays clips that are favorited or rejected

▶ Media: Displays clips that include video with audio, video only, audio only, or still images

▶ Type: Displays items that are auditions, synchronized, compound, multicam, layered graphic, or projects

► Stabilization: Displays clips that have excessive camera shake

► Keywords: Displays clips that contain all or any of the selected keywords

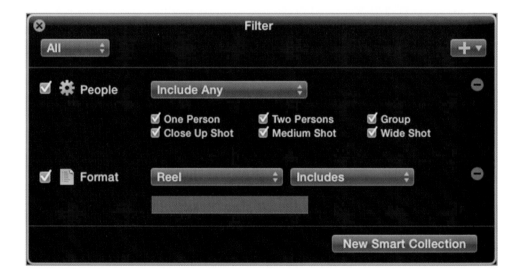

► People: Displays clips that contain all or any of the selected analysis keywords

► Format: Displays clips that include text that matches the Reel, Scene, Take, Audio Output Channels (number), Frame Size, Video Frame Rate, Audio Sample Rate, Camera Name, or Camera Angle fields

▶ Date: Displays clips in which the content was created or the clip was imported on a certain date or within a date range

▶ Roles: Displays clips assigned specific roles

Most of these filter rules allow you to perform inverse or negative searches of the set criteria (is not, does not include, and so on). Also, the Filter window itself offers a rule with two settings: The pop-up menu at the upper-left permits you to choose All or Any.

▶ All: All active criteria must be met for a clip to be displayed in the results.

▶ Any: If a clip matches any of the criteria, the clip will be displayed as a search result.

NOTE ▶ Setting the menu to Any typically yields more results than filtering by All.

Creating Smart Collections

Smart Collections are dynamic collections, unlike the static Keyword Collections. Keyword Collections are collections only if you manually add the same keyword to multiple clips, while Smart Collections automatically gather clips that meet all or some criteria you set.

For example, when applying analysis keywords, Final Cut Pro adds keywords to the clips based upon an analysis of their content. Then, Final Cut Pro creates Smart Collections to organize the analysis results. Although this automation is turned off by default, you may activate it at anytime during your workflow.

New clips imported to an event automatically appear in Smart Collections with matching criteria. This automation reduces the time and energy spent on organizing events. Through the use of a template library or event, an editor can save time by presetting Smart Collections on empty events.

The power and efficiency of the Filter window comes together with the New Smart Collection button at the lower-right of the window.

Clicking the New Smart Collection button creates a Smart Collection, a saved version of the Filter HUD's search parameters.

The collection appears in the Libraries pane, assigned to the active event. You may alter the criteria of the collection by double-clicking the Smart Collection's icon in the library.

Exercise 3.4.1
Filtering an Event

Now that you have a few ratings, keywords, and notes applied to some clips, you are almost ready to edit. But you're "almost ready" because you still need to search, sort, and filter your clip metadata to find the favored sound bites or B-roll gems among hundreds or thousands of clips.

1   In the Libraries pane, select the B-roll Keyword Collection.

This collection contains the B-roll footage you organized earlier by applying a combination of ratings, keywords, and notes. The Filter HUD provides the tools to zero in on those clips you'll need while editing.

2   In the Browser, from the Filter pop-up menu, choose All Clips.

3   In the search field, click the magnifying glass to open the Filter HUD.

Let's take the Filter HUD for a spin, experimenting with the different criteria settings.

4   In the Filter HUD's text field, type *heli* (an abbreviation for helicopter).

Immediately, the Browser updates to display the search results. They include all the clips in the selected collection that have the text *heli* in a text-searchable field. Now you'll locate any clips tagged as B-roll that were also sourced from an iPhone. These search terms exist as keywords in the library.

5   In the Filter HUD, click the Add Rule (+) button, and choose Keywords while watching the Browser's contents.

The clips displayed in the Browser do not change, but look at the added rule. The rule may be interpreted as, "Display all clips containing the text 'heli' and any of the keywords checkmarked below." Let's see what happens when you change just one small parameter.

6   In the Filter HUD, change the Keywords pop-up menu to Include All.

All the Browser clips disappear because no clip meets the criteria of having the "heli" text, and all the selected keywords.

7 In the Keywords rule, deselect all checkboxes except the B-roll and iPhone keywords.

Your search still returns no clips. But you know that you do have iPhone B-roll clips. To return useful results in this search, the iPhone footage needs to be tagged as B-roll.

8 In the Libraries pane, select the iPhone Keyword Collection.

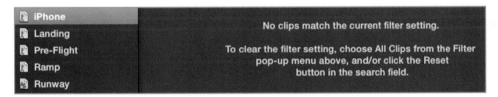

What happened to your iPhone clips? They're hidden because you have a search in progress, as shown in the search field at the upper-right of the Browser. The three iPhone clips do not match the search criteria. You'll need to clear the search field before you can proceed.

9 In the search field, click the reset button (X) to clear the field and the search criteria.

The iPhone clips return to view. The three clips in the iPhone Keyword Collection are currently tagged only with the keyword iPhone and not B-roll.

10 In the Browser, select the three iPhone clips, and drag them to the B-roll collection in the Libraries pane.

Now these three iPhone clips appear in both the B-roll and iPhone Keyword Collections. This is one of the big advantages of the database architecture in Final Cut Pro. Clips may exist in as many collections of a library as you want without duplicating the source media file.

▶ Using Inter-Library Copying

As you've learned, source media files needn't be duplicated when placed in multiple collections, even when those collections are within the same library. However, dragging a Browser clip from an event of one library to an event in another library does display a media management dialog with some additional options.

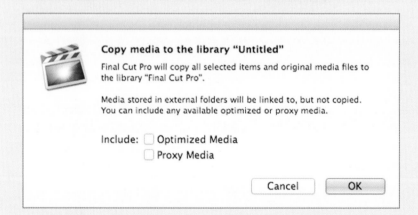

You'll learn more about this and other media management options in Lesson 9.

Exercise 3.4.2
Working with Smart Collections

With all the searching, sorting, and filtering power available in Final Cut Pro, you have the tools to create complex searches you can save for later referral during an edit. But saving a search as a collection is not the end of the story. Saved search collections are Smart Collections that automatically contain any clip in the event that matches the collection's search criteria.

To see this in action, let's create a Smart Collection that automatically collects any audio-only clips contained in the event. This is a very handy collection that some editors have built into a library template for use on every editing project.

1   In the Lifted library, Control-click the Primary Media event, and from the shortcut menu, choose New Smart Collection.

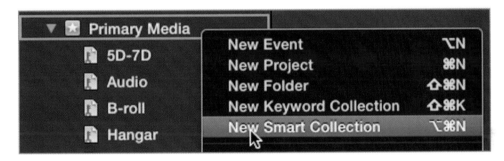

The new Smart Collection is created with Untitled as the default name. The Name field is highlighted and ready for you to input a more meaningful name.

2   Rename the collection *Audio Only*, and press Return.

3   Double-click the Audio Only Smart Collection to edit its filter criteria.

4   In the Filter HUD, from the Add Rule (+) pop-up menu, choose Media Type.

5   Using the Media pop-up menus, create this criteria for the collection: "Collect any clip that is an audio-only clip."

Immediately, the two music clips appear in the Audio Only collection. However, you may wonder why creating this collection was useful when an Audio Keyword Collection already existed.

6 In the Libraries pane, look at the icons for the Audio Keyword Collection and the Audio Only Smart Collection.

One looks like a key while the other resembles a gear, respectively. Clips must be added manually to the Keyword Collection. You are the key to creating Keyword Collections. When any audio-only clip is imported into the event, that clip automatically appears in the Audio Only Smart Collection. Final Cut Pro does the grinding gear work, processing the metadata. Let's see that in action.

7 To the left of the toolbar, click the Media Import button.

8 In the Media Import window, navigate to the FCPX Media folder you previously downloaded for this book.

9 Inside the FCPX Media folder, navigate to the LV1 > LV SFX folder, and then select the **Helicopter Start Idle Takeoff** audio file.

10 Click the Import Selected button.

11 Set the Import Options dialog as shown, and then click Import.

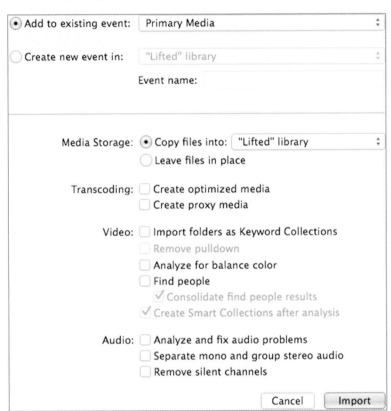

The import happens very quickly, so you can immediately verify the results.

12 Click between the Audio Keyword Collection and the Audio Only Smart Collection while noting the difference in the Browser.

The audio-only sound effect clip you imported was automatically placed into the Smart Collection. So with some pre-post planning, you could create a series of Smart Collections in a library template that would auto-collect clips based on a wide range of metadata.

Exercise 3.4.3
Detecting People and Shot Composition

Some analysis tools can create their own Smart Collections. One tool that performs two types of analyses is Find People, and you can apply it at any time during your workflow.

This tool is extremely sophisticated, although the results may appear obvious in this exercise. The goal is to understand how to access the analysis tools on existing clips and the potential results when performing a Find People analysis.

For this exercise, you will perform a Find People analysis. What you need to know is that you should also select the "Create Smart Collections after analysis" options. Without the Create Smart Collections option selected, the results will not be automatically visible.

1   In the Primary Media event, select the Interview Keyword Collection.

2   In the Browser, select clips **MVI_1042** through **MVI_1055**.

3   Control-click any one of the selected clips, and from the shortcut menu, choose "Analyze and Fix."

A dialog appears with very familiar options and one extra option. The extra option is to perform an analysis for stabilization and rolling shutter.

4   In the "Analyze and Fix" dialog, select "Find people" and "Create Smart Collections after analysis," and then click OK.

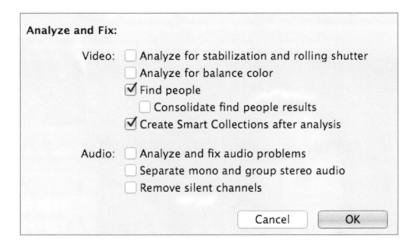

When a background task such as an analysis is underway, a progress report appears to the left of the Dashboard.

The Background Tasks indicator showing the progress is actually a button you can click to display more information.

5   In the Dashboard, click the Background Tasks button.

The Background Tasks HUD appears with more details about the tasks Final Cut Pro is performing behind the scenes.

As the analysis progresses, a People folder appears in the Primary Media event.

6 Click the disclosure triangle to display the People folder's contents.

In its analysis of the selected clips, Final Cut Pro determined that the clips were framing the subject as a medium shot and that the clips contained only one person. Here's a list of the possible results when performing a Find People analysis:

Framing	People
Close Up Shot	One Person
Medium Shot	Two Persons
Wide Shot	Group

These analysis keywords are huge time-savers when deadline is approaching. When you need one more B-roll clip that is a single of the interviewee framed as a wide shot standing next to the helicopter in the hangar recorded on the 5D, you can find it thanks to the user, camera, and Final Cut Pro applied metadata. That's the sweet moment in editing with Final Cut Pro. Think about the story, not the clip.

Reference 3.5
Roles

An additional, even stronger set of metadata controls are available in Final Cut Pro: roles. Roles enable *grouping* inside an editing project. Roles may be used to modify Timeline playback, for the organization of similar clips within the Timeline, and to create *stems* on export. Roles allow you to aggregate items such as the primary language audio into one role and the secondary language audio into another role, and then in two simple clicks you are hearing one while disabling the other.

> **NOTE** ▸ Roles, like keywording, yield greater benefits the earlier you add them to your workflow.

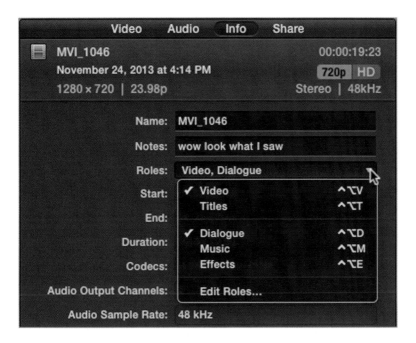

Roles are divided into two groups: Video and Audio. As shown in the preceding image, some default roles are created for you in every editing project. You can manually add both roles and subroles to this list. Subroles are specialized subsets of the roles. Under the Titles role, you may want to create a subrole for the primary distribution language and additional subroles for the secondary distribution languages. When you're ready to distribute your finished edit, you will then be able to quickly switch from the graphics intended for one language to the set of graphics intended for the second language.

Exercise 3.5.1
Assigning Roles

Roles, when assigned to Browser clips, carry into editing. Roles may assist during the edit by, for example, allowing you to disable all sound bite audio when you need to focus on the ambient sound. A simple, deselected checkbox and you've got the mix-minus you need. In the Browser or during the edit, roles can be assigned to a clip or a batch selection of clips. Before you start assigning roles, let's look at how to create them.

1   Choose Modify > Edit Roles to open the Role Editor.

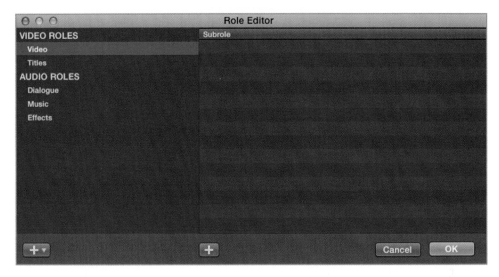

For this editing project, you will be utilizing the Video, Dialogue, Music, and Effects roles. During the edit, you will also isolate the natural, or ambient, sound recorded by the cameras' onboard microphones. These "nats" audio clips add to the realism and help draw the viewer into the visuals. The nats will be treated separately from any sound effects added later.

2   In the Role Editor, click the Add Role (+) pop-up menu to add a role.

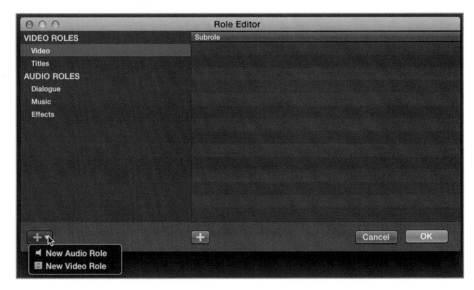

3   From the pop-up menu, choose New Audio Role.

The new role appears and is awaiting a new name.

4   Rename it *Natural Sound*, and press Return. Click OK.

With the roles set up, let's assign them to batches of clips using multiple methods. We'll start by using a menu command.

5   In the Libraries pane, select the Primary Media event's Audio Only Smart Collection.

6   In the Browser list view, select the Helicopter sound effect. Because this is a sound effect, assign the Effects role to the clip.

7   Choose Modify > Assign Roles > Effects.

To see that the clip received the role assignment, check the inspector.

8   Open the inspector, if necessary, by clicking the Inspector button, or by pressing Command-4.

9   Click the Info button to open the Info inspector, if necessary.

The Info inspector displays some basic metadata about the selected clip.

10   Verify that the Roles pop-up menu is set to Effects.

Assigning Additional Roles

You're now ready to assign additional roles. Leave the Info inspector open—you can assign roles and verify their assignment in the inspector.

1   In the Audio Only Smart Collection, select the two music clips, Tears of Joy-Long and Tears of Joy-Short.

In the Info inspector, the top portion recognizes that you are inspecting two items. The roles are currently set to Dialogue.

2   Using the Roles pop-up menu in the Inspector, assign the two clips to the Music role by choosing Music from the pop-up menu.

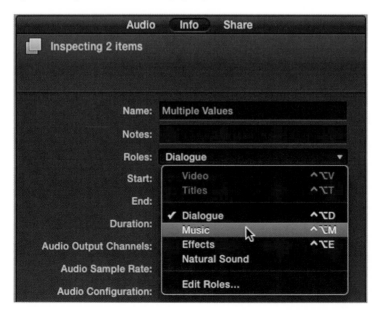

With the music clips, only one role is needed as the clips are audio only. Let's take a look at the B-roll clips, which are assigned Video and Audio roles.

3   In the Libraries pane, select the B-roll collection.

4   In the Browser, select one clip, and then press Command-A to select all the B-roll clips.

   The Inspector recognizes that you are about to modify multiple clips.

5   In the Info inspector, from the pop-up menu, choose the Video and the Natural Sound roles to assign those roles to the selected clips.

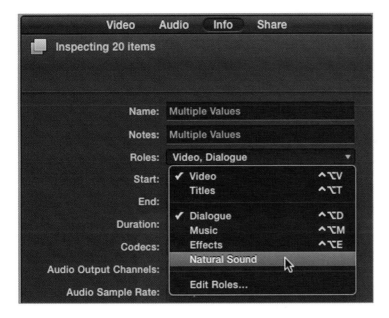

Let's also take this opportunity to get granular with the metadata. Since you have all the B-roll clips selected, you can create and assign a B-roll Video subrole.

6   In the Info inspector, from the Roles pop-up menu, choose Edit Roles to open the Roles Editor.

You will be adding a subrole to the Video role, so verify that Video is selected.

7   With the Video Role selected, click the Add Subrole (+) button at the lower-center of the window.

8   Rename the subrole *B-roll*, and press Return. Click OK to close the window.

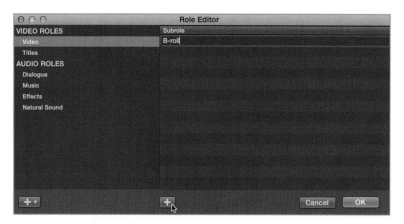

9   To assign the new Video subrole to the selected Browser clips, from the Roles pop-up menu in the Inspector, choose Video > B-roll.

You have one more assignment to make for the interview clips. You will also process these as a batch.

10 In the Libraries pane, select the Interview collection.

11 In the Browser, select one of the interview clips, and then press Command-A to select all the clips in the collection.

12 In the Info inspector, verify that Video and Dialogue are selected.

That's all the clips you need to modify for now. You've successfully assigned metadata to your clips. In Lesson 4, you will utilize that metadata to start your edit.

Lesson Review

1. When applying keywords to a clip, may keywords be overlapped?

2. Which inspector lets you add notes to a clip?

3. All clips start with which rating assigned?

4. What default filter setting prevents Rejected clip ranges from appearing in the Browser?

5. You are trying to locate a clip you imported into the library. How can you locate it?

6. What procedure is necessary to search an event using a combination of keywords?

7. How do you edit the criteria rules for an existing Smart Collection?

8. At what point in the workflow may a clip be assigned a role?

Answers

1. Yes

2. The Info inspector

3. Unrated

4. Hide Rejected

5. In the Libraries pane, select the Library. From the Filter pop-up menu, choose All Clips. Clear the Browser's search field.

6. Keyword combinations are searchable only by clicking the magnifying glass in the search field and using the Keywords criteria rule in the Filter HUD.

7. In the Libraries pane, double-click the Smart Collection.

8. Clips may be assigned a role at any time in the workflow. However, roles assigned to clips shortly after import are carried with the clip throughout the editing workflow.

Lesson **4**

Making the First Edit

After importing and organizing, the story elements sit as clips in the library, ready for editing. The editing phase of the post-production workflow involves crafting a story from the library clips into a project or timeline.

The first edit, or *rough cut*, of a project involves some or most of the major tasks from the remainder of the post-workflow. An edit of the project is created; it's trimmed down for timing, pacing, and conciseness; additional elements such as music may be added; and then the project is shared out of Final Cut Pro for client or producer approval.

You are ready to embark on the post-workflow with the Lifted project. In this lesson, you will assemble the interview sound bites and the helicopter B-roll to form the story. You'll trim the edits to remove any extraneous content, and then add a music clip. Lastly, you will export this first edit of the project as a file that is playable on a Mac, PC, smartphone, or tablet.

GOALS

► Create a project

► Add and rearrange clips within a primary storyline

► Ripple and Roll trim clips

► Blade, replace with gap, ripple delete, and join through edit

► Perform connect edits

► Create and edit in a connected storyline

► Adjust audio levels

► Share the project to a media file

Reference 4.1
Understanding a Project

The editing phase occurs in a *project*—a timeline-based container of sequentially arranged clips that tell a story. Projects are simple or complex timelines depending on the technical depth of the story.

Finished project for Lesson 4

Projects are stored within individual events in a library: the super-container of your Final Cut Pro editing project that makes loading/unloading and transporting all your clips, events, and projects for a show, client, or movie much more convenient.

Events may contain as many projects as you need. For example, a news editor may need three projects for the VO (voiceover), the package, and the teaser. A documentary editor could easily use 10 to 30 projects when breaking down an edit by segment, creating a variety of video news releases, posting online teasers, and developing various versions of the documentary based on running time and/or content.

You already have the Lifted library with two events of clips. Let's edit.

Exercise 4.1.1
Creating a Project

To start the first edit, you must create the project. A couple of clicks and you've got yourself a starting project.

1   In the Lifted library, Control-click the Primary Media event, and from the shortcut menu, choose New Project.

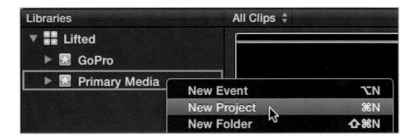

The Project Properties dialog opens to the default automatic settings.

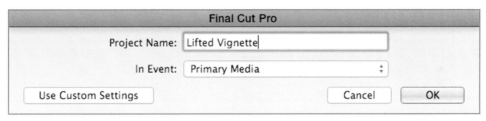

NOTE ▶ If your dialog opens to the custom settings, click the Use Automatic Settings button.

2   For the Project Name, enter *Lifted Vignette*.

3   Click the In Event pop-up menu.

In Event specifies the event in which to save the project you are creating. The pop-up menu displays the events available in the open libraries.

4   Ensure that the In Event pop-up menu is set to Primary Media, and click OK.

The project is created and saved in the Primary Media event.

5   If necessary, in the Lifted library, select the Primary Media event.

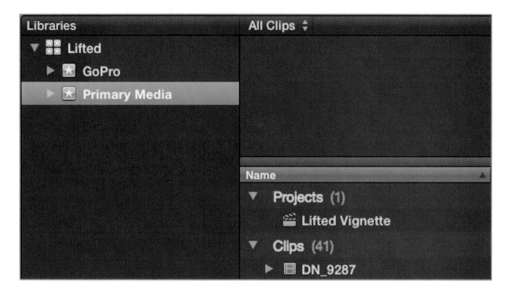

The project appears at the top of the Browser.

6   Double-click the project to open it in the Timeline.

The project displayed in the Browser

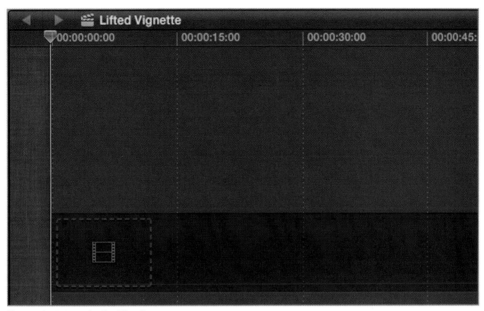

The project open in the Timeline

NOTE ▶ See Lesson 10 for more information about the automatic vs. manual project settings.

Reference 4.2
Defining the Primary Storyline

Every project in Final Cut Pro is based around the primary storyline, identified by the dark stripe across the Timeline. The primary storyline contains the clips that drive your project. For a documentary, a combination of sound bites and a narrator's VO could constitute the primary storyline. For a project that starts with a montage, you could consider placing the music intro in the storyline followed by the on-camera host. The primary storyline is flexible content-wise.

By default, clips in the primary storyline interact with each other and incoming clips. This interaction is similar to that of two magnets: attraction or repulsion.

Dragging a clip to the end of a project

The storyline appends the clip to the project

When you drag a new clip from the Browser to the far right of the project, that clip is attracted to the end of the primary storyline, and "magnetically" snaps to the preceding clip.

Dragging a clip to a project for insertion between two storyline clips

Positioning the clip on the storyline clips reveals an insert bar, and a gap for the clip is created.

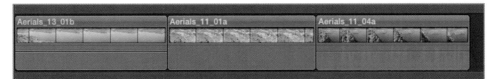

The clip is wedged between the storyline clips.

Dragging a clip between two existing clips creates a repulsion that pushes the existing clips far enough apart to insert the new clip.

These two behaviors form the basic concepts of the magnetic storyline: As you add clips, shift clips around to change their order, or remove clips, the magnetic storyline keeps the clips snapped together, ensuring that the clips play back-to-back in a continuous stream.

Knowing the basic concepts of a primary storyline as the magnetic backbone of a project, you can start assembling your first edit.

Exercise 4.2.1
Appending the Primary Storyline

You are ready to edit your first clips into the Lifted Vignette project. Because this project is sound bite–driven, you will edit the sound bites into the primary storyline. Let's first alter the interface so you can see as many clips and notes as possible in the Browser.

1   If necessary, in the Browser, select the list view.

2   With the Interview collection selected in the Libraries pane, click the Hide Libraries button.

3   Drag the toolbar down to create more vertical room in the Browser.

Expanding each clip listing reveals the favorites you marked previously, along with the notes you applied to each clip. You'll use these to create the rough cut of the sound bites. Remember that "great passion" sound bite that Mitch started with when you were marking favorites? Let's search for it.

4   In the Browser search field, type *passion*.

As you begin to type, the Browser updates immediately with the matching results: **MVI_1042** and **MVI_1055**.

5   In the Browser select **MVI_1042**, and skim the clip to review the marked favorite.

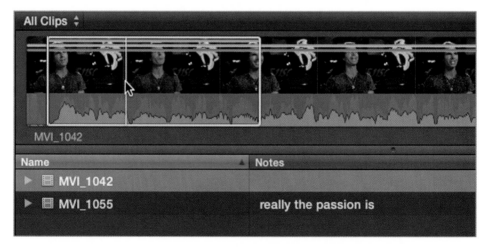

As you skim the clip, notice that its audio is pitch corrected, which allows you to quickly review the clip's contents at variable speeds while maintaining the aural clarity of its contents.

NOTE ▶ You may also review the clip by pressing the navigation controls: the Spacebar and the J, K, L keys.

Your search results include a second clip tagged with the word *passion*.

6   In the Browser, play **MVI_1055**, and review its contents.

With a little *trimming* later in the edit, both sound bites could fit back to back into your storyline. Let's edit these into the project as the first two sound bites.

7   In the Browser, select the favorite with the "passion when kid" note listed under **MVI_1042**.

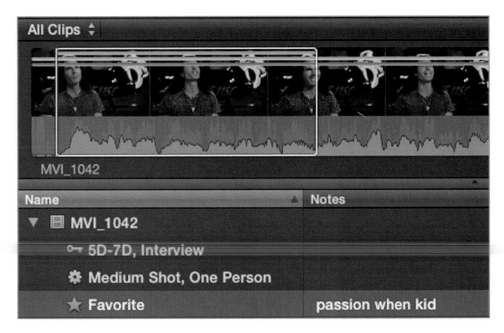

8   Click the Append button, or press E, to add this clip selection to the project.

The clip's selection is edited into the primary storyline. The E stands for "End." No matter where the skimmer or playhead is currently located in the project, you can press E to quickly edit the active Browser selection to the end of the storyline.

Currently, the playhead is at the end of MVI_1042. The playhead always jumps to the end of the clip you append edited to the project. This default playhead behavior in Final Cut Pro anticipates your next edit. But what happens if you move the playhead before the next append edit? Let's find out.

9   Move the playhead to the left by clicking the empty gray area above MVI_1042.

This cues the playhead over MVI_1042, which you can see in the Viewer. Now you will append edit with the playhead placed in the middle of MVI_1042 and observe the results.

NOTE ▶ Depending on your display's resolution, your clip may appear short and shoved to the left of the interface. After clicking to move the playhead in the previous step, press Shift-Z to fit the project within the Timeline. Alternatively, you could drag the Zoom slider at right to change the zoom setting.

10   Returning to the Browser, notice the Used entry under MVI_1042.

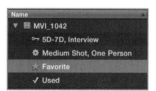

The Used listing identifies the clip's selection used in the open project. As that was the only favorite for that clip, you will go to the next clip for the next edit.

11 In the Browser, select the "really the passion is" favorite in the **MVI_1055** clip, and then press E to append this clip to the end of the storyline.

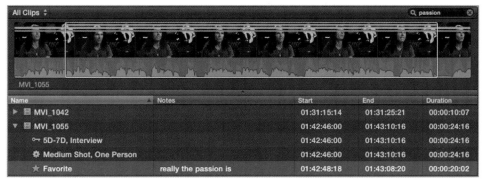

Clip selected in the Browser

Clip append edited into the primary storyline

That was quick. The clip was edited to the end of the storyline immediately following **MVI_1042**. The playhead's position had no impact on the append edit. You are two sound bites into the edit with several more to go. You could continue with this one-at-a-time approach to editing, but Final Cut Pro offers a slightly faster edit method.

NOTE ▶ If the previous edit caused the **MVI_1042** clip to not be visible in the Timeline, you need to change the zoom setting. Click once in the Timeline, and press Shift-Z or adjust the Zoom control at right.

Appending a Batch Edit to the Primary Storyline

You can use the append function to edit more than one clip at a time into the primary storyline. As you are building your first edit, you will be looking for your next clip in the Browser. Append allows you to remain in the Browser and storyboard the next few clips with one edit. This batch editing technique is a fast and simple way to edit several clips into your project at once.

1   In the Browser, switch to filmstrip view.

Currently, you are looking at two clips that were identified in your earlier search. You'll need to clear the search field to reveal the rest of the sound bites.

2   In the Browser, click the Reset button (X) in the search field to clear the previous search.

The remaining clips in the Interview collection appear. You may select multiple sound bites to append at one time, and the order in which you select the clips is the order they will be edited into the project.

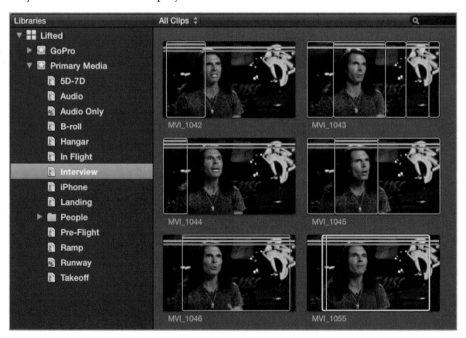

3   If desired, you may increase the size of the filmstrips by changing the Clip Appearance's Clip Height slider.

4   In the Browser's filmstrip view, click within the first green range in **MVI_1043**.

The favorites you marked earlier appear as green stripes that you may use to quickly select the favorited ranges.

5   Command-click the following clips in this order to add them to the selection: **MVI_1046**, **MVI_1045**, and **MVI_1044**.

6   Press E to perform an append edit.

The clips appear at the end of the project in the same order you selected them in the Browser.

7   To see the entire project within the Timeline, click once in the Timeline gray area, and press Shift-Z.

> ▶ **How Did Final Cut Pro Know Where to Put the Clips?**
>
> If you have prior editing experience, you may have noticed that you didn't need to assign tracks, position the playhead, or set a start point to make this edit. The append edit function efficiently takes legacy overwrite editing to the next level.

Playing the Project

To play the project, you may press the Home key to cue the playhead to the beginning of the Timeline; but on Apple Wireless Keyboards and laptops, the Home key is not labeled.

1   Hold down the fn (function) key at the lower left of keyboard, and then press the Left Arrow key to simulate pressing the Home key on your keyboard.

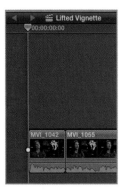

The playhead is now cued to the beginning of the project.

2   Press the Spacebar to start playback.

Playback will stop when the playhead reaches the end of the project.

NOTE ▶ When loop playback is enabled (by choosing View > Playback > Loop Playback), your project will not stop automatically but will repeat over and over until you manually stop playback.

Exercise 4.2.2
Rearranging Clips in the Primary Storyline

The sound bites don't quite flow yet. It's time to rearrange them into an order that more fully supports your storyline. Working in a storyline makes such changes incredibly easy. Just drag a clip to a new location in the Timeline, wait for the interface to preview the results, and then release the mouse button.

1   In the project, select the fourth clip, **MVI_1046**.

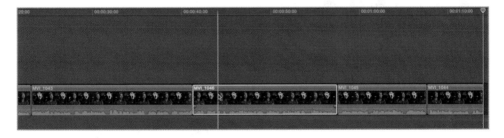

The playhead must be located over this clip to preview it. Your playhead is currently located at the end of the project. You do not need to move the playhead because the skimmer relocates the playhead if the skimmer is visible when you start playback.

2   Move the mouse pointer slightly to verify that the skimmer is active.

The skimmer extends vertically up to the timestrip across the Timeline pane, the same as the playhead; however, the skimmer does not have an arrowhead on top as does the playhead.

Skimmer (left) compared to playhead (right)

3   Press the Spacebar to play the clip.

The playhead relocates to the skimmer's position and the clip plays. **MVI_1046** starts with Mitch saying, "At the end of the day." It sounds as if that phrase should be placed nearer the end of the storyline.

4   Drag **MVI_1046** toward the end of the storyline, but don't release the mouse button just yet.

5   Position the clip so that a blue clip box appears in the primary storyline after **MVI_1044**. Release the mouse button.

MVI_1046 is edited in as the last clip in your storyline.

Some extra words, phrases, and syllables remain in your clips. One clip may cut Mitch off too early. That's OK. We'll trim those troubled frames later in this lesson. For now, let's try moving another clip in the storyline.

6   Locate **MVI_1044**, which is now the second clip from the end of the project. Drag the clip between **MVI_1043** and **MVI_1045**.

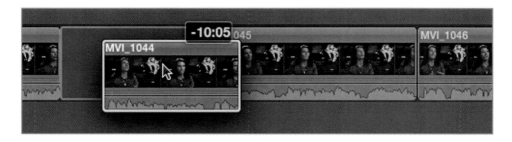

As you drag **MVI_1044** between the two clips, an insert bar appears. If you continue to hold the clip in that position, **MVI_1045** will slide to the right to allow **MVI_1044** to drop into place. The magnetic storyline enables these quick, reorganizing edits as you explore your story flow.

NOTE ▶ While dragging a clip, the delta, or timing change, of the clip's position within the Timeline appears above the clip.

Reference 4.3
Modifying Clips in the Primary Storyline

When reviewing the storyline's flow, an additional clip or two may fill in story gaps. The flow may be disrupted by extra words or sounds at the start or end of a sound bite. Thanks to the magnetic properties of the storyline, the solutions to these problems are painless.

The append edit added the selected clip or clips to the end of the storyline. Sometimes a clip needs to be placed between those appended storyline clips; an insert edit will wedge a browser clip between two storyline clips.

The trimming tools allows you to remove, or add, an extra breath, sound, word, or movement from or to a clip. Final Cut Pro includes several trimming tools. The basic trim tool you'll learn in this lesson is called ripple trim.

The ripple trim allows you to remove media from a project clip, frame by frame if desired. The ripple trim also allows you to insert media to a project clip.

Whether you're performing an insert edit or a ripple trim in the storyline, the adjoining clips in the storyline stick together. Remove a clip and the subsequent clips move forward and hook up to the previous clip. Insert a clip between others and the subsequent clips move right to make room.

Exercise 4.3.1
Performing Insert Edits

When you dragged **MVI_1044** to its new location, you performed an insert edit. Clips to the right of the new clip slid right to make room, while clips to the left retained their positions. Previously, you marked another sound bite as a select that needs to be added to the project. In this exercise, you will insert this clip into the project, but without dragging it.

1   In the Browser, switch to thumbnail view, then perform a search for *awe*.

The search identifies one clip, **MVI_1043**. The filmstrip displays two favorite ranges within the clip.

2   In the Browser, skim the second favorite of **MVI_1043**.

Depending on your display's resolution, you may have difficulty skimming the clip at a speed that makes the audio intelligible. Expanding the filmstrip by zooming in will help you skim the clip.

3   Drag the Zoom slider to right until the zoom scale reads 5s.

4   Skim the second favorite in **MVI_1043** again.

At this scale setting, each thumbnail in the filmstrip represents five seconds of source media. This time you can identify the sound bites by listening to the pitch-corrected audio. Notice the torn edge on the left end of the row. That indicates the clip continues from the previous line of thumbnails. The start and end of the clip are represented by a solid edge as shown on the right side of the filmstrip.

5   In the clip's filmstrip, ensure that the second favorite range is selected.

Next, you need to choose where this clip belongs in the storyline by cueing the play-head to the desired location.

6   In the Timeline, skim between **MVI_1043** and **MVI_1044**.

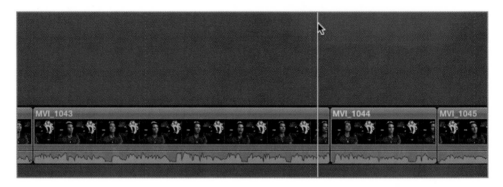

MVI_1043 must be edited between those two clips with frame accuracy. To help you precisely place the playhead on the edit point between the two clips, you can turn on snapping.

At the upper-right of the Timeline locate the Skimming, Audio Skimming, Audio Soloing, and Snapping buttons.

7   If necesssary, click the Snapping button to turn on snapping, or press N.

8   Skim over several clips and edit points within the project.

Notice that the skimmer jumps to the edit points. To prepare for the insert edit, you need to cue the playhead to the desired edit point.

9 Snap the skimmer to the edit point between **MVI_1043** and **MVI_1044**, then click here to cue the playhead.

NOTE ▶ The edit point between is the start frame of the right clip (the starting clip), and not the end frame of the left clip (the ending clip). A "start bracket" is overlaid on the clip to visually identify that the playhead is on the start frame.

The "L" bracket indicates this frame is the start point.

10 In the Browser, verify that the clip's second range is still selected.

11 In the toolbar, click the Insert edit button, or press W.

The second select of **MVI_1043** is placed into the project between the two storyline clips, and a missing sound bite becomes part of the storyline.

Exercise 4.3.2
Rippling the Primary Storyline

When you pulled your select sound bites in Lesson 3, you included some extraneous material. (The reason you left some extra material in your favorites will become apparent during this exercise.) However, everyday editing is all about trimming down to create a more concise story, or padding the story to extend its length. You will now learn how to use ripple trimming to remove that extra content, and also how to reinsert content when you trim off too much.

NOTE ▶ Because Final Cut Pro is context sensitive, you may not have to activate the Trim tool. The Select tool automatically switches to the Trim tool's ripple function when necessary.

1   Locate the playhead at the end point of **MVI_1055**, the second clip in the project.

Some extra content, where Mitch says, "Uh, so," needs to be trimmed, leaving a new end point after Mitch says, "Whole new look."

Before you perform this bit of clip trimming, zoom in on the edit so that you may operate the tools with greater precision.

2   With your skimmer or playhead cued around the end of **MVI_1055**, press Command-= (equals sign) to zoom into the Timeline.

As you zoom, the thumbnails and waveforms expand to reveal where the trim should occur. The "uhh, so" phrase is displayed as the peaks of waveforms at the end of the clip. Those need to be removed. You can approach this edit in several ways. In this exercise, you will use the ripple trim function without getting the Trim tool.

3   Identify the new end point by cueing the playhead before Mitch says, "uhh, so" at the end of **MVI_1055**.

Locating the playhead at the desired trim point allows you to use snapping to make an exact trim with the default Select tool. This tool automatically changes function based on its location in the Timeline.

4   In the Tools pop-up menu in the toolbar, verify that the Select tool is chosen, or press A.

5   In the Timeline, place the mouse pointer over the end point of the clip.

6   Without clicking, slowly move the mouse pointer back and forth across the edit point between the two clips' edit points.

Notice how the pointer icon changes as the mouse pointer moves from one side of the edit to the other. The changing icon indicates that the Select tool automatically becomes the ripple trim tool.

The ripple trim icon has a small filmstrip that always points toward the clip you will trim. Because you want to change the end point of **MVI_1055**, the filmstrip must point left toward the clip.

7   With the ripple trim's filmstrip pointing toward the left, drag the end of the clip until it snaps to the playhead.

8   Review the edit you completed by playing this portion of the Timeline.

You easily changed the end point of the clip, thereby removing the extraneous content. The ripple trim also moved all the following clips earlier in the Timeline to fill in for the removed content. Now you'll trim off the start of the same clip.

9   Scroll left in the project and adjust the zoom level of the Timeline to see the start point of **MVI_1055**.

10   Play the start of the clip to identify the new start point before Mitch says, "And really the passion."

You will cue the playhead here between Mitch saying, "of film" and "And really." Ideally, you will find a frame for an edit that has the interview subject appearing with eyes open and mouth closed. In this clip, you'll find such a frame just as Mitch finishes the word "film."

11 With the playhead parked at the new start point's location, place the Select tool over the current start point of the clip.

This time, the filmstrip of the ripple trim pointer will point to the right toward **MVI_1055**.

12 Drag the start point of **MVI_1055** and snap it to the playhead.

When ripple trimming a start point, you may notice that the clip to the left appears to move. However, the clip did not move because it still starts at 0:00. As you trimmed content from the beginning of **MVI_1055**, the clip's duration shortened, the following clips rippled left in time, and the Timeline timecode shifted accordingly.

Using the Keyboard to Ripple Trim an End Point

Sometimes the mouse or trackpad does not offer sufficiently fine control to perform a trim without setting an extreme view or altering your System Preferences. Fortunately, you can use keyboard shortcuts for greater precision.

1 Locate the end point of the second, shorter **MVI_1043**; and cue the playhead before Mitch utters an extraneous "so." Ordinarily, you might press Command-= (equals sign) a few times to zoom your view into the edit.

Because you have heard this interview already, you know that Mitch runs words and sentences together, thereby making this edit more difficult. Let's turn to keyboard shortcuts to help trim this clip.

2   Select the end point of the second **MVI_1043**.

With the end point selected, you can use keyboard shortcuts to trim the clip one frame at a time.

3   Press the , (comma) key multiple times to ripple trim, removing content frame by frame.

4   If necessary, press the . (period) key multiple times to insert content frame by frame.

5   Skim to just before the edit point, and then play back the project to check your results.

This trim edit will take a few tries to perfect, but let's leave it for now and move on.

6   Proceed through the project removing extraneous clip content. When you're finished, the project should resemble the following table:

Lifted Vignette Edit in Progress

Clip	Start dialogue	End dialogue
MVI_1042	Flying is	a little kid
MVI_1055	And really the	whole new look
MVI_1043	One thing that	what we're shooting
MVI_1043	As I'm technically	what we're experiencing

Lifted Vignette Edit in Progress

Clip	Start dialogue	End dialogue
MVI_1044	You know it's	opener for me
MVI_1045	Every time we may be	see or capture
MVI_1046	At the end of the day	adventure I went on

NOTE ▸ You may hear a slight click or pop on some of your edits. You'll learn to resolve those errors later in this lesson.

Lifted Vignette in progress

Reference 4.4
Timing the Primary Storyline

Every edit in a project is based upon the primary storyline. Up to this point, the concern has been to place the select sound bites into the project and organize them to reflect the story structure. Now that the structure has been established, the task switches to adjusting the timing and pacing. The sound bites should not be a hailstorm of thoughts spewed at the viewer, but should flow like everyday conversation.

The first technique to pacing the sound bites involves a gap clip, which is an empty clip container in the Timeline. Gap clips may be applied as placeholders until additional material arrives, such as more B-roll content, clips from a hard-to-schedule interview, or a late shipment of second unit content. Gap clips are also used as the spaces, pauses, and breaths that enhance your story flow.

The second technique to pacing the sound bites involves removing segments of a clip or entire clips. The Blade tool segments a clip to remove one or more clip ranges from the project. Each time you blade a clip, you create a *through edit*.

A through edit marks the clip into segments without breaking the clip into two physical clips. If you blade that clip a second time, you mark it into three segments with two through edits. You can rejoin these segments if you inadvertently blade the wrong frame. The repair is called a *join through* edit.

When you are ready to delete a segment, you can do so in one of two ways. Simply pressing the Delete key performs a ripple delete. The selected clip segment is removed, and the subsequent clips slide left to occupy the Timeline position of the deleted segment.

Blade to segment unwanted content

Select segment for removal

Press Delete to ripple delete.

The second delete method is a replace with gap. This deletion, performed by pressing Shift-Delete, removes the selected segment and leaves a gap that occupies its former position in the Timeline. As a result, the following clips do not ripple, but remain in place.

Blade to segment unwanted content.

Select segment for removal.

Press Shift-Delete to replace segment with a gap clip.

Exercise 4.4.1
Inserting a Gap Clip

Currently, your project sound bites are sequenced very tightly. This breathless stream of consciousness does not lend itself to clear storytelling. Let's separate some of these clips so the storytelling relaxes a bit.

1   Park the playhead between **MVI_1042** and **MVI_1055**.

Placing a gap clip here allows Mitch to take a breath. Don't worry about the visual break. The B-roll clips you will add later can fill in those pauses.

2   To insert a gap clip, choose Edit > Insert Generator > Gap, or press Option-W.

A three-second clip is inserted between the two clips at the playhead location. Those three seconds may be a little too long for this edit. As with any other clip, you may ripple trim a gap clip to adjust its duration.

3   Place the mouse pointer over the end point of the gap clip. Ensure that the ripple trim's filmstrip is pointing left, and then drag the end point to the left.

As you drag, the clip's new duration and the delta (the amount you have changed the clip's duration while dragging) appears above the edit.

4   Trim the gap clip to a new duration of one second, thereby removing two seconds from its length.

5   Skim to just before the gap clip, and play back to review the edit.

That's not bad. It allows just a moment for your audience to understand the who, what, and where of Mitch's comments. Let's repeat that for the next edit.

6   Advance the playhead to the next edit by pressing the Down Arrow key.

The playhead jumps to the edit between **MVI_1055** and **MVI_1043**.

Mitch is offering more details in **MVI_1043**, so placing a longer gap before this clip may help transition the audience into this sound bite.

7   With the playhead cued, press Option-W to insert a three-second gap clip.

8   Review the edit.

Now that you have silence between the two sound bites, you may discover the "breath" at the end of **MVI_1055**. As you proceed with your edit, you will probably notice more of these fine details.

9   If necessary, adjust the end or start points surrounding the gap clips to tidy up the trimmed clips.

You are listening for extra syllables or breaths to remove. For example, you would trim the end point of **MVI_1055** to the left a few frames to remove the breath.

These gap clips won't necessarily remain at the durations you just set. They may flex as you continue to build the story...or tear out parts of it.

Exercise 4.4.2
Blading and Deleting

The Blade tool allows you to quickly break a clip into smaller sections to be moved else-where or completely removed from your story. In the first instance of **MVI_1043**, some pauses in Mitch's interview can be removed to tighten the edit.

1   Play the project, and locate the point at which Mitch says, "And film at the same time, (breath) uhhm," in the first **MVI_1043**. This occurs about four seconds into the clip.

2   Cue the playhead after the breath and before the "uhhm."

You will blade the clip here to divide it into two segments. You will then blade the clip again after the "uhhm" to separate this sound from the good content that occurs before and after it.

3   From the Tools pop-up menu, choose the Blade tool, or press B.

4   With snapping turned on, move the Blade tool over the **MVI_1043** clip and toward the playhead until it snaps to the playhead.

5   With the Blade tool snapped to the playhead, click to segment the clip at this edit point.

You can choose the Blade tool while still using the Select tool. Let's switch to the Select tool to blade on the other side of the "uhhm."

6   Press A to choose the Select tool.

Remember, A stands for arrow. Because the Select tool is already located next to the edit you just made, the ripple trim icon may appear.

7   Press the Right Arrow key—and the Left Arrow key, if necessary—to advance the playhead to after the "uhhm" and just as Mitch is starting the word "you're." Instead of choosing the Blade tool, let's use its keyboard shortcut.

8   Without moving the mouse, press Command-B to blade the clip at the playhead.

The single clip is now three segments. You need to remove the middle segment.

Remember, there are two types of clip deletion. Let's use both to see the difference between them.

9   Select the middle clip segment, and press Shift-Delete.

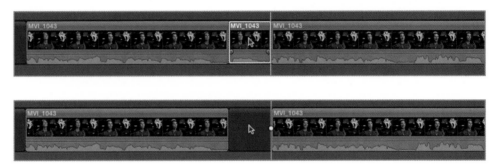

The clip segment is replaced with a gap clip. Called a "replace with gap" edit, this edit type is also known as a lift.

10   Press Command-Z to undo the previous edit.

11   Reselect the "uhhm" clip segment, if necessary, and press Delete.

The segment is removed, and the following clips slide to the left to replace it.

12   Play the edit and listen to the results.

The current second clip might sound like the first word is cut off a bit, what is commonly referred to as an *upcut*. In addition to that concern, does the breath at the end of the first clip distract and call attention to the edit? Or, does the breath naturally flow into the next clip?

13 Using the ripple trim techniques you've learned, clean up the edit to smooth the audio transitions between these two new neighbors.

You may first want to remove the breath at the end of the first, or ending clip. You may also need to insert or remove frames to the start point of the second clip, the starting clip. Refer to Using the Keyboard to Ripple Trim an End Point in this lesson to review ripple trimming.

Visually, this edit is a *jump cut*. A jump cut occurs when similar but nonsynchronized content appears to jump in space and time at an edit point. The B-roll you will add in the next section will hide this error.

Exercise 4.4.3
Joining a Through Edit

In the previous exercise, you used the Blade tool to divide a clip into segments. The resulting through edits may be easily repaired if you made them in error or change your mind about splitting up a clip.

1 In your project, locate **MVI_1044**.

2 In the Tools pop-up menu, choose the Blade tool, or press B.

3 Skim toward the end of the clip just after Mitch says, "New," and then pauses.

The audio waveform displays a definite pause, represented as a "valley" in the waveform.

4 Click in this waveform valley to blade the clip and create a through edit.

5   The through edit point appears as a dashed line. Because we really did not want to split this clip, you are going to rejoin the through edit.

6   Press A to choose the Select tool.

7   With the Select tool, click the through edit point (dashed line) to select it.

Only one side of the through edit will be selected with the Select tool active. That's OK.

8   Press Delete.

The through edit point is removed and the two segments are rejoined into one clip.

Exercise 4.4.4
Refining Some Sound Bite Edits

Before progressing to the next layers of B-roll and music, let's polish the "technically flying in awe" section of the project by adjusting the sound bites' contents and pacing.

Currently, the second instance of **MVI_1043** ends with the word "shooting," which does not flow smoothly into the next clip. This occurs at roughly the 40-second mark in the Timeline.

Earlier, you trimmed off Mitch saying, "so." You could use that here to blend into the next sound bite.

1   Place the skimmer so that the ripple trim appears with the filmstrip pointing left at the end of the second instance of **MVI_1043**.

2   Ripple trim the end point of the second instance of **MVI_1043** to the right to insert roughly 11 frames of content.

3   Review the edit.

That created a nice story flow.

The end of the third instance of **MVI_1043** will be a little tougher to get a "clean" ending; that is, a natural-sounding ending when you are actually cutting the sound bite off mid-sentence. The clip's current end point is at "experiencing," which doesn't sound right. Let's trim that end point to a little earlier in the sentence.

4   Ripple trim the end point to the left roughly one second.

The clip should now end after Mitch says, "filming," and most likely has an extra syllable or two that need to be removed.

5   With the end point still selected, press the comma (,) and period (.) keys to nudge trim frame by frame, refining the edit point.

This trim edit may take a few moments to get the right frame for the end point. That frame is going to be right on the "g" of "filming."

As for **MVI_1044** and **MVI_1045**, these two get the axe. For timing purposes, let's leave these out of the story for now.

6   Select both clips, and press Shift-Delete to replace both clips with a gap clip.

7   Trim the gap clip to a duration of three seconds.

Trimming creates room for a natural sound break and music swell before Mitch segues into the next sound bite.

With these edits in place, you have built the sound bite foundation for your project. Take a moment to review your story.

Lifted Vignette's sound bite-driven primary storyline

Reference 4.5
Editing Above the Primary Storyline

The primary storyline has established the content foundation, timing, and pacing for the project. It's time to see what those sound bites are discussing. At this stage, you'll edit B-roll clips into the project by placing them above the primary storyline, and connected to it.

With these B-roll edits, your editing approach changes to a "lane" above the primary story-line. Clips in a lane outside the primary storyline are vertically connected back to the primary storyline, thereby establishing a synchronized relationship in this project between the sound bite and the B-roll. When Mitch says "helicopter," your audience sees a helicopter.

These connections keep clips synchronized even when a ripple edit occurs in the primary storyline. An upstream ripple that shifts a sound bite's timing in the project will also shift the B-roll clips connected to that sound bite. The connection ensures that the sync is maintained by shifting the connected clips the same amount. You first establish the connection and then Final Cut Pro maintains it so your focus may be on the rest of the story edit.

In the following exercises, you will connect B-roll clips to the sound bite–driven primary storyline you've already edited. Then, you will trim these connected clips and observe their unique trimming behaviors.

Exercise 4.5.1
Adding and Trimming Connected B-roll

B-roll is the editor's friend. Sometimes referred to as *cutaways*, B-roll clips allow you to smooth discontinuity in your primary storyline, and in this project they will help you hide the jump cuts and soften the audio edits made to the sound bites. Furthermore, good B-roll content may also include great natural sound audio, or *nats*. An editor can use the nats to cover a tight audio edit, such as the one you now have with the word "filming."

Let's start by resetting the interface and searching those keywords you applied earlier to quickly locate B-roll of a hangar door opening.

> **NOTE ▶** For the purpose of training, we'll start at the beginning of the project and continue forward by adding B-roll content. However, an actual workflow could begin by adding B-roll anywhere within your project.

1   In the Browser, click the Show Libraries button.

2   In the Lifted library, select the Hangar Keyword Collection.

To ensure that you are seeing all the hangar clips, double-check the Browser's sorting and filtering options.

3   In the Browser, from the pop-up menu, choose Hide Rejected; and then ensure that the search field is clear of any criteria.

4   From the Action pop-up menu in the Browser, set Group Clips By to None and Sort By to Name.

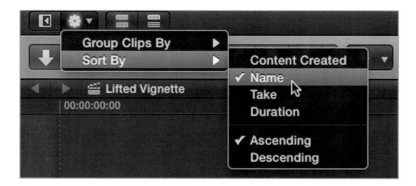

5   If necessary, drag the toolbar up to open more vertical room in the Timeline.

6   In the Browser, adjust the Zoom control to All.

With the environment properly set up, you will search for the first clip of the hangar door opening.

7   In the Lifted library, verify that the Hangar Keyword Collection is selected.

The Browser displays the clips you previously tagged with the Hangar keyword. The first clip you want is **DN_9390**.

8   Skim the clip to refamiliarize yourself with its contents.

This clip starts in the dark before the hangar door opens. Mitch walks in from the left, crossing to center to preflight the helicopter. The clip is currently 13 seconds long. Let's trim the clip down before connecting it to the primary storyline.

9   In **DN_9390**, mark a start point when you first hear the hangar door motor.

10 Mark an end point when Mitch drops down to inspect the camera.

The clip is ready to edit into the project.

11 In the Lifted Vignette project, cue the playhead to the beginning of the Timeline.

Cueing the playhead tells Final Cut Pro where the hangar clip belongs time-wise in the Timeline. In this case, locating that point is easy because it will be the first shot in the project.

You will edit this clip into the project so that we hear Mitch speaking while watching the hangar clip. You can do this by connecting the video clip in a higher lane.

12 In the toolbar, click the Connect button, or press Q.

The hangar clip is stacked into a lane above the first sound bite. Let's review the edit to see the results.

13 Cue the playhead to the beginning of the project, and play the Timeline.

You see the hangar and hear the hangar motor while also hearing Mitch's sound bite. The video hierarchy rule makes the video in a higher lane visible, while mixing and playing all the audio content in the clips.

Connecting the Second B-roll Clip

As you can see, the **DN_9390** clip extends over the second sound bite. That's OK for now, so let's look at the next B-roll clip to add to the project.

1 In the Browser, skim **DN_9465**.

In this clip, Mitch enters the hangar from the right side, approaches the helicopter, and then kneels to inspect the camera. Although Mitch enters from the opposite side of the hangar, you can set a start point as he's kneeling to inspect the camera. With finessing, this clip can be made to match the previous shot of Mitch approaching the helicopter.

2 In the Browser, mark a start point when Mitch has already started to kneel to inspect the camera.

Now you need to locate the Timeline point at which this clip can be matched to the previous edit.

3 Cue the project playhead over **DN_9390** where Mitch has started to kneel at the helicopter's camera.

4   Click the Connect button, or press Q, to make a connect edit.

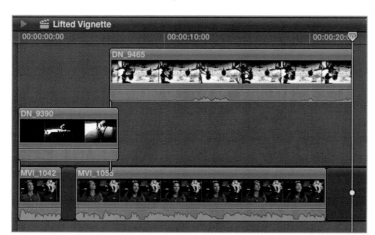

The second B-roll clip stacks into a higher lane above the previous edit. When two connected clips will impact one another, Final Cut Pro automatically avoids a "clip collision" by moving one of the clips to a different lane. The edit still cuts to the second B-roll clip at the connection point.

5   Review the edit to see the results.

Does the action of Mitch kneeling flow from one clip to the other? If not, this situation is easily corrected.

6   Place the mouse pointer over the center of the **DN_9465** clip and drag it to the left or right until the action of Mitch kneeling appears to be one smooth movement.

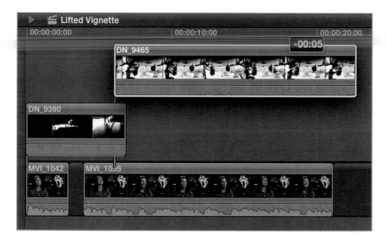

Once **DN_9465** is in place, you can ripple trim the end of **DN_9390** to lower **DN_9465** into the same lane.

7   Ensure that snapping is turned on (the Snapping button in the Timeline is blue).

NOTE ▶ Press N to turn snapping on and off.

8   Drag the end point of **DN_9390** to the left until **DN_9465** drops into the same lane.

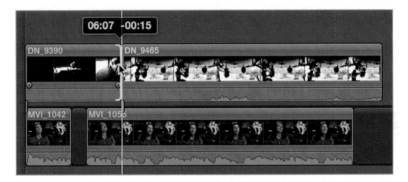

With snapping turned on, the end point of **DN_9390** will snap to the start point of **DN_9465**.

Notice that **DN_9465** extends down the Timeline. We'll trim that clip after connecting a third B-roll clip.

Connecting the Third B-roll Clip

Let's connect one more B-roll clip before analyzing what you've created.

1   In the project, cue the playhead over clip **MVI_1055** when Mitch says "nobody."

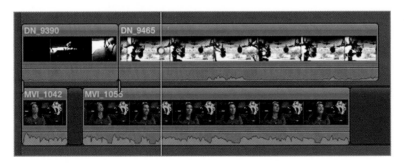

You're telling Final Cut Pro to make a precise start edit based upon the contents of the primary storyline. Now let's find a clip for that edit.

2   In the Browser, locate clip **DN_9470**, a close-up of Mitch inspecting the camera.

3   Mark a start point about halfway through the clip as Mitch turns the camera counter-clockwise.

4   Set an end point as Mitch's face moves halfway behind the camera.

5   Press Q to connect this clip to the primary storyline at the playhead.

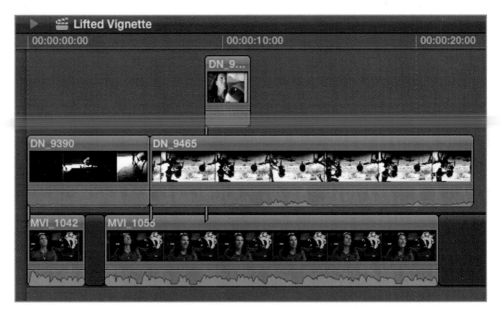

Although the edit cuts nicely to the close-up, in your Timeline, **DN_9465** resumes playing after the close-up ends.

6   Trim the end point of **DN_9465** to the start of **DN_9470** so that the two B-roll clips are sequential.

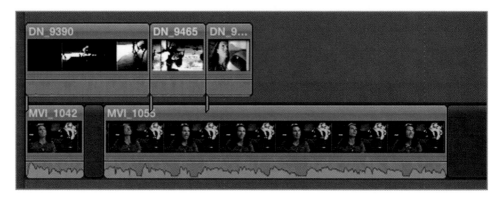

Now **DN_9465** doesn't give an encore performance.

Exercise 4.5.2
Understanding Connected Clip Sync and Trimming Behaviors

Each of the three B-roll clips has a vertical connection point that synchronizes it to the primary storyline. These vertical relationships remain intact even when you alter the primary storyline. Let's see how this works.

In the project, notice the vertical spikes that extend from the B-roll clips to the sound bites in the primary storyline. Those are the connections you established by making a connect edit.

If a sound bite moves within the Timeline, that movement will also be applied to any connected clips.

1   Drag the middle of **MVI_1042** to the right until the clip is located after **MVI_1055**.

Notice that **DN_9390** was relocated with the sound bite, and the other two B-roll clips also slid to the left to remain synchronized with their connected sound bite.

2   Press Command-Z to undo the previous edit.

Connected clips are still independent clips that can be moved away from their synchronized, primary storyline clip.

3   Drag the middle of **DN_9465** to the right until it connects after **DN_9470**.

DN_9465 establishes a new connection with the primary storyline.

NOTE ▸ Every clip outside the primary storyline must connect to the primary storyline.

4   Press Command-Z to undo the edit.

Final Cut Pro will maintain the synchronization of connected clips until you change the connection point or tell Final Cut Pro to ignore the connection.

Overriding the Connection

After connecting your B-roll clips, you may realize that you need to move a sound bite elsewhere in the primary storyline, but also need to leave the connected B-roll clips in place. The B-roll story you've created works great, but you've discovered your project is running too long. Or, you may want to experiment with a different arrangement of the sound bites without disturbing the B-roll order. You can temporarily suspend a connected clip's sync point while adjusting the primary storyline clip.

1   In the project, position the mouse pointer over **MVI_1042**.

2   Hold down the ` (grave accent) key, and drag **MVI_1042** after **MVI_1055**.

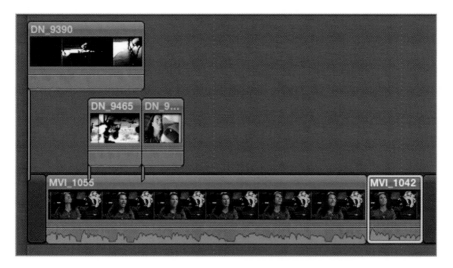

When you press the grave key, the pointer becomes a crossed-out connection symbol. Dragging a clip while holding down the grave key tells Final Cut Pro to ignore any connected clips during that edit.

The **DN_9390** B-roll clip remains in place while the sound bite is moved later in the primary storyline. When the move is completed, the **MVI_1055** sound bite slides to the left along with its two connected B-roll clips. Final Cut Pro automatically bumps **DN_9390** to a higher lane to avoid a collision with the two oncoming B-roll clips. Rather than canceling the edit due to a potential clip collision, Final Cut Pro maintains sync and shifts the clips vertically out of the way of one another.

3   Press Command-Z to undo the edit.

Connected clips help your editing by maintaining the sync between clips you established when initially making the edit. Final Cut Pro lets you change your mind while maintaining that sync, or will sync to a different clip if you desire.

Trimming Connected Clips

Unlike the sound bites in the primary storyline, connected clips are independent of other connected clips and do not have a horizontal relationship with them. As a result, performing a trim edit on a connected clip produces results different from applying a trim edit to a clip in the primary storyline.

1   Place the Select tool over the end point of **DN_9390**.

Notice that a filmstrip does not appear on the trim icon as it would when trimming a clip in the primary storyline. You cannot ripple trim connected clips because no horizontal relationship exists between them.

2   Drag the end point to the left to trim the clip.

Only **DN_9390** was affected by this trim edit.

3   Press Command-Z to undo the edit.

This default behavior of Final Cut Pro is not necessarily a bad thing because you may want connected clips to remain independent of other connected clips. However, when it is desirable, you can establish a horizontal relationship between connected clips.

Reference 4.6
Creating a Connected Storyline

When B-roll clips are connected to the primary storyline, the B-roll takes over the video storytelling of the project. When reviewing the project, you may want to shift the B-roll timing to better align the visuals with the audio-driven storyline. Because each connected clip is independent, trimming one B-roll clip does not ripple trim to affect the others. The vertical relationships of each connected clip isolates it from adjacent clips.

However, an editor may establish horizontal relationships between connected clips by placing them within a *connected storyline*. Doing so creates a horizontal relationship between the grouped connected clips, reducing their individual vertical relationships to a single connection between the connected and primary storylines. Furthermore, by creating a connected storyline, you gain access to several trimming options such as ripple trim.

A connected storyline is a container identified by a gray handle across the top of the grouped clips. This handle is the selection point when you want to apply an edit to the connected storyline. To insert edit a clip into a connected storyline, you must select the storyline's handle, and not the clips within the storyline.

Creating a connected storyline is as simple as selecting connected clips and instructing Final Cut Pro to group them as a storyline. However, not all connected clips may be added to a group. Only connected clips that can exist in the same lane without overlapping may be converted into a connected storyline.

Exercise 4.6.1
Converting Connected Clips into a Connected Storyline

You can create a connected storyline comprising the first three B-roll clips in two easy steps.

1   Select the three connected B-roll clips at the start of the project.

2   Control-click any one of the three, and from the shortcut menu, choose Create Storyline, or press Command-G.

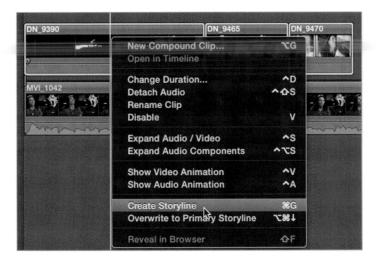

Notice the gray bar or handle above the clips that becomes the outline of a container surrounding the clips. Now that the clips are contained in a storyline, you can ripple trim them.

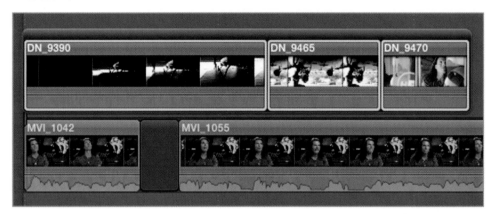

3   Place the Select tool over the end point of **DN_9390**.

The ripple trim icon appears with the filmstrip.

4   Drag the end point to the left to shorten the clip, but do not release the mouse button yet.

A few things for you to notice. First, the two following B-roll clips ripple along with the trim. The storyline established a horizontal, magnetic relationship similar to the primary storyline clips.

Second, as you ripple trim the edit point, a *two-up display* appears in the Viewer. The area to the left shows the new end point of the hangar door opening clip while the right shows the existing start point of **DN_9455** recorded from under the helicopter. The two-up display allows you to see both sides of the edit so you may match the action between the two clips.

5   Referencing the two-up display, ripple trim the end point of **DN_9390** appearing on the left to match the action appearing on the right in the Viewer's two-up display.

Enclosing connected clips in a storyline gives you the advantages of a storyline's magnetic properties when trimming and rearranging the B-roll clips.

Another trim tool similar to ripple trim is roll trim. Whereas ripple trim modifies the duration of one clip (and potentially the project's duration), the roll trim modifies the adjoining points of two clips, not affecting other clips or the total project duration. The roll trim achieves this net-zero duration change by trimming the opposing edit points in opposite directions: inserting frames at one edit point while removing the same number of frames from the adjoining edit point.

In the edit you just completed, the roll trim is handy for fine-tuning the cut's trigger. With the ripple trim, your focus was on continuity of action at the edit. Now that the continuity is in place, you may need to adjust when the cut happens. Should the cut to the shot underneath the helicopter occur as Mitch reaches for the camera, while Mitch is dropping down, or even after Mitch has stopped moving? The roll trim allows you to explore all of those options.

6   From the Tools pop-up menu, choose the Trim tool.

The roll trim function requires that the Trim tool be selected when working with storyline clips.

7   Place the Trim tool over the edit point between **DN_9390** and **DN_9465**.

With the Trim tool on the edit point, the tool becomes the Roll trim with filmstrips pointing at both clips to indicate that the end point of **DN_9390** and the start of **DN_9465** are about to be changed.

8   Drag to the right until Mitch has squatted down, which you can see in the Viewer two-up.

9   Drag back to the left and decide where within the action to cut between the two clips.

The roll trim allowed you to move the edit to find the best cut point between the two clips. This roll and the earlier ripple trim worked because the clips are enclosed in a storyline. Connected clips do not interact with other connected clips editing-wise. Grouping them together in a connected storyline brings the trimming and magnetic properties of the primary storyline to these clips.

Exercise 4.6.2
Appending Clips to a New Connected Storyline

In this exercise, you will create a connected storyline, and append additional B-roll clips to it. This editing method offers the speed and convenience of the batch and ripple trim techniques that you previously performed on the primary storyline.

1   In the Libraries pane, select the Pre-Flight Keyword Collection.

2   In the Pre-Flight collection, find **DN_9455**.

This clip shows Mitch getting into his helicopter, and is the first of a series of clips depicting the preflight and startup.

3   In **DN_9455**, mark a start point just before Mitch appears in the frame. Set an end point after Mitch is in the helicopter.

Next you need to define where this clip goes timing-wise within the Timeline.

4   In the project, cue the playhead after Mitch says, "has been shot on the ground."

You'll connect the first clip of this series of B-roll clips at this point.

5   Click the Connect button, or press Q to make the edit.

NOTE ▸ To enable the Connect button when it is dimmed, move the mouse pointer back into the Browser to activate the Browser pane. The Q keyboard shortcut works with the button dimmed.

To quickly set up an append edit for the following B-roll clips, you will convert this one clip into a storyline.

6   Control-click **DN_9455**, and from the shortcut menu, choose Create Storyline, or press Command-G.

The clip is now contained in a storyline. To make additional edits to this storyline, you must select the storyline's handle rather than the clip inside.

7   Click the storyline's handle to select it.

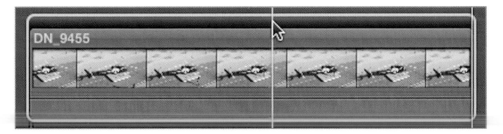

When you select its handle, the storyline is outlined in yellow. The goal is to efficiently add the subsequent B-roll clips to the selected storyline.

8   In the Browser, locate **DN_9446**.

9 Mark a start point on the jib's first take of Mitch's feet on the pedals. Set an end point after the jib movement ends for that take, leaving the clip duration at approximately six seconds.

10 Press E to append this clip to the end of the selected storyline.

NOTE ▶ The highlighted storyline is dimmed because the Browser is the active pane if you are skimming the Browser before pressing E.

You also can batch edit clips into this storyline.

11 Mark the following ranges for each listed clip:

Clip	Start	End	Result
DN_9453	Start of third take tilt/pan on Mitch	End of tilt/pan move to panel	
DN_9454	Flips switch and the displays change	Releases switch and displays change again	

Clip	Start	End	Result
DN_9452	Before rotors start turning	End of clip	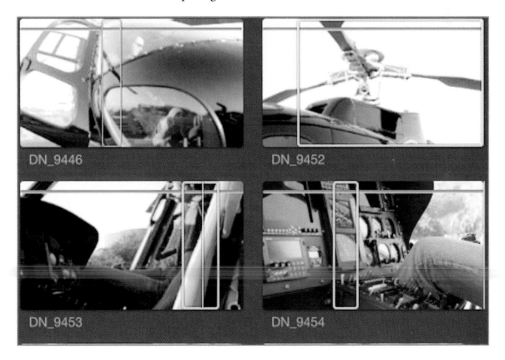

After marking these three clips, you can select all three for the append edit into the DN_9455 and DN_9446 storyline, which we'll call the Preflight storyline.

12 With DN_9452 still selected, Command-click the ranges you marked for DN_9454 and DN_9453 to select the three clip ranges.

DN_9446

DN_9452

DN_9453

DN_9454

13 In the project, ensure the gray handle of the Preflight storyline is still selected.

Make sure you select the gray handle and not DN_9455 or DN_9446. The outline will be yellow if the Timeline pane is active, or dimmed if the Browser is active.

A selected storyline in the active Timeline pane

Storyline selected but Timeline pane is not active.

14   Click the Append button, or press E, to append the three clips to the selected storyline.

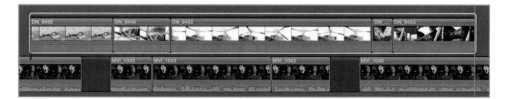

The clips are added to the selected storyline in the order you selected them.

NOTE ► With the Timeline pane active (move the skimmer into the Timeline to make it active), press Command-– (minus sign) to zoom out the Timeline view.

Editing Within a Connected Storyline

Because these clips are now inside a storyline, rearranging and ripple trimming them is a breeze.

1   Drag **DN_9452** to the end of the Preflight storyline after **DN_9454**.

Next you'll ripple trim each of these storyline clips to reduce their durations. The goal is to finish playing the first four clips in this storyline by the end of the **MVI_1055** sound bite. There's a lot of content to remove!

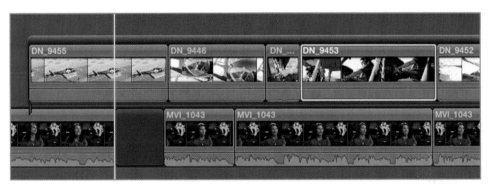

No joke. The selected clip, **DN_9453**, should end a few moments before the end of **MVI_1055**, where the playhead is located in the previous image. This is a common editing scenario and the reason why you batch edited the clips into the storyline. The durations you marked earlier in the Browser were set to narrow down the clips to the needed content. But the timing of these clips with the sound bite and to each other is what determines their final durations and positions.

The art of editing is the art of compromise. You need to present just enough information for the viewers to understand the actions they are seeing and tell the story. You want to present these four preflight actions while Mitch is talking about the whole new look of shooting something from the air. When he finishes that statement, the rotors start turning and the helicopter takes off. The compromise to make that edit happen is to adjust the timing of not only these preflight clips to Mitch's sound bites, but also adjust the earlier hangar storyline clips' timing to the sound bites. Don't be afraid to look at previous edits when trying to make up time in a project.

Let's first gain a few seconds by trimming the hangar storyline.

2   In the hangar storyline, ripple trim the start point of **DN_9390** so the clip begins with just a sliver of light visible through the hangar door.

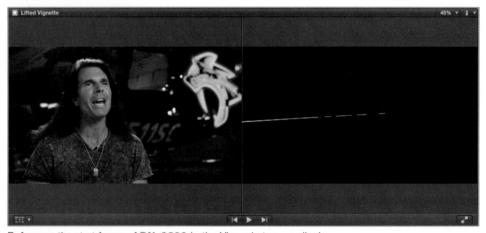

Reference the start frame of **DN_9390** in the Viewer's two-up display.

After trimming the start of **DN_9390**, the start of **MVI_1042** is now visible. You can drag the hangar storyline to realign it with the beginning of the project.

3   Drag the storyline to the beginning of the project.

Remember the gap clip you previously added to the beginning of the primary story-line? You can gain some additional time by lengthening that gap clip. Increasing its duration allows you to shift the start of the Preflight storyline earlier in relation to the sound bite **MVI_1055**.

4   In the primary storyline, drag the end point of the first gap clip to the right to a dura-tion of about 2:15.

NOTE ▶ You may need to disable snapping to get the desired duration. Press N while dragging the edit point to disable snapping without releasing the mouse button, and then enable snapping for the next step.

The hangar storyline now ends and Mitch's interview video becomes visible as he says, "Nobody." Mitch needs to be on camera for a short time to accommodate a graphic you will add in a later lesson, so you will leave a few seconds of him visible. The Preflight storyline can now start a little earlier.

5   Drag the Preflight storyline so that its first clip starts at the "standpoint" audio cue.

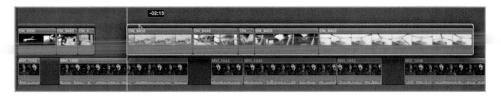

That edit gained you another two seconds, more or less. But more trimming is still needed.

DN_9455 is much too long. When you review the clip's content, you see that the real action occurs at the end of the clip when Mitch gets in the helicopter. Cutting the clip duration to that last action will make the shot more interesting and gain you time.

When you trimmed the start of **DN_9390**, you did so using the Select tool and moving the entire storyline to the beginning of the project after the trim. This time, you'll save a step by performing a ripple trim using the Trim tool.

6   From the Tools pop-up menu, choose the Trim tool, or press T.

7   Drag the start of **DN_9455** to the right, but don't release the mouse button yet.

As you drag with the Trim tool, the two-up display appears in the Viewer. The area on the right shows the new start point you are setting for **DN_9455** with the Trim tool.

8   Referencing the right frame of the Viewer's two-up, drag the start point until you see Mitch stepping on the skid to get in the helicopter. Release the mouse button.

Now you'll trim the end point of **DN_9455** to tighten the shot.

9   Drag the end point of **DN_9455** to the left until the two-up display shows that Mitch just got into the helicopter.

The end result is a clip just over two seconds long. That's quite a bit of tightening for that clip. Let's shorten **DN_9446**, too.

10   Using the Trim tool, drag the start point of **DN_9446** right until the two-up display in the Viewer shows the body of the helicopter at the bottom of the frame blocking the transport cart from view.

11 Now trim the end point of **DN_9446** to realize an overall clip duration of two seconds.

NOTE ▶ Don't forget to disable snapping using the N key, when necessary.

The next clip should be **DN_9453** followed by **DN_9454**. Because these two clips are inside a storyline, this involves only a simple rearrangement of the two clips.

12 Switch to the Select tool, and then drag **DN_9453** left to insert the clip before **DN_9454**.

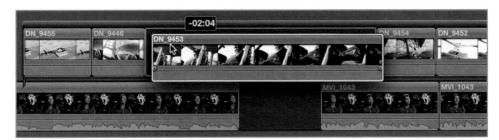

13 Staying on **DN_9453**, trim the start point to where Mitch is centered in the image and starts to reach forward.

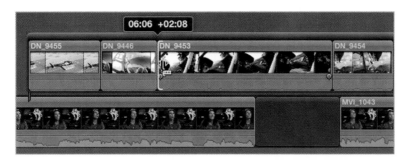

14 Trim the end point to a clip duration of around 1:20, the point at which Mitch has his fingers on a switch and drops his hand to a "wrist low" position.

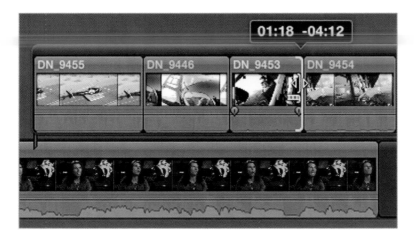

To create the pacing and the feel that Mitch is starting the engine, you will cut from this movement to a closer "throwing the switch" shot.

15   In **DN_9454**, trim the start point to where Mitch's hand is still open before pointing and throwing the switch.

NOTE ▶ This may require dragging to the left to add frames.

16 Trim the end point to realize about a 1:15 clip duration ending while Mitch is holding the switch.

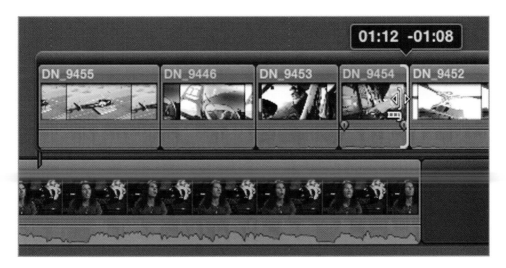

Finally, you'll trim the clip of the helicopter rotors starting to move.

17 Trim `DN_9452`'s start point so the rotors have already started to turn. Trim the end point to a clip duration of about two seconds. Review the edit.

You have just one more B-roll storyline to go!

Creating and Editing the Third Connected Storyline

Use the following tables to create and trim the third Takeoff storyline.

> **NOTE ▶** Don't forget that you have two events in the Lifted library that contain clips for this project. Also remember that dragging a range point displays the range's duration.

1   Mark each clip as detailed in this table:

Clip	Keyword Collection	Start	End	Result
DN_9463	Takeoff	Before forward movement	Exits frame	
DN_9415	In Flight	A couple of seconds before the mountain is behind the helicopter	Duration of five seconds	
GOPR1857	In Flight	Two seconds before Mitch stretches his arm out behind seat	Duration of five seconds	
IMG_6493	Flight Controls	Just before hand leaves shot and lens flare ends	Duration of four seconds	
GOPR3310	In Flight	Last third of clip; before Mitch leans forward into sunlight	Duration of five seconds	

Clip	Keyword Collection	Start	End	Result
DN_9503	In Flight	Halfway point; helicopter behind tree	Helicopter exits frame	DN_9503
DN_9420	In Flight	Helicopter is just off screen	Helicopter exits frame	DN_9420

2   With the clips' start and end points marked, Command-click them in the order they are listed in the table.

NOTE ▶ Selecting the Lifted library in the Libraries pane and selecting a smaller Clip Height in Clip Appearance may ease this process.

3   In the project, cue the playhead immediately after DN_9452, if necessary.

You will perform a connect edit first to place these clips in the project, and then group these clips into a connected storyline.

4   Click the Connect button, or press Q, to connect edit the selected clips into the project.

Now that the clips are part of the project, you can group them.

5   In the project, select the connected clips you just added. Control-click any one of the selected clips, and from the shortcut menu, choose Create Storyline, or press Command-G.

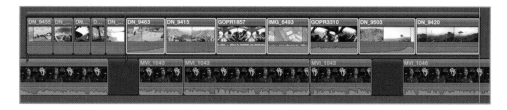

The clips are grouped into a connected storyline, the third such storyline in your project, which we'll refer to as the Takeoff storyline.

You have two more B-roll clips to add, you also have some very loud nats on a couple of B-roll clips, but let's take a break from B-roll to add a music clip, and align some edits to it.

Reference 4.7
Editing Below the Primary Storyline

Audio clips are typically edited "below the line" meaning physically beneath the video clips. In Final Cut Pro, you may place audio clips below or above the primary storyline. The vertical positioning of audio clips is not as critical as when prioritizing video clips because Final Cut Pro mixes together all audio clips—such as sound effects and music— and plays them simultaneously.

Exercise 4.7.1
Connecting a Music Clip

For this first rough cut, you will include a music clip that plays in the background during the entire edit. The music contains an apex moment towards the end that you will synchronize with a specific clip.

1   In the Audio Only Smart Collection, select the **Tears of Joy-Short** clip.

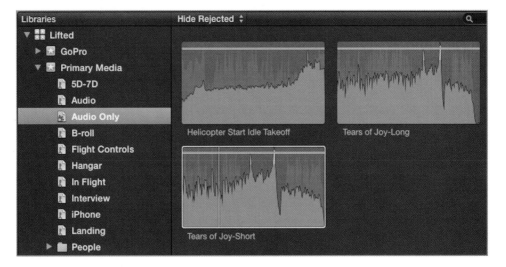

2   With the playhead cued to the beginning of the project, click the Connect button, or press Q.

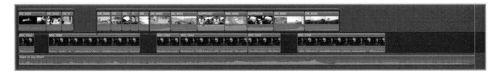

The music clip is added to the beginning of the project.

The music will be a little too loud, or *hot*. You can adjust its volume level in the Timeline. Every audio clip has a volume control: a black, horizontal line that overlays the clip's audio waveforms.

3 Move the Select tool over the volume control in the **Tears of Joy-Short** music clip.

The current volume level setting appears as 0 dB (decibels), which means that Final Cut Pro currently plays the clip at its original volume level.

4 Drag the Volume control down to around –15 dB to play the music clip at 15 dB below its original recorded level.

As with all the other clips, this is not the final volume setting for the music. This was simply a "sanity" adjustment so the rest of the audio clips are audible while editing. There is more audio work to be done.

Reference 4.8
Finessing the Rough Cut

Your project is racing to the end of this phase of the workflow. The details and adjustments you need to perform become more granular as you finish addressing the major editorial issues. You may still perform some major changes, but you should now see the light shining at the end of this editorial tunnel. At this stage, a project generally needs audio adjustments and a bit more trimming. By now, your project is definitely ready for a run-through with the slip trim.

The slip trim changes the content within the clip container. You change the start and end points of the content simultaneously revealing earlier or later source materials without changing the clip's duration or position in the project. Think of the clip as your iPhone and the clip content as the photos on your iPhone. When you want to see earlier photos, you swipe with your finger from left to right to pull the earlier photos into view. The reverse to see later content is to swipe right to left to pull that content into view.

Dragging right to slip earlier content into view.

While performing a slip trim, two-up display of the new start and end points appears in the Viewer. The two-up display shows your changes in real time as you drag the slip trim across the clip. When you release the mouse button, the clip is already updated in the project.

Slip trimming may also be used on audio-only clips. However, for smoothing out audio edits at this stage of the workflow, adding some transitions and audio fade handles will do the job. Every clip that contains audio content has fade handles to create audio envelopes for ramping.

Your project has a basic music bed, the B-roll edits, and even the sound bites positioned and trimmed to align them to visual or audio cues in other clips. For this first rough cut, you will adjust some clip positions and timings to coincide with the music clip's major moments.

Exercise 4.8.1
Adjusting the Edits

In **DN_9420**, the sunset shines dramatically through the helicopter's windows; and during the clip, the music swells to a climax. But we can do better. In this exercise, you will align those audiovisual moments for maximum effect.

1   In the project, select **DN_9420**, and skim to the first frame of the sun coming through the helicopter windows.

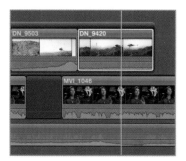

2   Press M to set a marker at that dramatic visual moment.

Marker appears under the
skimmer along the clip's top edge.

Now you need to set a marker on the music swell. Unfortunately, it's a little hard to hear while the previous sound bite is playing.

3   Select the music clip, and then click the Solo button, or press Option-S.

Only the selected audio clip is audible and in color while the nonselected clips' audio is muted and desaturated in the interface.

Now that you can hear the music clearly, let's place a marker on the music swell.

4   Using the Select tool, click the music clip, skim to the music swell, and then press M to set a marker.

5   With the marker set, click the Solo button again, or press Option-S, to disable the Solo function.

Now the task is to align those two markers. You'll perform two edits with the ripple trim: shortening the B-roll and extending the last gap clip to align the music swell with the sunset.

6   Ripple trim to remove a few frames from each clip of the Takeoff storyline. Your goal is to move the sunset marker closer to the music swell.

Here are some trim points to consider:

▶ Start of **DN_9463**: Could the helicopter already be in forward movement? You'll need to reposition the storyline after any adjustment to this point.

▶ **DN_9415**: Don't trim too much here. This is a "landscape" shot that needs time for the viewer to gain perspective.

▶ Start of **GOPR1857**: Trim to just before Mitch turns his head.

These edits should get you very close to aligning the markers.

7   Also using the ripple trim, push the last sound bite farther out by lengthening the gap clip. Insert enough frames so that the last sound bite starts when the music starts again.

You can finish aligning these markers using one or both of these methods: ripple trim more of the earlier B-roll clips, or slip edit the content of **DN_9420**.

Using the Slip Edit

The slip edit is a safe edit for setting the B-roll clips to their best content without disturbing other edits.

1   From the Tools pop-up menu, choose the Trim tool, or press T.

2   Move the Trim tool over the middle of **DN_9420**.

The Slip tool appears.

3   Drag **DN_9420** until the marker aligns to the music marker.

While dragging with the slip trim, a two-up display of **DN_9420** appears in the Viewer.

The image on the left shows the start point of the clip, while the right image shows the end point. The start and end points are updating in real time as you drag the slip trim. Although not particularly needed for this edit, the two-up display is great for ensuring that the best content is included between the displayed start and end points.

4   With the two markers aligned, play the entire project, slip trim at the ready, evaluating whether the B-roll clips are displaying their best contents within their current durations.

While you review the project, ask questions about the effectiveness of your results. Can you avoid the lens flare in the instrument/GPS panel shot? Should there be more lens flare content? Should the project show less of Mitch leaning back and pointing out the side window, or should you slip the clip to include Mitch pointing out the front?

Exercise 4.8.2
Adjusting Clip Volume Levels

The two basic rules of mixing audio are: Don't peak the meters; and if it doesn't sound good, change it. That change should not be a knee-jerk reaction. Don't get in the trap of continuing to boost the volume of a clip to make it louder than the other clips. If the sound bites are too quiet, you don't necessarily crank up the sound bites. Maybe you need to turn down the volume of the music or B-roll nats.

In this exercise, you will perform some simple volume level adjustments to ensure that the sound bites are clearly audible, and that the overall audio mix does not reach up to 0 dB on the Audio meters. A safe target is to not allow any of your loudest audio go above –6 dB on the meters.

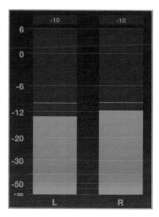

1   In the Dashboard, click the Audio Meter button.

The larger Audio meters open to the right of the Timeline. Although you'll delve deeper into audio mixing in Lesson 6, at the present you just want to ensure that your audio levels don't peak at or beyond the 0 dB mark.

You experienced changing the volume of one clip, the music clip, a few minutes ago. When you want to change the volume levels of multiple clips at once, you can use a keyboard shortcut to do so.

2   In the Takeoff storyline, select all the B-roll clips.

3   While watching the clips' volume controls, press Control-- (minus sign) and Control-= (equals sign) to lower and raise the volumes of the selected clips.

4   Continue playing through the rest of the project listening to the mix while watching the Audio meters. Select a clip or multiple clips, and use the volume control or the shortcut keys to keep the meters below 0 dB, and more importantly, so you can clearly hear Mitch talking.

The peak indicators, the thin lines left over from the highest meter reading should not go much over –6 dB.

▶ **Know Your Volume Controls**

A great practice to establish early on when dealing with audio is to understand that you have access to at least two volume controls. The volume level controls per clip in Final Cut Pro are the only ones that affect your audience. Turning down your Mac computer's volume or separate speaker volume control will not affect the volume in Final Cut Pro.

The built-in Mac speakers are good quality for a computer, but they won't do the job for professional editing. At the very least, you'll want to have good over-the-ear studio headphones, and at best, powered near-field loudspeakers. Audio monitoring equipment is a key investment that will add immeasurably to your final output's quality. Just because you're not listening on good equipment doesn't mean others won't either; viewers with high-quality equipment will probably notice audio issues you couldn't even hear.

Exercise 4.8.3
Connecting Two Additional B-Roll Clips

To complete this rough cut's B-roll edits, you've got two concluding B-roll clips to add. Currently, the sunset shines through the helicopter's windows at the music swell and grand pause. Then the music starts again, and Mitch begins his last sound bite. Time to land the helicopter "at the end of the day," and to fly off into the sunset when remembering the day's adventures.

1   In the GoPro event, locate a clip assigned the Landing keyword.

Looking in the Landing Keyword Collection of the GoPro event, you find **GOPR0009**.

2   In the Browser, skim to where the helicopter is completely visible in the frame, and mark a start point.

Although you just trimmed this clip, its duration is still almost 30 seconds. You might need only 10 of those seconds.

3   Skim **GOPR0009** and set an end point as the helicopter lands.

The duration should now be roughly 10 seconds.

4   Using the connect edit method of your choice, connect edit the landing clip to the primary storyline about where the music restarts. This will also be just as or slightly before Mitch starts talking. Play the results.

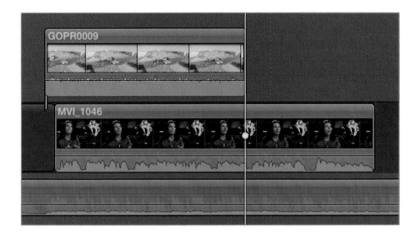

This edit feels choppy because the sunset clip cuts to black followed by another clip cutting in from black. Before fixing that, you have one more clip to edit into the project.

5   In the Browser, search for an In Flight B-roll clip that shows the helicopter flying off into the sunset. You should find **DN_9424**.

6   You will be trimming this clip to get it just right, but for now, set a start point before the helicopter enters the frame. You want that action to happen just as Mitch is finishing the last sound bite.

7   Connect edit **DN_9424**, "flying into the sunset," just as Mitch is saying, "Adventure I went on." Trim the clip to end after the music.

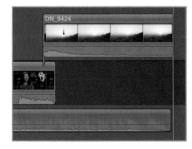

That works. To finish with this clip, give its content some breathing room by adding several seconds to the clip's start.

8   Drag the start point of the "flying into the sunset" clip, and extend the start point to the left to when Mitch says, "Wow."

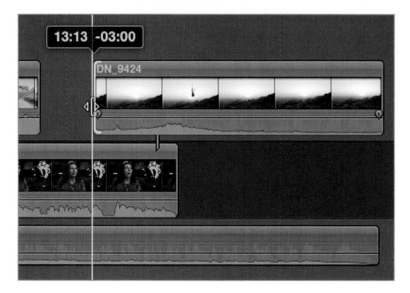

9   Since you just added these two clips, take a moment to adjust their audio levels to more closely match the previous adjustments you made to the other clips.

Great! All the clips for your first edit are in your project. A final refinement pass will soften some not-so-clean edits.

Exercise 4.8.4
Refining Edits Using Cross Dissolves and Fade Handles

Some of your audio edits may contain a click or pop at their start or end points. Every clip that has audio has the potential to "catch a click." A quick solution is to rapidly fade the audio in or out using a technique called *ramping*.

▶ **Catch a Click**

Pleasant sounding audio travels in a sine wave with a peak and a trough per cycle.

Each cycle of the waveform traverses the zero crossing point 2x as the soundwave peaks and then goes down to the trough and then repeats. When an audio clip has a start point that catches the audio soundwave anywhere other than at zero, you may hear a click as the playhead grabs on to the soundwave in progress.

1   At the end of the first sound bite, move your pointer over the audio waveform of **MVI_1042**.

Two fade handles, or "birds-eyes," appear at the ends of the clip. These envelope handles allow you to quickly or gradually ramp the audio into or out of the edit.

2   Move your pointer over the ending fade handle.

When positioned over the handle, the pointer changes to a pair of arrowheads point-ing left and right.

NOTE ▶ If you have difficulty seeing the fade handles, use the Clip Appearance button at the lower-right to increase the clip height. Also, you may select a larger waveform presentation.

3   Drag the fade handle to the left about five frames.

The number of frames to move is dependent upon how tight the edit is against "kid." You do not want to cut off the last word Mitch says.

4   Position the pointer over the beginning of the next sound bite.

5   Drag the fade handle right from the start point to add a small ramp into the clip's audio.

The clicks and pops are fading away. These audio ramps also soften the clip's entry and exit. When an audio clip was recorded in a noisy environment, a cut into or out of the clip will make the edit undesirably obvious as the noise pops into or out of the mix. In addition to audio edits, let's soften some video edits. A fade-in is not necessarily required if your edit starts with black. But the sunset clip definitely needs an easy, blending transition in and out.

For now, you will use a keyboard shortcut to apply the default transition: cross dissolve. When placed between two clips, a cross dissolve transition blends two images together by varying their levels of transparency. One appears to fade away while the other appears to fade into view. When applied to a single edge of a clip that does not adjoin another clip, the Command-T cross dissolve will either fade the clip in from black or fade out to black. A few cross dissolves placed into your project will smooth the clips' entries and exits.

6   Using the Select tool, click the start point of the sunset through the windows clip, and press Command-T to add a cross dissolve.

A cross dissolve with a one-second duration blends the previous shot into the sunset shot. This sets up the shot and begins to slow down the pacing for the ending segment.

NOTE ▶ Connected clips are automatically placed within a connected storyline when a transition is applied.

While you may apply many transition types and customizations here, let's add a few more cross dissolves to your project.

7   Select the end point of the sunset through windows clip, and press Command-T.

8   Select the start point of the **GOPR0009** clip, and press Command-T.

9   Review this transition by playing the project.

Notice that while the video is fading in from black, a momentary cut to Mitch on-camera appears as the helicopter landing clip continues to fade in. This occurs because the Mitch clip starts while the transition from black is still in progress.

10 You will need to either drag the **GOPR0009** storyline left until the transition does not overlap the Mitch clip, shorten the transition duration, or lengthen the gap clip to push Mitch's sound bite to start after the transition completes.

As easy as it is, selecting single points is tedious. Fortunately, you can apply a transition to both points of the same clip at once.

11 In the project, select the **DN_9424** clip, and press Command-T.

A cross dissolve is applied to both edit points, but the ending dissolve should be a little longer than the default duration of one second.

12 Place your pointer over the left edge of the transition in the project.

The pointer becomes a resize icon without a filmstrip. This allows you to set the transition's duration.

13 Drag the transition's start edge to the left away from the transition's center until the duration info indicates two seconds.

Now you have a slower fade to black at the end of the project.

14 Review your project, looking and listening for edits that could be softened with a cross dissolve or audio ramp. A quick tip while you are reviewing: When it comes to video transitions, less is more.

With a few audio ramps and a couple of video cross dissolves, your rough cut is ready to show to the client.

Reference 4.9
Sharing Your Progress

When a project is ready to be shared, the project is exported from Final Cut Pro. The Share pop-up menu includes several preset *destinations* for many popular delivery platforms.

The preset destinations include desktop formats such as Apple ProRes and H.264 as well as iOS devices; DVD/Blu-ray; and online services such as YouTube, Vimeo, and Facebook. These presets may be customized and additional presets added to this list within preferences. The destinations are even more customizable through the use of Compressor, the Apple batch transcoding application available in the App Store.

> **NOTE** ▸ Due to copyright restrictions, you cannot use the supplied media materials for any purpose other than performing the exercises in this book.

Exercise 4.9.1
Sharing an iOS-Compatible File

You've done a lot in this first edit of Lifted Vignette. In this and the previous lessons, you've gone through a typical post-production workflow using Final Cut Pro. Although it's not perfect, this rough cut must be shown to the client, the producer, or your colleagues attending an upcoming lunch meeting. The following exercise briefly describes exporting your project to a media file that is playable on a Mac, PC, smartphone, or tablet. Such media files are also acceptable for upload to most popular online, video-hosting services.

1   With the Lifted Vignette project open, ensure that no clip or range is selected in the project by pressing Command-Shift-A.

This keyboard shortcut deselects any selected items and clears any marked ranges, which is important because Final Cut Pro will share a range if one is selected instead of the entire Timeline.

2   In the toolbar, click the Share button.

The Share Project pop-up menu appears with a list of preset destinations. Most of these presets focus on delivering high-definition content to online hosting sites or to desktop, portable, and handheld devices. For this exercise, let's create a file that we can AirPlay to the conference room's projector by way of an Apple TV.

3   From the list of destinations, choose Apple Devices 720p.

The Share dialog that appears contains four main elements: a skimmable Preview area to verify the content for export, Info and Settings panes, and a File inspector that summarizes the exporting file's settings.

The Info pane displays the metadata that will be embedded into the file. This metadata will be visible in the exported media file's Info inspector when it is opened in QuickTime Player.

4   Set the following metadata information:

▶   Title: *Lifted-Rough Cut*

▶   Description: *A helicopter pilot and cinematographer describes his passion for sharing aerial cinematography.*

▶   Creator: [insert your name]

▶   Tags: *aerial cinematography, helicopters, aviation*

NOTE ▶ To enter the tag "tokens," type the tag's text followed by a comma, or press Return to close each tag.

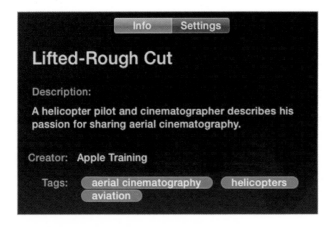

5   After entering the metadata, click the Settings tab to modify the file's delivery options.

By default, the selected destination preset automatically saves the file to your iTunes Library. You may alter this behavior in the "Add to playlist" pop-up menu.

6   From the "Add to playlist" pop-up menu, choose "Open with QuickTime Player."

NOTE ▶ If the Open With option lists another application, choose Other from the Open With list, select QuickTime Player from the Application folder, and then click Open.

In the Settings pane, the "Add to Playlist" line has converted to "Open with QuickTime Player."

7 Click Next.

8 In the Save As dialog, enter *Lifted-Rough Cut*, if necessary, and from the Where pop-up menu, choose Desktop. Click Save.

The Background Tasks button displays the progress of the share.

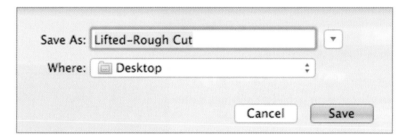

When the file has been shared, the file will automatically open into QuickTime Player and an OS X Notification will appear.

NOTE ▸ The QuickTime Inspector window is available by pressing Command-I in the QuickTime Player application.

9 Play the movie file in QuickTime Player.

If the file looks and sounds as expected, you have several options for delivering the file to Apple TV. Several of the options are available within QuickTime Player using OS X Share services.

10 To the right of the QuickTime Player transport controls, click the Share pop-up menu.

To Send the File to a	Use This Option
Mac	AirDrop
iPad, iPhone	Messages
Hosting service	Vimeo, Facebook, YouTube, Flickr

▶ If you have not set up these Internet accounts, OS X will prompt you to enter your username and password for the selected service.

▶ If you send the file to an iPad or iPhone using Messages, when the message arrives, simply choose to Save Video from the Messages Share button. The movie file will be available to share to AirPlay in the iOS Photos app.

▶ If you choose to use a hosting service such as Vimeo, you may access the file directly using the Apple TV Vimeo application.

Alternatively, you could use a file-sharing service such as Dropbox to transfer the file to your iPad or iPhone.

Using AirPlay with QuickTime Player

You may also stream the file from your OS X Mac to an Apple TV. However, you must use the correct video resolution. When you send your OS X desktop to the Apple TV, you may choose to send the full desktop resolution over AirPlay or restrict the desktop to the Apple TV resolution, which may be 1920 × 1080 pixels, compared to your video file, which is 1280 × 720 pixels in QuickTime Player. Forcing QuickTime Player to the desktop resolution will degrade the video playback quality. Here's how to maintain QuickTime Player at the movie file's resolution.

1   With the shared file still in QuickTime Player, click the AirPlay menu button.

2   From the "Connect to" options, choose the desired Apple TV.

The AirPlay menu button turns blue when connected to the AppleTV.

3   Once connected, click the AirPlay button again.

4   Under Match Desktop Size To, select the Apple TV.

5   Return to QuickTime Player by clicking the displayed video.

6   In QuickTime Player, choose View > Enter Full Screen, and then choose
    View > Actual Size.

Your video now appears on the Apple TV at its native 1280 x 720 resolution sur-
rounded by a black background.

NOTE ▸ If you have a 2nd Generation Apple TV, the video will fill the screen.

Congratulations on completing the first edit of the Lifted Vignette project. You have
gone from nothing to a rough edit in a short period of time. You created a project
and learned the various trim commands of append, insert, and connect to get clips
into a project. The rearranging of clips in the primary storyline introduced you to
the magnetic properties of a storyline. For the B-roll, you learned how to create connected storylines. A variety of tools for trimming clips and for softening the edits and
adjusting the audio levels rounded out the finishing tools. And finally, you learned
some ways to share the project out of Final Cut Pro. No matter which projects you
will edit in the future, every project will be edited using this same import, edit, and
share workflow.

Lesson Review

1. What do the Automatic Settings do when creating a new project?

2. Where are projects stored?

3. Which edit command is depicted in the following figure?

4. Which edit command is depicted in the following figure?

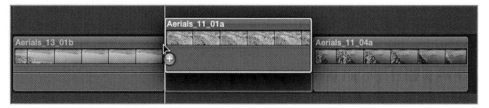

5. Which toolbar button performs an append edit?

6. What do the green, blue, and purple colored stripes overlaying the clip identify?

7. When in filmstrip view, which modifier key do you hold down to edit clips into the project in the order that you select the clips in the Browser?

8. When performing an insert edit, what marks the Timeline location for the edit: the playhead or the skimmer?

9. Identify the trim type used in the following figure.

10. Which two interface items provide additional skimming precision in the Browser?

11. What does the Viewer overlay in the following figure indicate?

12. With the primary storyline determining the project's timing, what generic clip can be inserted to "create" time between storyline clips?

13. In the scenario shown below, what type of edit was performed in one command?

Before

After

14. Identify the edit functions indicated by the mouse pointer in the following figures.

A

B

C

15. To append edit a clip into a connected story, what must be selected and what must not be selected before pressing E?

16. What does the −15 dB indicate in the following image?

17. Identify the interface element that displays the Audio meters.

18. Describe what will occur during playback of this transition.

19. Which interface element lets you export an iOS- and AppleTV-compatible file of your project?

Answers

1. They conform the project's resolution and frame rate to the first video clip added to the project.

2. Projects are stored within a designated event.

3. Append

4. Insert

5.

The Append edit button

6. Favorite, user-applied keyword, and analysis keyword

7. Command

8. The skimmer, if active; otherwise, the playhead

9. Ripple trim

10. The Zoom slider allows you to see more clip content horizontally, and Clip Appearance permits you to increase clip height and hide and view waveforms.

11. The playhead or skimmer is cued to the start frame of a clip.

12. A gap clip

13. Replace with Gap or Lift edit (keyboard shortcut: Shift-Delete)

14. A: Ripple; B: Roll; and C: Slip

15. The connected storyline's handle must be selected, but not the clip's handle inside the connected storyline.

16. The audio volume control has been lowered to play the audio clip −15 dB quieter than the audio clip's recorded level.

17.

Show/hide the meters in the Timeline pane

18. The **GOPR009** clip will fade in from black; but halfway through the transition, Mitch's interview will suddenly cut in and be visible until the GoPro clip becomes fully opaque.

19.

The Share
pop-up menu

Revising the Edit

The second editing pass is all about implementing changes: the notes from the producer, comments from the client, issues you notice after getting some sleep and taking a fresh look. One or all of these feedback channels will influence the choices you make during this second pass. Editing is all about resolving creative differences, making compromises, and balancing art and reality. Speaking of reality, you also have a schedule and a budget to meet. How creative can you be in X number of days with only Y dollars?

Since our sample client is imaginary, let's be optimistic. Happily, the notes you've received commend you for a "nice job" on the first edit of Lifted Vignette. The client likes the edit; so much so, they have ideas—one of which is excellent. The client located some aerial clips that weren't submitted. He would like you to work in some of those aerial shots and make the project a little longer.

GOALS

▶ Define and distinguish the two types of project duplication

▶ Understand the replace edit options

▶ Use the Dashboard for playhead positioning

▶ Use markers for clip synchronization and task notes

▶ Create and edit with an audition clip.

▶ Refine project using trim to playhead and trim to selection

In this lesson, you'll explore a different workflow for the primary storyline. Although you could leave the primary storyline as-is for this revision, let's explore the tools and features that allow you to change, shift, and regroup your previous edits. You will change the driving content of the primary storyline to a longer cut of the music while creating a relationship between the music and sound bites. You'll incorporate some gyro-stabilized aerial footage to visually support the sound bites. Adding more good music and B-roll will allow you to spread out the sound bite sections a little and open up some breathing room.

While performing this second pass, you will learn about replace edits, auditions, markers, and trimming to the playhead or a range. It sounds like a lot to explore, but these tools are easy to learn and a snap to use. All the metadata organization you did earlier will pay off. In addition, the Magnetic Timeline, connected clips, and storylines allow you to experiment with story flow and make big structural changes easily and painlessly. Once again, Final Cut Pro lets you focus on the artistic aspect of storytelling by helping you execute the technical aspects.

The Lifted Vignette rough draft

Reference 5.1
Versioning a Project

Before you begin a rework of the rough cut, we need to discuss versioning, which is simply copying or duplicating a backup version of your project. You could do this regularly at editing milestones (rough draft, musical edit, color grading) to create a just-in-case backup copy, or when you wish to experiment and want to preserve a "safe" version of the previous edit. Final Cut Pro allows you to make as many versions as you need to complete your project, creating either a snapshot or a duplicate.

Duplicate Project as Snapshot

The favored method for its speed and simplicity, creating a snapshot is like taking a digital picture of your project. A snapshot is a unique "freeze" of the project at the time the snapshot was made. That freeze may represent a milestone moment you want to save. Or, a snapshot may be used as a creative or experimentation edit, leaving the original project safe and sound. The contents of the snapshot are independent of changes made to the project and any duplicate versions of the project.

The text "Snapshot" is auto-appended to the project name.

Duplicate Project

A duplicate is a little more robust and lively. A duplicate is great for backing up, archiving, and sharing a project. When a project is duplicated, there are special situations where a change to a specific clip type (compound clips, for example) affects the same clip in the other versions, but not the snapshots.

Exercise 5.1.1
Snapshotting a Project

Your project has reached the first edit milestone. You are ready to dissect it in some areas and build the next version. But first, you will make a snapshot to back up this version of the project for later reference, and create a Smart Collection to gather this and future snapshots.

1   In the Primary Media event, locate the Lifted Vignette project.

2   Control-click the Lifted Vignette project. From the shortcut menu, choose "Duplicate Project as Snapshot" to create a current snapshot of your project.

You now have a snapshot of the project at this milestone. To help keep things organized, you will create a Smart Collection for the project and snapshots.

Creating a Projects Smart Collection

This Smart Collection will automatically collect the projects and snapshots you will create throughout the rest of this book.

1   In the Lifted library, Control-click the Primary Media event, and from the shortcut menu, choose New Smart Collection.

An empty Smart Collection appears in the Libraries pane of the Primary Media event. The collection is named Untitled, but you can rename it.

2   Select Untitled for editing, enter *Projects*, and then press Return to accept the new name.

Now you must assign rules to the collection that will determine how it gathers projects.

3   In the Libraries pane, double-click the Projects Smart Collection to open the Filter window.

In Lesson 3, you added search criteria in this Filter window. You'll now do the same for this Smart Collection.

4   From the Add Rule (+) pop-up menu, choose Type.

5   In Type's two pop-up menus, create the criteria Type Is Project.

Your Projects Smart Collection will now gather your projects and snapshots as you craft the story.

6   Close the Filter window.

You will continue editing with the Lifted Vignette project with the knowledge that you have this and future snapshots as points of return in case the client changes his mind or a file is accidentally deleted.

Reference 5.2
Lifting from a Storyline

In a second pass edit, the editing needs can vary widely. The first edit may have nailed what the client wanted, so you can jump right to cleaning up the edit and exporting for distribution. More commonly, you'll embark on a second pass edit that may require some editorial changes, possibly major, which reroute the flow of the piece. Whichever editing strategy you must accept during the second edit, Final Cut Pro will keep everything in sync. The Magnetic Timeline, connected clips, and storylines you created during the first pass will pay off when you're moving and refining elements in this second pass.

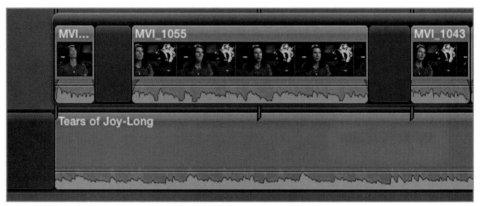

Sound bites replaced with music in primary storyline

The music and sound bites will drive this second edit. Because you are going to explore a variation of the workflow, you will lift the sound bites out of the primary storyline, and replace them with a longer version of Tears of Joy. Even this somewhat radical change will be surprisingly easy because Final Cut Pro will maintain the sync of all the connected clips and storylines.

Additional storylines of aerial media

You will add the aerial media depicting expansive landscapes: shots that scream out for the crescendo of a musical score. You'll see how weaving sound and image together in Final Cut Pro can be a joy for the editor.

Exercise 5.2.1
Lifting Clips Out of a Storyline

Replacing primary storyline sound bites with music sounds like a daunting task, but have no worries. Final Cut Pro will do the hard work for you.

1   In the primary storyline, select **MVI_1042**, and then Shift-click the last sound bite at the end of the storyline to select all of the sound bites and gap clips.

2   Control-click any one of the selected sound bites, and from the shortcut menu, choose Lift from Storyline.

The sound bites and gap clips move out of the primary storyline, and into a new connected storyline that we'll call the "sound bite storyline." In their places, one big gap clip is placed inside the primary storyline. As you learned earlier, Final Cut Pro avoids clip collisions by pushing the existing second lane clips and storylines up to the third lane. The project plays back in the Viewer exactly as it did before the lift edit. Now your project is ready to receive the new music into the primary storyline.

Reference 5.3
Replacing a Clip

Sometimes a clip doesn't work out, and must be replaced with another clip. Or perhaps a structural change requires exchanging one clip for another. Final Cut Pro includes five versions of the replace edit. Right now, we'll discuss the top three: Replace, Replace from Start, and Replace from End. All three commands become choices when you drag a replacement clip to a project clip.

The Replace command places the total duration of the Browser clip into the storyline. If the Browser clip is longer than the project clip it's replacing, the project clip expands to receive the longer clip. If the Browser clip is shorter, the project clip's duration decreases.

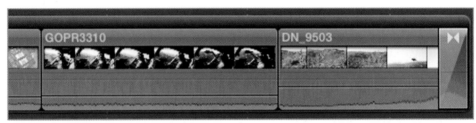

The Timeline clip's three-second duration

The seven-second Browser clip overrides the Timeline clip's three-second duration.

"Replace from Start" and "Replace from End" place the Browser clip within the duration of the current project clip. If the Browser clip is longer than the project clip, the Browser clip is truncated. "Replace from Start" aligns the start points of the two clips, and then truncates the end of the Browser clip. "Replace from End" aligns the end points and then truncates the start of the clip.

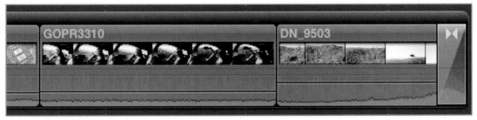

The Timeline clip's three-second duration

The three-second Timeline clip overrides the Browser clip's seven-second duration when "Replace from Start" or "Replace from End" is used.

If the Browser clip has insufficient content to fill out any of the three replace edits, Final Cut Pro performs a ripple trim, shortening the clip. If source media is available in the clip beyond the selected range, that extra media is used to avoid shortening the clip.

The three-second Timeline clip is shortened by the replacement one-second Browser clip.

Exercise 5.3.1
Replacing the Primary Storyline

You've already lifted the sound bites out of the primary storyline. Let's first delete the old music, and get ready to add the longer version.

1   In the Lifted Vignette project, select the existing music clip, and then press Delete.

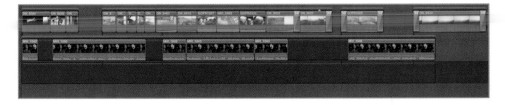

The shorter music clip is now gone. The project is ready for the new, longer music clip, which will replace the primary storyline's gap clip.

2   In the Primary Media event, select the Audio Only Smart Collection and locate **Tears Of Joy-Long**.

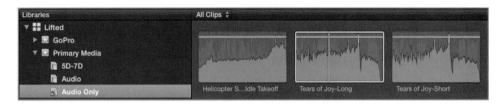

3   Drag the **Tears of Joy-Long** music clip from the Browser to the gap clip in the primary storyline. When the gap clip is highlighted in white, release the mouse button.

4   A shortcut menu appears. Because you want the entire music clip used for this replace edit, choose Replace from the shortcut menu. Play the project to hear the results

The gap clip is replaced. You now have a new score for your project, and a loud score it is. You can fix that quickly.

5   Lower the volume level of the new music clip by approximately –12 dB by placing the Select tool over the volume control (the horizontal line) in the audio waveform, and dragging down.

NOTE ▶ Press Shift-Z to fit the entire project in the Timeline pane.

cadence. So you can see and hear the music, let's make the audio waveforms bigger and hide the video thumbnails

9   In the Timeline's Clip Appearance window, select the first clip display option. Then click back in the Timeline to close Clip Appearance.

Now you can see what you are hearing.

10   Listen to the music around the Timeline's 28-second mark as displayed in the Dashboard.

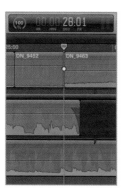

Prior to this point, the piano carries more of the melody in the verse. At around 28 seconds, the strings take over and soar above the piano. That flight of melody in the chorus calls out for the flight of the helicopter.

11   As the chorus takes off at 28 seconds, place a standard marker named *takeoff*.

Remember, "who's got the ball?" You'll need to select the music clip to intercept the clip in the pre-flight storyline from receiving the marker.

12 Continue listening to the music while setting the following markers:

Music-Based Markers

Timecode	Marker Name	Marker Type
~1:17	Swell	Standard
~1:31	Sunset	Standard

13 Click the Solo button to return to monitoring all audio.

14 Also before continuing, reset Clip Appearance to the third display option.

15 Set these additional markers:

Content-Based Markers

Timecode	On Clip	Marker Name	Marker Type
~0:15	MVI_1055	Add a Title	To-do
~0:27	DN_9452	Speed and SFX	To-do

Take a moment to look at the various views of the Tags Index while changing the filter controls. You will find the various markers you've created listed in the indices.

Reference 5.5
Using the Position Tool

The Position tool overrides a storyline's magnetic properties and allows a clip to be moved horizontally much like a connected clip, but with slightly destructive properties. A story-line clip, dragged with the Position tool, erases any existing clips and gaps that it contacts, leaving a new gap clip. The Position tool is in a constant overwrite state. Overwrite editing allows one clip to erase the contents of another clip by dragging.

The Position tool is very handy when you are locked-to-time, as in a commercial spot, and need to edit within a storyline without rippling the adjoining edits.

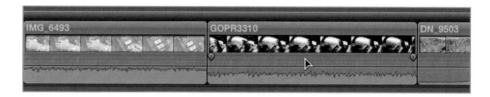

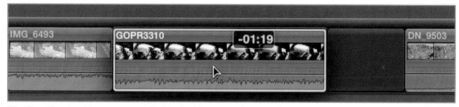

The Position tool leaves a gap behind while removing earlier content.

Exercise 5.5.1
Realigning Sound Bites and B-roll to Music

Before returning to the editing tasks, let's get a feel for the difference between the Select and Position tools. Select is magnetic while Position is not. Dragging a clip with the Select tool uses magnetic attraction or repulsion to keep clips attached to each other horizontally within a storyline. Dragging a clip with the Position tool "bulldozes" over adjoining clips, leaving a gap clip in place of the existing content.

1   In the Timeline, drag the middle (not the edges) of the **MVI_1055** sound bite to the left.

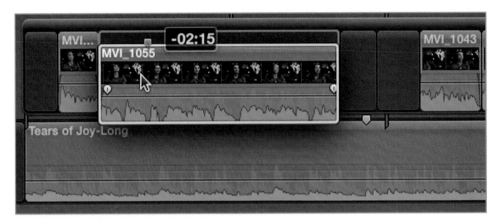

The sound bite swaps position with the gap clip before it. That's the expected magnetic behavior.

2   Press Command-Z to undo the edit.

Repeat the same edit, but this time using the Position tool.

3   From the Tools pop-up menu, choose the Position tool, or press P.

4   Once again, drag the **MVI_1055** sound bite slightly to the left in the storyline.

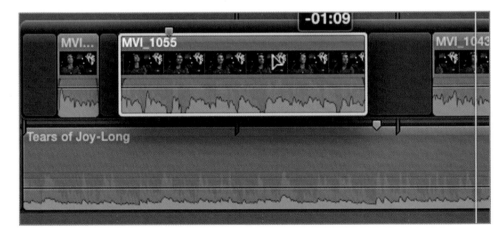

The gap before the sound bite becomes shorter.

5   If you don't see the difference between this behavior and the behavior when using the Select tool, press Command-Z to undo the edit, and try again while carefully watching the back end of **MVI_1055**.

When you drag a clip with the Position tool, a new gap clip or growing gap clip is left behind. Let's use the Position tool to adjust the timing between the second sound bite and the start of the music chorus. You want the sound bite to finish close to the takeoff marker you added earlier.

6   Using the Position tool, realign **MVI_1055** to end just to the left of the takeoff marker.

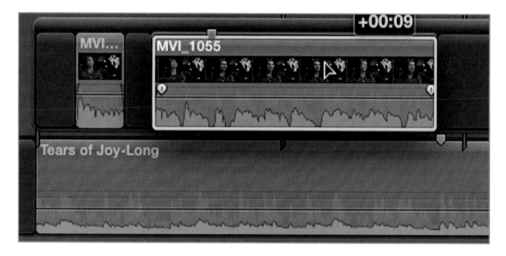

NOTE ▶ Depending on your earlier edits, this may entail dragging **MVI_1055** right to end closer to the marker.

7   Choose the Select tool, or press A.

You will use the Select tool after your takeoff marker to make room for the takeoff and new aerial B-roll. To fit with the music and open that room, the second set of sound bites will start after the eighth bar of the chorus (approximately 44 seconds into the Timeline).

8   Park your playhead on the music downbeat where Mitch says, "Inspired by, making sure," at approximately 44 seconds.

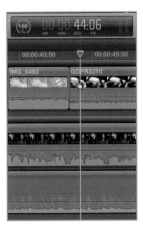

This is during or after the eighth bar of the chorus, just where you want to begin the next set of sound bites.

9   Using the Select tool, ripple trim the gap before **MVI_1043** to push the sound bites to the playhead.

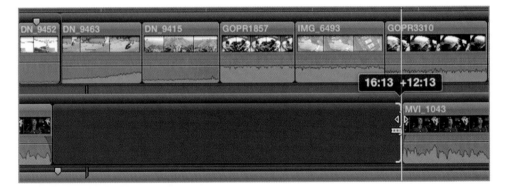

Don't worry about the B-roll. Just as you did during the first pass edit, your task is to interweave the new sound bite audio story with the music story. When that's done, the B-roll will flow together smoothly.

Breaking Up and Adding New Sound Bites

With more time available in the project, you can slow Mitch down a bit by breaking apart existing sound bites and adding more gap clips. You will also add some additional sound bites. Let's start by using roles to focus on the sound bite audio.

1   In the Roles Index, deselect the video, music, and natural sound roles.

The video clips, the music clip, and the natural sound clips are disabled in the project, which lessens the distraction of the video and other audio edits and allows you to concentrate on the sound bites.

NOTE ▸ If you find some clips are still audible when you expected them to be muted, check the clip's assigned roles in the Info inspector. Reassign the role, if necessary.

2   In the second instance of **MVI_1043**, cue the playhead after Mitch says, "Imagery of what you're shooting."

The playhead "ball" indicates the clip under the playhead that will receive the next edit. Because you want to blade the sound bite, you will need to select it.

3   Select the sound bite beneath the playhead. Press Command-B to blade the sound bite at the playhead.

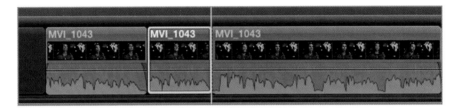

NOTE ▶ If the skimmer is active, you may place a cut where you didn't intend it. If so, press Command-Z to undo the edit, press S to disable the skimmer, and repeat the edit.

To create a pause, you'll use the Position tool.

4   Select both sound bites after the cut you just made.

5   Press P to choose the Position tool, and then drag the two sound bites to the right about 12 frames.

The existing **MVI_1046** is the sound bite that goes after the big musical crescendo as the sunlight shines into the helicopter. Let's push that clip into position to make room for the new sound bites.

6   Using the Select tool, ripple trim the gap clip before **MVI_1046** to push it to the last section of the music. The ripple trim should be approximately 15 to 20 seconds.

You've created a large gap that is ready to receive the two additional sound bites. The first should be placed roughly three seconds after the end of **MVI_1043**, at approximately

...pes here as a favorite. Let's search for

...in the Browser's search field, type *new*.

...favorite range appears on this clip.

...ipe. Press / (slash) to preview the range.

...re Mitch says "virtually," and an end

...e this clip in the sound bite storyline at

11 Leave the playhead cued, select the storyline handle, and then press D.

The sound bite is placed on top of the gap clip in the connected storyline. The edit does not ripple any other clip.

One more sound bite to go. Again, you'll place the new clip about three seconds after the sound bite you just added.

12 With the playhead at the end of **MVI_1044**, press Control-P.

The Dashboard lights up awaiting your time entry for moving the playhead. You want to move the playhead three seconds down the Timeline. You can do so using the + (plus sign) key.

13 Press the + (plus sign) key, and type *3.* (3 period), and press Return.

The playhead advances three seconds and is ready for the sound bite.

14 With the Interview Keyword Collection still selected, change the search text to *capture*.

MVI_1045 appears in the Browser because you previously assigned the word "capture" to the clip's notes.

15 In the Browser clip, click the green favorite stripe, and then press / (slash) to preview it.

16 Overwrite edit this clip into the sound bite storyline by selecting the storyline's handle, and press D.

17 In the Roles Index, re-enable the video, music, and natural sound roles. Review the last edit you performed with all audio and video clips enabled.

Let's move this last edited sound bite closer to the big musical crescendo.

18 Using the method you prefer, move MVI_1045 so the clip ends just before the Sunset marker you set earlier.

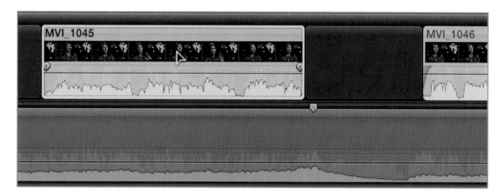

You performed quite a few edits already in this lesson. And not only edits. You added some markers to serve as editing notes. You also began exploring the Timeline Index and roles. Don't forget, this lesson started with moving the sound bites out of the primary storyline to be replaced by a new music clip. With the connected clips, story-lines, and magnetic timelines that Final Cut Pro watches over, you should feel enabled in your projects to push and pull things around throughout the Timeline.

Reference 5.6
Working with Auditions

When your editing project involves on-camera talent, that talent may be directed to per-form the same dialogue multiple times, each time with a different interpretation. When it comes time to edit those takes, many editors cut the performer's first take into the project and review it. Then they replace edit the second take into the project—which requires finding the second take, dragging it to the first take, and selecting Replace—and review it. The editor tediously has to repeat this process to evaluate every additional take.

The Audition feature in Final Cut Pro allows you to bundle those multiple takes into one clip that you can cut into your project. Then you can evaluate several performances by switching from take to take, and not performing multiple edits.

To select a take, the Audition window presents all the takes in a simple carousel display. Clicking a take thumbnail or pressing a keyboard shortcut performs the replace edit. And using a preview mode, you may cycle through every take during a playback loop.

Exercise 5.6.1
Repositioning Storylines and Deleting Within

Before you create and start editing with auditions, you'll need to make some Timeline changes to prepare for the audition clip. Final Cut Pro makes this easy; just remember to zoom in so you can see everything that is happening. Starting from the beginning, make these changes in anticipation of new aerial clips.

> **NOTE** ▶ Don't forget to toggle snapping on or off with the N key as needed while editing, and remember to zoom in to the edits for a detailed view. You may zoom by dragging the Zoom slider or by pressing Command-= (equals sign).

1   Trim two seconds from the first gap clip in the primary storyline.

This shifts the music, sound bites, and the Preflight and subsequent B-roll storylines, and keeps them in sync.

The start of the Takeoff storyline is DN_9463. This clip should start on the takeoff marker you set earlier.

2   Dragging the takeoff storyline's top handle, align the storyline with the major musical downbeat that occurs around the 26-second point in the Timeline. That point should be at the takeoff marker.

The second B-roll storyline, pre-flight, shifted up and now overlaps the takeoff storyline.

Depending on earlier edits, your takeoff storyline may already align with the marker. If so, you may skip to step 4.

3   Drag the pre-flight storyline to the left until it drops down because it no longer overlaps the takeoff storyline. With snapping turned on, ensure that the two storylines abut each other.

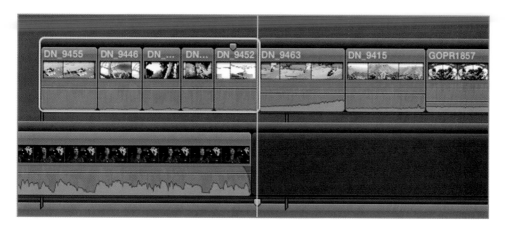

After the takeoff storyline, you'll want to quickly cut in an aerial shot, so let's remove and relocate some of the next B-roll clips.

Clip **DN_9415** will be removed from this pass. Perform a replace with gap deletion to leave a gap clip for the next series of edits.

4   Select **DN_9415**, and press Shift-Delete.

A gap clip replaces the deleted clip. You will use this gap as a reference point for the next edit series.

Exercise 5.6.2
Importing the Aerials

For the Lifted Vignette project, you will create an audition clip to edit all the new aerial clips into the project as a single clip. You will then cycle through those aerial clips within the audition clip to find the desired shot.

To prepare for this exercise, you must import the aerial media source files and organize them as library clips. The steps are abbreviated here because the entire process should take less than five minutes to complete.

> **NOTE** ▶ If you need a refresher on importing clips, review Lesson 2.

1   Open the Media Import window.

2   Navigate to your downloaded FCPX MEDIA > LV2 > LV Aerials folder.

3   Select the LV Aerials folder, and click Import Selected.

4   In the Import Options dialog that opens, set the following:

   ▶   Add to the existing Primary Media.

   ▶   Select to leave files in place.

   ▶   Select "Import folders as Keyword Collections."

   ▶   Deselect all other analysis options.

5   Click Import.

The aerial clips are placed in an LV Aerials Keyword Collection within the Primary Media event.

Exercise 5.6.3
Working with an Audition Clip

The Audition feature is a great way to review multiple takes, and even completely different clips. You will use it in this exercise as one approach to adding clips to a project. Let's start by building an audition clip in the Browser.

1   In the Browser, select all six aerial clips.

2   Control-click any one of the selected clips, and from the shortcut menu, choose Create Audition to create an audition clip.

The audition clip appears in the Browser. The audition clip is identified by the "spotlight" icon in the upper-left of its thumbnail. There are quite a few B-roll additions, deletions, and repositions to make. The audition clip will serve as an in-line browser of the aerial clips.

Experiencing the Audition Window

Let's take the audition clip for a spin by inserting it into the various B-roll storylines.

> **NOTE** ▶ The steps in this part of the exercise and in following exercises may feel as if you've lost control of the edit. However, Final Cut Pro will keep everything in sync.

1   In the Browser, click the audition clip's spotlight badge to open the audition window.

The Audition window appears showing the current pick. The pick is the currently active clip within the audition clip.

2   Press the Left or Right Arrow keys to cycle through the clips within the audition clip.

NOTE ▸ Alternatively, you may click the next thumbnail to select a different clip.

Notice that the selected clip's name and duration appears in the window. The audition clip works by performing a replace edit for you.

3   Using the Audition window, select `Aerials_11_02a` as the pick, and click Done.

The Audition window closes leaving the new pick in the audition clip. This canyon clip is currently 39 seconds in length. Let's cut that down to about six seconds.

4   With the audition clip (the one with the spotlight badge) selected in the Browser, create an approximately six-second clip starting around timecode 54:00.

NOTE ▸ The clip's timecode is visible in the Dashboard while you skim the clip.

5   From the Browser, insert edit the audition clip after `DN_9463`. Remember, you must select the storyline's handle before clicking the Insert button, or pressing W.

An audition clip performs a replace edit using the duration of each clip at the time you created the audition clip. Because you marked a duration of only one clip in the audition clip, the other aerial clips will ripple the B-roll storyline when they are selected as the pick.

6   Open the Audition window in the Timeline by clicking the spotlight icon next to the clip's name.

As you cycle the window between the alternate takes, the clip's duration is rippling the storyline.

7   Cycle the audition clip back to **Aerials_11_02a**.

This operation may seem a little hazardous to perform within a Timeline in which you've spent some time to "lock" sync specific clips to other clips. The subsequent storyline clips will realign after you trim the pick to the needed replacement duration.

▶ **Avoiding an Audition-Induced Ripple**

You may use a storylined audition clip without causing a ripple edit sync panic. The "Lift from Storyline" command gets the clip out of the storyline as a connected clip, leaving a gap. Now, as a connected clip, the audition's duration change is independent. After selecting the pick, and trimming the audition to the gap clip's duration, you have the option of returning the clip to the storyline or leaving it as a connected clip.

▶ **Relocating a Connection Point**

A connected clip or storyline defaults to a connection point at the start point of the clip/storyline. You may reset this connection to anywhere within the clip/storyline. The new connection point is defined by Command-Option-clicking the bottom of the clip (or top of a clip if below the primary storyline).

Connecting storylines at different points is slightly different in that you Command-Option-click the storyline's handle to set a new connection point.

Reference 5.7
Trimming the Tops and Tails

Whether you are working with a connected clip or a clip in a storyline, you may also use the "top and tail" trimming tools that support three trim methods.

The first two methods are "top the head" and "trim the tail." If you have extraneous material to remove from the start of the clip, park the playhead on the first frame you want to keep, and then use the Trim Start command. To trim material at the end of the clip, place the playhead after the last frame you want to keep, and use the Trim End command.

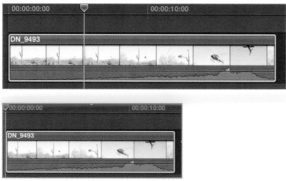

Trim Start to playhead

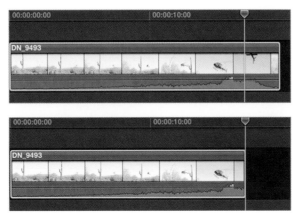

Trim End to playhead

The third method trims "top and tail" simultaneously using "Trim to Selection." You use the Range Selection tool, or mark start and end points with the help of clip skimming, to select the material you want to keep, and then "Trim to Selection" to delete the extraneous content outside that selection.

Trim to the selected range

Trim Start, Trim End, and "Trim to Selection" may be used during playback. This gives you real-time editing in context.

Exercise 5.7.1
Trimming the Aerials

You will continue using the audition clip to add the aerial B-roll clips. You'll trim those clips using the "top and tail" commands: Trim Start, Trim End, and "Trim to Selection."

1   From the Browser, select the audition clip, drag it to the gap after your first audition edit, and perform a replace edit.

2   Open the Audition window by selecting the second instance of the audition clip, and pressing Y.

3   Press the Left or Right Arrow keys to select **Aerials_13_02a**. Click Done.

For the moment, you will trim end **Aerials_13_02a** to the start of the sound bite.

4   Cue the playhead to the start of the sound bite.

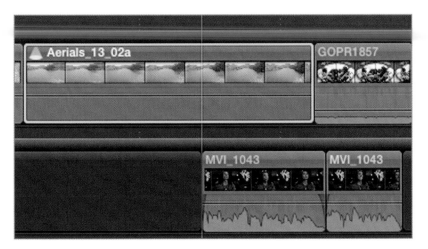

5   Select **Aerials_13_02a**, and press Option-] (right bracket).

The end of the clip is trimmed to the playhead, and the rest of the storyline ripples.

Let's add another clip here. You'll set up a pattern where the helicopter performs a low pass to "buzz the camera" before returning to Mitch's sound bites.

6   In the Browser, locate clip **DN_9493**. Mark an end point for the clip when all that's visible in the Viewer is the helicopter's tail.

7   Back up the playhead about three seconds, and set a start point.

8   Insert the trimmed **DN_9493** between **Aerials_13_02a** and **GOPR1857**.

The helicopter should buzz the camera before the sound bite plays. You can quickly trim the two aerials to place the loudest waveform of **DN_9493** before Mitch starts talking.

9   Select **Aerials_11_02a**, and start playback at the beginning of the clip. Look for a visual cue or listen for a musical hit that would make a suitable end point.

This point could be visually where the dry stream bed is about to reach the bottom of the screen. Musically, the edit could be at the start of a bar.

10 Park the playhead at the end point you've identified, verify that the clip is selected, and press Option-] (right bracket).

11 Trim a second or two from the end of Aerials_13_02a by once again listening and watching for an appropriate end point.

The loudest waveforms in DN_9493 probably occur just before the sound bite starts, so you can trim frames (or seconds) from the start of that clip.

12 If necessary, trim some additional frames from (or to) Aerials_11_02a, Aerials_13_02a, and/or DN_9493 to position the "buzzing" waveform before the sound bite.

13 Lower the volume of DN_9493 to –15 dB.

This is not the final mix level, but merely an adjustment to tame this audio content and avoid sonic aggravation until you remix the audio in Lesson 7. Also, the end of this clip is abrupt and overlapping the sound bite. In Lesson 6, you'll add a transition and split the audio to blend this clip into the next clip. You'll also adjust the clip so it carries the viewer into the sound bite.

Continuing to Add B-roll

Still more to go in this second edit pass. You've explored the theory and the tools. Now it's down to the physical work of assembling the edit.

1   Cue the playhead between **GOPR1857** and **IMG_6493**, and select the storyline's handle.

2   In the Browser, locate the B-roll clip **IMG_6486**. From the beginning of the clip, mark a 2:10 duration.

3   Press W to insert the clip into the takeoff storyline, and then lower the clip's volume level.

4   For **IMG_6493**, ripple trim the clip, if necessary, so that the clip ends with Mitch's hand and arm out of the clip, but before the camera starts to pan.

In Lesson 6, you will create a composite "split screen" of the next clip, **GOPR3310**, and an aerial clip. In anticipation of that composite, let's trim **GOPR3310**.

5   Ripple trim **GOPR3310** to a duration of 8:10.

There's more to add to the project. But, like a typical house remodel, there are some more old things that have to be removed to make room for the new.

Removing a Transition and Moving Clips

In the first edit pass, you applied some transitions to quickly smooth out some start and end points. One of those is now in the way and must be removed.

1   Use the Select tool to select the transition between **DN_9503** and **DN_9420**.

2   Press Delete.

NOTE ▸ Press the "Big Delete" or Backspace key. Do not press the small Forward Delete key found on full-size keyboards.

A couple of B-roll clips toward the end need some attention. Both of these clips, **GOPR0009** and **DN_9424**, should be moved to the Timeline's final sound bite.

3   Using the storyline's handle, drag **GOPR009**, the helicopter landing, above **MVI_1046**. Continue dragging to align the start transition with the music as it restarts after the big musical hit and the moment of silence.

4   Also using the storyline's handle, drag **DN_9424**, the flying-into-the-sunset clip, over **MVI_1046**. Continue dragging to align the peak of the audio waveform to occur just after the sound bite ends.

DN_9420 is the sunlight-through-the-windows clip. You may recall the great music hit that would sync well with this clip. That hit is the apex of the music.

Not only can you see the largest peak in the music waveform, but you also placed **MVI_1045** so it already ends with the musical hit.

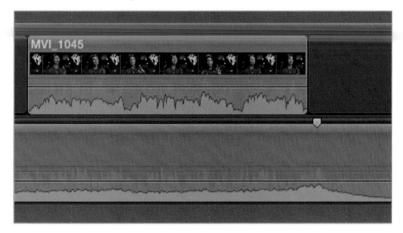

5   From the Takeoff storyline, drag **DN_9420** toward the largest peak in the music clip. Because you want **DN_9420** to reposition, drag the clip, and not the handle, so that you pull the clip out of the storyline. Use the markers you set earlier to align the visual effect to the musical hit.

Aligning the Bites and Bits

There are several edits to go in this pass; however, you've learned the necessary tools and workflow to tell your story. Storytelling is not only about describing actions in a linear format, but video storytelling looks for ways to enhance the story with both video and audio accents.

To start this series of edits, you want to establish a pattern. Previously, you edited **DN_9493** to low-pass over the camera before Mitch started talking again. You are going to create the same edit again with **DN_9503** and **MVI_1044**. However, currently this edit has little useable clip content to make the edit. For the transition to occur correctly, there must be overlapping media. The sound bite must start at minimum when the transition above starts. You'll achieve this overlap by creating more useable content by trimming the start of **DN_9503** and adjusting the gap's duration.

> **NOTE ▶** Don't forget to zoom in on the edits. Position the skimmer over what you need to zoom in on in the Timeline and then use the keyboard shortcut Command-= (equals sign) to zoom in for a detailed view of the edit.

1   Ripple trim the end point of the gap preceding **MVI_1044** so that **MVI_1044** starts aligned to the start of the transition.

Depending on your earlier edits, you may have not been able to complete the previous step, or aligning the start points of the clip and transition resulted in a very short gap.

2   If you need to lengthen **DN_9503** to increase the gap and ensure that the transition is over **MVI_1044**, ripple trim frames to the start of **DN_9503** by dragging left.

Dragging left with the Ripple tool on the start of **DN_9503** will supply the additional media.

3   Adjust the gap clip's duration under **DN_9503** to align the start of **MVI_1044** to the start of the transition in **DN_9503**.

You have three more B-roll clips to edit from the aerials audition clip. The three start during the **MVI_1044** sound bite.

4   From the Browser, connect edit the aerials audition clip to **MVI_1044** when Mitch says "new" a second time.

5   Within the audition clip, select **Aerials_13_01b** as the pick.

As it is, this clip is rather dull. But you haven't yet seen a reveal to the lake that occurs later in the clip. Right now, you will just place the clip for timing. In Lesson 6, you'll apply a speed change on the clip that will rush to that reveal. However, let's create a reminder to do this.

6   Click in the gray area above the storylines to ensure that no clip is selected.

7   Skim over the first half of **Aerials_13_01b**, the run-over-the-desert audition clip, and press M twice.

A standard marker is set, and the Marker window appears.

8   Name the marker *speed to reveal*, change the marker type to to-do, and then click Done.

A new to-do reminder is created (and one less sticky note is tagging your display). Let's get back to chopping the desert run audition clip down to size.

9 In the Timeline, blade the desert run audition clip at the start point of **MVI_1045**, but don't delete the second half.

You can use this second half of the audition clip to select the second B-roll clip.

10 Switch the second audition clip you just created to **Aerials_11_01a**.

The clip is much too long, but you can take advantage of that to find the range you need.

11 If necessary, from the View menu, enable clip skimming.

With clip skimming turned on, you can solo the audio and video of a clip. The skimmer is contained to the clip you are skimming, providing a skimmer solo option. No matter where the clip is in vertical relationship to other clips, the clip skimmer solos that clip's contents.

12 Clip skim **Aerials_11_01a** to a Dashboard timecode of ~37:00. This is the source timecode of the clip. Press I to mark a start point.

13 Continue clip skimming to the right until the Dashboard reads 42:00. Mark this as the end point by pressing O.

Now you will perform a "Trim to Selection" to remove the extraneous material outside that range.

14 Press Option-\ (backslash).

Because this is only a connected clip, it comes to rest at the range's location rather than sliding left to the head of a storyline.

15 Using the Select tool, snap the clip to the end of **Aerials_13_01b**, which is toward the left.

Now you need one more copy of the audition clip for the third aerial clip in this series. You can make that copy from the existing Audition clips in the Timeline.

16 Option-drag a copy of the Aerials audition clip off of itself, and release the mouse button before releasing the Option key.

This technique duplicates the clip, creating a copy you can place elsewhere in the Timeline.

17 Snap the copied clip to the end of the audition clip from which you just copied.

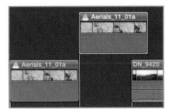

18 Change the pick of this third audition clip to **Aerials_11_03a**.

19 Clip skim this audition clip and then set a start point at 1:42:00 and an end point at 1:46:00. Press Option-\ (backslash) to "top and tail" the clip to the marked range.

20 Snap this trimmed clip to the end of the Aerials_11_01a clip.

21 Trim the end of Aerials_11_03a to create a clean snap to DN_9420.

Because you will later add transitions to the four clips you've been modifying, you can prep them by placing them in a storyline.

22 Create a storyline using the four clips, starting with Aerials_13_01b and continuing through to DN_9420.

Only one more quick tweak to the last sound bite in the project is needed.

23 Ripple trim the end point of the gap before MVI_1046 to push the sound bite's start point after GOPR0009 has fully transitioned onscreen. Play the project.

As you watch your project, you'll notice a few things that aren't fully realized. You still have to add sound effects, apply some speed changes, place some transitions, mix the audio, and create that split-screen clip. These will be enjoyable edits you'll experience in the following lessons.

But look at what you've accomplished on this second pass. To experience a different workflow approach, you lifted the sound bites out of the primary storyline to be replaced by a longer music clip. You shifted and created some additional connected storylines for grouping the B-roll. You created an audition clip to house the similar aerial clips. That audition allowed you to stay in the Timeline when working with the aerial B-roll rather than digging back into the Browser to get the clip you need. You made some big changes, but Final Cut Pro has made those changes easy.

Your current Timeline

Lesson Review

1. Describe the results of using the following commands: Duplicate Project as Snapshot, and Duplicate Project.

2. Which replace edit command replaces the project clip using the duration of the browser clip: Replace, Replace from Start, or Replace from End?

3. Identify and define (from left to right) the four buttons in the following figure.

4. What action results from the displayed indication in the Dashboard?

5. Where do you find a list of all markers used in a project?

6. What command was invoked in the displayed project?

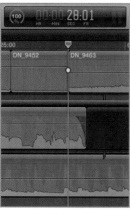

7. Which tool repositions storyline clips relative to time allowing a clip to overwrite other clips?

8. Where may you assign a role to a clip?

9. What types of clips may go into an audition?

10. What icon badge identifies an audition clip?

11. What command was used in the scenario shown below?

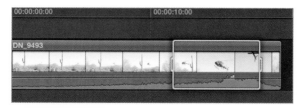

Answers

1. Duplicate Project creates a "live" version that updates its compound and multicam clips used in other projects. Duplicate Project as Snapshot produces a complete freeze of the project at the time of the duplication.

2. The Replace edit command

3. Skimming (S): Enable/disable the video skimmer.
    Audio Skimming (Shift-S): Enable/disable audio skimming (skimming must be enabled).
    Solo (Option-S): Monitor the audio playback of the selected clip(s).
    Snapping (N): Magnetically align the skimmer/playhead while dragging to the start of clips, keyframes, and markers.

4. The playhead will move three seconds to the left. This adjustment was performed by pressing Control-P.

5. The Tags Index found in the Timeline Index pane

6. The Solo command, Option-S

7. Position tool

8. Roles may be assigned in the Info inspector or in the Modify menu.

9. Commonly used for multiple takes of an on-camera performance or of an audio-only VO, the audition clip collects whatever clip types you add to the audition.

10. A spotlight badge identifies and is an access point to an audition clip.

11. Trim to Selection, Option-\ (backward slash)

Enhancing the Edit

The second pass at revising your project has led to this enhancement pass. Not every project will need the techniques presented here, while other projects may require all of them. Regardless of how much work remains to be done, a third enhancement pass is when your creativity may flourish—not just while polishing your edit, but also when covering a production or post-production error.

The Lifted Vignette project received some significant revisions in second pass. Now you will insert the necessary speed effects, apply visual effects to enhance an image or two, and further unify your story elements by adding more transitions. You'll learn how to composite two clips, and then collapse that composite into a manageable compound clip.

GOALS

► Vary the playback speed of clips

► Modify the look of clips with effects

► Utilize transitions

► Adjust transform and compositing controls

► Create compound clips

Reference 6.1
Retiming Clips

Speed effects can serve many purposes in a project. For instance, you might want to suggest the compression of time in a training video to more quickly demonstrate the entire action of a time-consuming process. The slightly faster playback speed can demonstrate that process without boring your viewers. Speed effects can also exert an emotional impact. In a narrative piece with a character or narrator reflecting on past events, slowing the playback speed may visually heighten the emotion expressed in the voiceover.

Regardless of your reason for applying a retiming effect, always make sure that you do have that reason. Using speed effects merely for the sake of adding an effect will distract viewers, and distance them from your storytelling.

You already applied a constant speed change to a clip when you previously reversed playback of the first clip, the reflection of the hangar door opening. That speed change was very easy to apply by choosing Reverse Clip from the Retiming pop-up menu. The Retime Editor set the clip to play at normal speed, but backward.

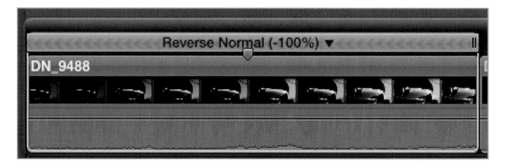

However, Final Cut Pro includes many more retiming options than simply playing a clip in reverse. The Retiming pop-up menu and the Retime Editor feature several retiming presets we'll explore in this lesson.

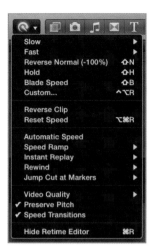

Exercise 6.1.1
Setting a Constant Speed Change

In your Lifted Vignette project, several clips require a speed change effect. You placed to-do markers on them as a reminder that they needed later attention. Let's review that to-do list in the Timeline Index; but before you make any more changes to this project, take a snapshot for later reference and to save as a backup.

1   With the project active in the Timeline, choose Edit > Duplicate Project as Snapshot, or press Command-Shift-D.

2   In the Timeline pane, click the Timeline Index button, or press Command-Shift-2, to open the Timeline Index.

You may need to reset the Index to view the Tags pane that filters the to-do markers.

3   In the upper section of the Timeline Index, click the Tags button.

4   In the lower section, click the Incomplete To-Do Items button (the third button from the right).

The index now lists the to-do markers you created during your previous edit passes.

5   In the Timeline Index, select the to-do marker titled "Speed and SFX."

The marker on **DN_9452** is selected, and the playhead is cued to the clip.

6   Play the clip to recall that it shows the helicopter starting up.

What if this clip started a little bit faster? Inherently, the clip's content is accelerating. You could give it a little boost to get the rotors up to speed faster for the next clip where the helicopter is taking off.

7   Select the clip, and then press Command-R to display the clip's Retime Editor.

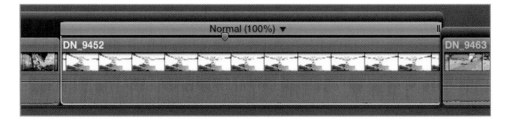

Every clip has an associated Retime Editor you may view to see if any adjustments have been made. As indicated by the stripe, the clip currently plays at normal, 100-percent speed.

Setting Playback Speed Manually

A retiming effect can realize more emotion from a clip's contents; make a shot usable within continuity; or create a noticeable, visual effect. The Retiming pop-up menu and a clip's Retime Editor, "the stripe," include several presets to get you started creating the effect you need. To understand the power of the Retime Editor, you'll try the manual adjustments.

1 At the right end of the Retime Editor for **DN_9452**, drag the retiming handle right and left while watching the stripe's speed indicator.

The clip's duration changes as the speed value changes. When you drag the retiming handle to the right, the Retime Editor indicates that the clip will play slower than normal speed and the clip's duration lengthens. When you drag the handle to the left, the clip will play faster than normal and the clip's duration shortens.

Be aware that this is not a ripple trim. Despite the speed change, the clip's end point remains the same. The frame cadence is altered to implement the new speed settings. In a nutshell, a clip at 100-percent speed plays frames 1, 2, 3, 4, and so on, just as the clip was recorded. When you play the clip at 200-percent speed, the clip skips alternate frames and plays frames 1, 3, 5, and so on. The side effect of skipping frames is that the clip's duration is shortened; however, the start and end points don't change.

Before you continue, you should reset the clip to normal, 100-percent forward speed.

2 With **DN_9452** selected, from the Retiming pop-up menu, choose Reset Speed.

By dragging the retiming handle, you may alter the duration or the playback speed of a clip. But you may also change speed using another manual method that utilizes a numeric entry.

3 In the Retime Editor, click the Speed pop-up menu.

The Speed pop-up menu contains some of the same options as the Retiming pop-up menu, including the Custom speed option.

4 From the Speed pop-up menu, choose Custom.

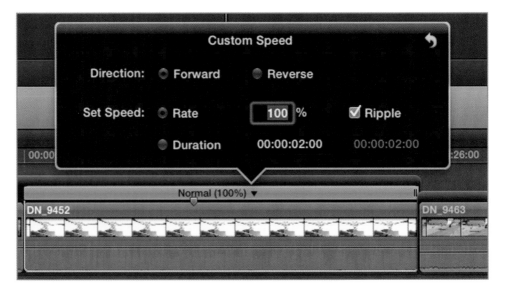

The Custom Speed window opens.

Here you may numerically enter a playback rate for a clip or the desired duration, and allow Final Cut Pro to calculate the necessary speed change. For **DN_9452**, you want to play the clip faster. Because the clip duration is already set as needed, you'll adjust the rate.

5 In the Rate percentage field, type *200*, but don't press Return yet.

Look at the Ripple checkbox. When it is selected, clips after the retimed clip and in the same storyline will shift to the left to ensure that a gap clip is not created. When the checkbox is deselected, the speed change will create a gap clip so that subsequent clips do not shift. In this edit, you do not want to create a gap clip, so leave Ripple selected.

6   Ensure that Ripple is selected, and then press Return.

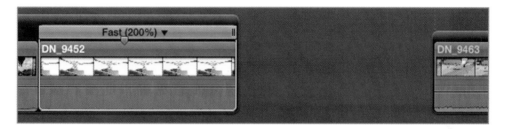

The clip shortens to half its original length because you entered a 2x playback speed. However, you need the shot to play as fast as it does now, but continue until the beginning of **DN_9463**.

NOTE ▶ Click outside the Custom Speed window to close it.

Previously you adjusted the retiming handle at the right end of the Retime Editor to change a clip's duration by varying its playback speed. Trimming the clip, however, changes the clip's duration by trimming its content, as you have already done several times.

7   With the Select tool, extend the clip's end to the right until it snaps into place against **DN_9463**. Preview the results.

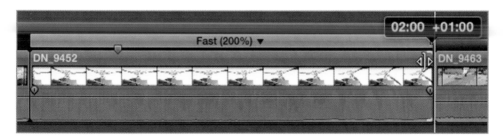

That's not quite dramatic enough. We want to see the power of a turbine-powered helicopter. Let's redo the Speed change to 500%. That should get those rotors turning.

8   In the Retime Editor, click the Speed button, select Custom, change the Rate to 500%, and then press Return.

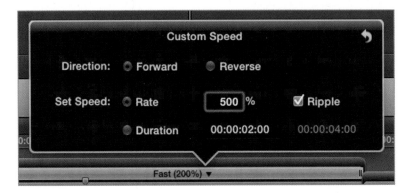

The clip shortens again. You can ripple trim to lengthen the clip, which adds content to the clip.

9   Drag the end point of **DN_9452** to snap against the start point of **DN_9463**.

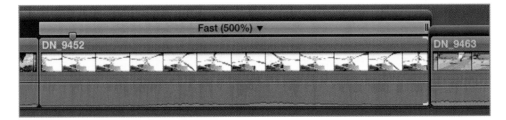

That's more like it. The helicopter is about to take flight, and the rotor blades visually convey that speed. Now you've applied two constant speed effects to your project. With the helicopter starting clip, you may notice the "sound effect" provided by the crew. It's not quite the real, mechanical sound, so you'll later insert a different sound effect.

Exercise 6.1.2
Editing with Blade Speed

Another retiming effect, the variable speed change, applies at least two different playback rates within a single clip. This effect requires dividing the clip into segments, one for each speed rate. **Aerials_13_01b** is the perfect clip for this effect. It shows the helicopter racing above the desert and then flying over the cliff, revealing the lake.

Right now, this clip is trimmed to the necessary story duration, but including more of the clip would be better. To perform this edit and apply the effect, you need to see the entire clip to identify the speed segments. Although you could temporarily ripple trim the clip to extend it to its full length, here's another method.

1   Using the Timeline Index, locate **Aerials_13_01b**, which has the "speed to reveal" to-do marker.

2   In Lifted Vignette, Control-click **Aerials_13_01b**, and from the shortcut menu, choose "Lift from Storyline."

You used this edit function in Lesson 5 to move sound bites out of the primary storyline. In this context, the function displays the aerials clip above the connected storyline; and as in the primary storyline, the clip is replaced with a gap clip to mark its location and duration. You may now adjust the clip's duration without disturbing other clips in the storyline.

You could drag to extend the **Aerials_13_01b** end point to view the entire clip; or you could change the clip's duration numerically, as you will do here.

3   With **Aerials_13_01b** selected, press Control-D.

The clip's current duration appears in the Dashboard. You may recall that the source clip is rather long, so entering a new, longer duration will include the "reveal" of the lake.

4   Without clicking (because the Dashboard is already prepared to receive a new value), enter *45.* (four five period), and press Return.

Aerials_13_01b lengthens to 45 seconds. Skimming the clip shows the reveal to the lake. You will use the Blade Speed option to "break" the clip into speed segments.

You will tie together two elements with these speed segments: the music and the visual reveal. The first speed segment will play the clip at normal speed, which is the clip's current status. So, what you are first looking and listening for is where to start the speed change and place the second speed segment.

Close to the end of the MVI_1044 sound bite, Mitch says, "eye opener." Let's use that as the kickstart for the speed change.

5   Cue the playhead where Mitch says, "eye opener."

6   Select Aerials_13_01b, and from the Retiming pop-up menu, choose Blade Speed, or press Shift-B.

The clip's Retime Editor opens, indicating the two speed segments you created. The start of the second speed segment identifies where in the shot (flying over the desert) and when in the sound bite's audio ("eye opener") the speed change will occur.

Starting at this segment, you will accelerate the playback to the point in the clip where the helicopter reaches the edge of the cliff and the lake is revealed. That's where you'll start a third speed segment.

7   With the second speed segment started, cue the playhead where the helicopter has gone halfway over the cliff. Press Shift-B.

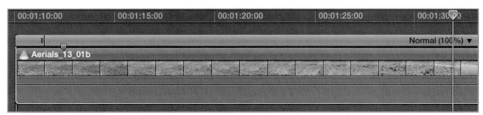

Before Blade Speed

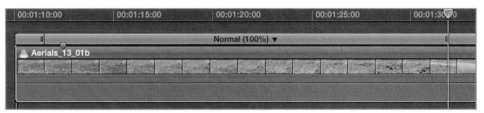

After Blade Speed

You've established what you want to see at the start of the third segment. Now you're ready to set the speed change in relation to the music. You will locate in the music where the speed change to the third segment occurs. Earlier, you created a marker named Swell. You may use the Timeline Index, set to All tags, or reference the nearby marker in the Timeline to locate the music swell.

8   Cue the playhead to the musical swell at roughly 1:15 in the project.

Setting the playhead at this musical hit identifies a reference point for the end of the second speed segment.

9 At the end of the second speed segment, drag the retiming handle to the left until it aligns to the playhead.

Review the whole clip to watch and listen as the helicopter races across the desert floor and the lake is revealed with the musical hit.

Working with Speed Transitions

While reviewing the effect, you may notice an acceleration into and deceleration out of the second speed segment. Although the acceleration is effective at the start of the segment, you would like a more abrupt change in speed to coincide with the lake reveal.

NOTE ▶ If necessary, zoom into the second speed segment.

The speed segments include speed transitions that control the speed change between segments. And, of course, they are adjustable.

1 Move the mouse pointer over the left edge of the second speed transition.

2 Drag the left edge of the transition toward the center of the transition until its left half is removed.

When you examine the edit, you'll see that a deceleration transition is still present, but it does not occur until the point at which you speed bladed the clip.

3   Vary the duration of the speed transition's right half to alter the deceleration and see how it impacts the dramatic relationship between image and music. Is the abrupt drop from jet speed to walking speed a good thing?

     After reviewing an edit, if you decide that you speed bladed at the wrong frame, you can still adjust where the transition occurs relative to the content.

4   Double-click the junction between speed segments 2 and 3.

The Speed Transition HUD opens.

NOTE ▶ If the HUD does not open, press Command-Z until at least one of the speed transitions reappears, and then double-click the transition.

In the Speed Transition HUD, you can enable or disable both sides of the speed transition. You'll also find the Source Frame Editor here, which allows you to roll edit the clip within the speed change without changing the speed segment.

5   Deselect the Speed Transition checkbox, and then click the Source Frame Edit button.

The source frame editor appears as a film-frame icon. The editor roll edits the content between the two speed segments, changing the end frame of the left speed segment while changing the start frame of the right speed segment.

6   Drag the source frame's film-frame icon left and right until the Viewer displays the cliff frame at which you want the speed change to occur.

7   Double-click the source frame icon to close the editor.

Now, you'll need to perform some cleanup edits to trim the end point of Aerials_13_01b to the duration of the gap clip so that the clip visually fits back into the storyline.

8   Cue the playhead to the start point of the next clip, Aerials_11_01a.

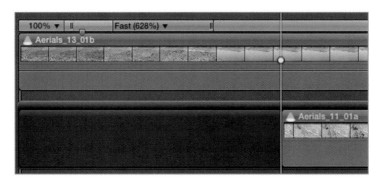

9   With the playhead and skimmer cued, press Option-] (right bracket).

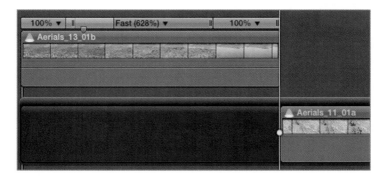

Aerials_13_01b is trimmed and ready for reinsertion into the storyline. The magnetic nature of storylines makes this easy.

10 Drag Aerials_13_01b down and to the right until an insert bar and subsequent blank space appears, then release the mouse button.

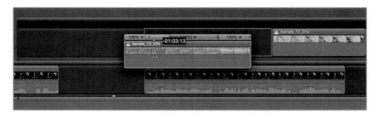

11 Select and delete the gap clip from the storyline.

12 With `Aerials_13_01b` selected, press Command-R to close the Retime Editor.

The clip is returned to its original location in the storyline. Furthermore, the lake reveal is synced with the audio cues.

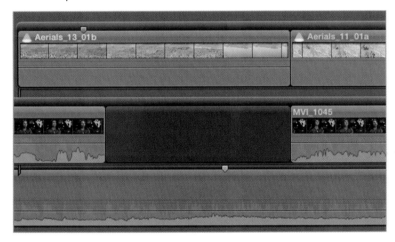

Reference 6.2
Working with Video Effects

Sometimes a clip needs the extra visual punch of a video effect or a color grade. A video effect could be a vignette to direct the viewer's attention to the center of the image. A color grade could increase (or decrease) the contrast to look as if the clip came from an old movie.

Final Cut Pro includes over 200 video and audio effects. Plus, the number of available third-party effects is growing every day. You may even create original effects and share them with fellow Final Cut Pro users.

All video and audio effects are displayed in the Effects Browser. In its left sidebar, effects are organized into video and audio subcategories. A search field at the lower end of the browser supports text-based searching for effects.

Exercise 6.2.1
Experimenting with Video Effects

Applying an effect is simple. First, select one or more destination project clips. In the Effects Browser, double-click the desired effect to apply the effect, which is now ready for additional customization.

In Lifted Vignette, let's apply a vignette effect to the last shot of the helicopter flying into the sunset.

1   Skim to and select the last B-roll clip, DN_9424.

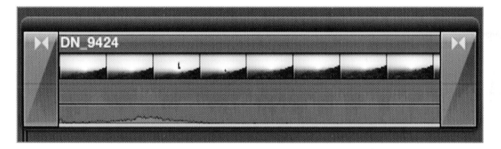

This clip may be enhanced by applying a vignette that darkens the corners of the image.

2   In the Effects Browser, ensure that "All Video & Audio" is selected in the sidebar, and search for *vignette*.

Two effects appear. You may preview each effect by skimming its thumbnail in the Browser.

3   Skim the Vignette and the Vignette Mask effects.

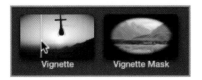

You do not need a mask version of this effect, so the regular Vignette effect will do.

4   Skim over the Vignette effect again, and then press the Spacebar to start playback.

You see a live preview of the Vignette effect applied to DN_9424. Some settings specific to this Vignette effect may be modified. To do so, you must first apply the effect to a project clip.

5   Ensure that DN_9424 is selected, and then double-click the Vignette effect.

NOTE ▶ Alternatively, you may drag an effect to a Timeline clip.

With the playhead cued over the clip, the results are visible in the Viewer. A key thing to remember when working with effects is to cue the playhead over the clip you are altering. You will then immediately see the results when you modify the effect.

Modifying an Effect

With the effect applied, you may adjust its settings in the Video inspector. Remember that the settings for effects, transitions, and titles are available only after the effect is applied to a Timeline clip.

The available adjustments will vary depending on the effect. Some effects have only two or three parameters, while others have dozens. You may change these parameters to customize the effect for a specific clip, as you've started to do with the Vignette applied to the last clip. Because exploring and experimenting is so easy and reversible, you're missing an opportunity to discover the possibilities if you don't tweak a parameter or two.

1   Open the Video inspector by clicking the Inspector button, or pressing Command-4.

2   In the Video inspector, accessed by selecting the Video button at the top of the Inspector pane, Vignette is listed in the first category, Effects.

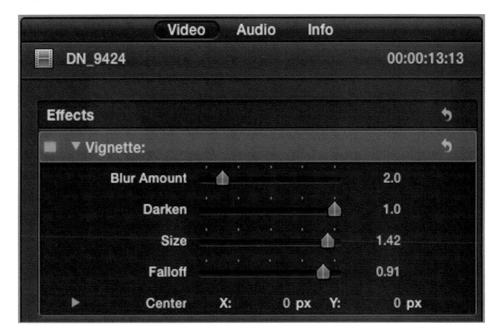

The Vignette parameters appear in the Video inspector because you selected the clip with that effect at the end of the previous exercise.

NOTE ▶ If Vignette is not listed, ensure that the playhead is over **DN_9424** and that no other clip is selected.

3   Drag the fourth slider, Falloff, left to a value of 0.57.

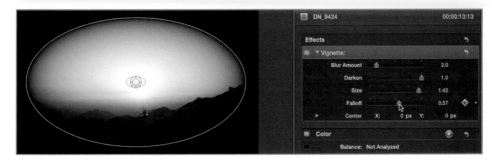

The Vignette collapses, shrinking the viewable portion of the clip. That may be too much falloff. But before addressing that, let's tweak some other parameters. Some of those parameters are adjustable in the Viewer and Inspector, while others are adjustable only in the Inspector.

4 In the Viewer, adjust the inner-concentric oval.

The image updates in the Viewer as the Size and Falloff parameters update in the Video inspector.

After you've experimented with an effect, you may want to reset the effect and start over. Reset buttons are available in the Inspector to the right of the effect.

At the upper-right of the Vignette effect are two hooked arrow Reset buttons. Clicking the lower one resets the current effect, in this case, Vignette. Clicking the upper Reset button resets all the parameters of every applied effect.

5 In the Video inspector, click the current effect Reset arrow (the lower one).

The Vignette effect returns to its default settings. Since trying one effect is so easy, let's now see how easy it is to try a couple of effects at once.

Stacking Effects

You can apply more than one effect to a clip. You should not go overboard by applying 20 to 30 effects to a clip without reason, but two or three may be called for in your project. Some effects are corrective effects. Depending on a clip's content, it may need a few corrective filters. Other effects function as decorative filters that add a visual style to an image.

One technique when using multiple effects is to change their stacking order in the Inspector. When you apply an effect to a clip, the effect is added to the bottom of the Effects category in the Video inspector. The order in which the effects appear in the Video inspector may affect their impact on the final image.

1   With **DN_9424** selected, ensure that the Video inspector is still visible.

2   In the Effects Browser, clear the previous search text, then locate and double-click the Aged Paper effect.

The sunset image appears to be part of the texture from the Aged Paper effect.

In the Inspector, notice the layering order of the effects. Vignette is first applied to the image and then Aged Paper is applied to the composite of the clip and Vignette. Let's make a change to see the impact of the layering order.

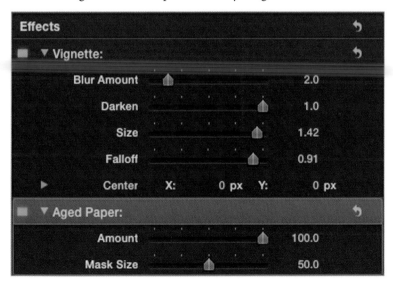

3   On the Vignette effect, drag the Blur Amount slider fully to the left and then fully to the right.

Notice that the paper texture does not get blurry. That's because Vignette is applied first followed by Aged Paper.

4   Adjust the Vignette effect's Falloff parameter to 0.57 again.

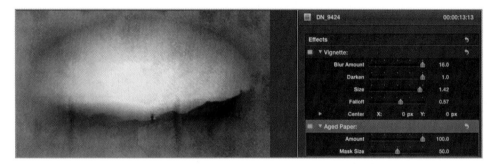

The look of the Aged Paper is slightly affected as you are compositing the two effects together, but the Blur Amount and Falloff are affecting just the Vignette. The Aged Paper effect is composited or added on after the Vignette effect. Let's reverse their compositing order and analyze the results.

5   In the Inspector, drag Aged Paper upward on top of Vignette. The Vignette effect automatically drops down to allow Aged Paper to go first.

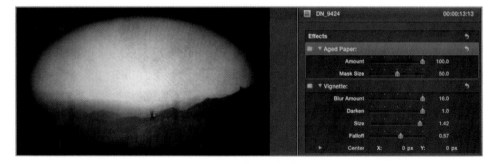

Notice the huge difference as Vignette is composited onto the Aged Paper effect.

6   In the Inspector, drag the Vignette's Blur Amount and Falloff sliders to their left and right extremes.

Now these parameters deeply affect the Aged Paper's look.

Effects are processed starting with the top effect, and then move through the stack in a top-down manner. The bottom-most effect can dramatically alter everything done previously.

Deleting Effects

An effect may be disabled or deleted in the Inspector. If you think you may later need a particular effect, disable it. If the results of that effect didn't suit your project at all, delete it. In the current project, Aged Paper is highly deletable.

1   In the Video inspector, select the Aged Paper effect.

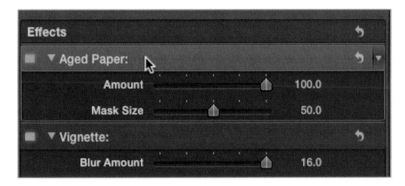

2   Press Delete.

> **NOTE ▶** Ensure that you press the Delete (Backspace) key, not the little Forward Delete key which deletes the clip.

The effect is removed from the clip. If you wanted to disable an effect, you could have deselected the checkbox to the left of the effect's name.

3   Reset the Vignette's parameters to default using the Reset arrow.

You'll leave the Vignette applied at its default settings.

Exercise 6.2.2
Creating a Depth of Field Effect

GOPR0009 has a couple of distracting natural elements in the foreground. A simple solution would be to use the Transform controls to enlarge the image and crop out those distractions. But, let's try combining filters with a copy of the clip to create an effect that will make those elements less distracting: a far-focused, shallow depth of field. You will blur the parapet wall to remove focus from those foreground elements.

1   In the Lifted Vignette project, back up to **GOPR0009** where the helicopter is landing at the end of the day.

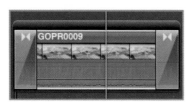

To blur the foreground slightly, you'll need to copy the clip. The original will provide the normal background while the copy will be partially blurred and composited above the original clip. The partial blur involves a *mask* to identify the parapet to be blurred while leaving the rest of the image in focus. To get started, you will copy and paste the clip on top of itself.

2   Cue the playhead to the start point of **GOPR0009**.

You want to use a clean copy of the clip with no transitions.

3   Select and delete any transitions applied to **GOPR0009**.

4   Select the clip, cue the playhead to the start point of the clip, and then press Command-C to copy it.

5   Press Command-V to paste the clip copy into the project directly above the existing clip.

As with any connected clip, the highest video clip is the clip visible in the Viewer. You are about to composite the two clips so that portions of each will be simultaneously visible.

NOTE ▸ If the skimmer is active in the Timeline, the clip will paste at the skimmer's location.

Creating a Mask

A mask shape identifies the visible area of the upper clip that will be the foreground. The parts of the image outside the mask will be transparent and allow the lower clip to show through as the background. You will define the foreground, the parapet wall, in the upper clip using the Mask effect. You will find this easier to do if you reduce the Viewer zoom level and disable the lower clip.

1   In the Viewer, from the Zoom pop-up menu, choose a value less than the currently displayed zoom level.

For example, if the zoom currently reads 60%, choose 50%. Doing so will display some space around the Viewer's image in which you can adjust the mask.

2   Select the lower **GOPR0009**, and from the shortcut menu, choose Disable, or press V.

Nothing changes in the Viewer because the upper clip is still the currently visible image. That's about to change.

3   Select the upper, visible clip to prepare it for the mask.

4   In the Effects Browser, search for *mask*.

Four masks are displayed in the Effects browser: Circle Mask, Image Mask, Mask, and Vignette Mask. Mask is the effect you want to use here.

5   Double-click the Mask effect to apply it to the selected project clip.

You see a masked GoPro clip foreground playing over the sound bite of Mitch. That's OK. The disabled lower clip will hide Mitch from view when re-enabled. You will drag the four control points of the Mask effect to outline the wall and roof.

6   Drag the lower-right control point down and slightly to the left to where the wall flashing intersects the bottom edge of the image.

NOTE ▶ Overshooting the image allows you to see the composite and accurately place the mask.

7   Drag the lower-left control point to the lower-left of the image's corner.

8   Drag the upper-left control point to the left and down to where the top of the wall's flashing intersects the left side of the image.

9   Finally, drag the upper-right control point to the apex of the wall's corner, just below the landing pad.

You've defined the mask for the composite of the roof and wall. Now you'll composite the correct two clips and apply the depth-of-field effect.

NOTE ▸ The wall is not quite square, but the Blur effect should cover it.

Compositing the Mask Effected Clip

Time to re-enable the lower GoPro clip and apply the Gaussian Blur effect to the upper wall-only clip. The final composite will help direct the viewer's eyes past the wall.

1 Select the lower GoPro clip, and press V.

   The two clips are composited in the Viewer, but there isn't much to see until you apply the blur effect.

2 With the upper GoPro clip selected, search for and apply the Gaussian effect.

   With the blur applied, you may want to realign your mask to more accurately match the wall.

3 If necessary, select the upper GoPro clip, and then drag the mask's control points to adjust the mask borders.

NOTE ▶ If the control points are not visible, in the Video inspector, select the Mask effect.

4   After setting the mask, adjust the Gaussian Amount slider to around 17 to make the effect a little more subtle.

5   To see the image before and after the effect is applied, deselect the checkbox next to the Gaussian Blur effect. Make sure you re-enable the effect when you're done.

The viewer's eyes are now more likely to go to the helicopter than the wall. In a moment, you'll reapply the transitions to smooth the entry into the clip.

Reference 6.3
Working with Video Transitions

In the syntax of video, transitions can help indicate a change in time and/or place: A slow dissolve sustains the emotional impact of the tragedy-just-happened into a scene a year later as the character returns to the tragedy site to find closure. Or, a soft-edge wipe carries the viewer across the galaxy from C3PO and R2D2 on the Millennium Falcon to Darth Vader overseeing construction of the Death Star. As effective and versatile as transitions are, you do have to be careful when adding them. While these visual devices can link storytelling elements across time and space, they can easily become disruptive and confusing when overused.

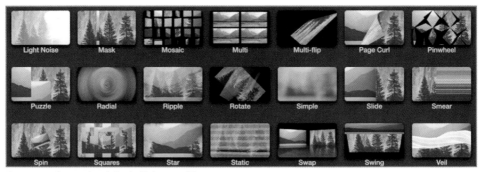

Just a small sample of the built-in transitions

With so many transitions available in Final Cut Pro, you may be tempted to use too many transition types within a single project. You should resist the temptation, and use transitions consistently within a project. Too much variation in transition types may lower a project's perceived production values.

You don't know what to avoid until you've at least seen or experienced other transitions. Let's look beyond the cut and cross dissolve transitions to see the other possibilities. You'll start by learning the three ways a clip or an edit point may receive a transition.

Exercise 6.3.1
Experimenting with Transitions

You'll find that applying and modifying transitions is similar to applying and modifying effects, although there is a difference when selecting clips versus edits points.

A transition between two clips involves two edit points: the end of the previous clip and the start of the next clip. Here's how Final Cut Pro sees and applies the transition to the edit points:

As you've already experienced, selecting an edit point applied a transition between the selected and adjacent points.

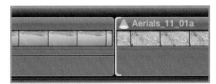

A selected edit point...

...applies the transition to that point

Faster than working with one edit point at a time, selecting a clip applies the transition to both ends of the clip.

When you are creating a montage or collage edit, selecting all your Timeline clips and then pressing Command-T places the default transition, Cross Dissolve, on every edit point.

Let's see a few cross dissolves in action in your project.

1   Select the start point of **Aerials_11_02a**, at around 0:30 in the project.

A dissolve applied to this first aerials clip will transition the viewer from the interview clips in the hangar and the takeoff B-roll to the "landscape" clips. It's a nice setup to glide the audience into the aerial clips.

2   Press Command-T to apply the default cross dissolve transition.

The cross dissolve appears with a one-second duration and gently invites the viewer to fly along. To return to the interview, you'll apply a cross dissolve to the end of the clip with the helicopter buzzing the camera, at about 0:42 in the project.

3   Select the end point of **DN_9493**, and press Command-T.

The transitions you've applied soften the visual edits. The audience is gliding along, in and out of the interviews with associated B-roll, and the music with connected aerials.

Defining Media Handles for Transitions

So far, your transitions were easily applied due to the existence of media handles. When you trimmed down the clips, you told Final Cut Pro to ignore the rest of the clip's source media. That remaining content is referred to as the clip's *media handles*, the source media that exists beyond a clip's start and end points.

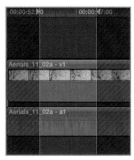

The left and right hashed sections represent the media handles.

When an edit point is set to the beginning or end of the clip's source media, no media handle is available to use with a transition, but that doesn't mean a transition cannot be applied. A transition may be applied when no media handle exists. Final Cut Pro will do it, but your content may suffer.

Final Cut Pro visually indicates whether a selected clip or edit point does or does not have a media handle. The clip's edit points are bracketed in yellow or red brackets. A yellow bracket indicates at least a two-frame media handle for a transition. A red bracket indicates the absence of a media handle.

Let's get back to the project to see these red and yellow brackets and learn how Final Cut Pro addresses a red-bracket, no-media-handle situation.

1   Select the end point of **Aerials_11_02a**, and then select the start point of **Aerials_13_02a**.

Something looks a little different here. The end point displays a yellow bracket indicating the presence of a source media handle after the end point. The start point, however, displays a red bracket indicating that no media handle is available prior to the clip's start point.

2 Press Command-T to apply the default cross dissolve.

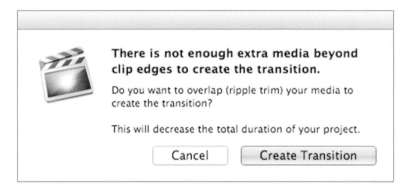

A warning dialog points out that the clip lacks adequate media handles for this transition. Final Cut Pro can complete the transition request only by performing a ripple trim.

3 Click the Create Transition button while watching the Timeline.

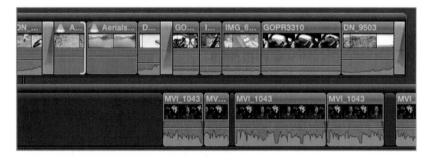

Note the rippling shift to the left in the storyline. To permit the transition, you agreed to ripple trim the clip to create a media handle. In response, Final Cut Pro created the transition by eating away some of the selected content. The following figures show the edit before and after the transition. Before the edit, no media handles were available on the lower, starting clip.

Before the transition

After the ripple trim to
apply a transition

The application moved the clip to fall under the transition, but that also affected the positioning of later clips. In some cases, that's not a bad thing. In this project, the ripple trim results in a potentially undesirable edit, which is why the warning dialog appeared. That undesirable edit is the adjusted timing that determines when the next cross dissolve occurs along with the timing of the sound bite and the music. And a second affected edit is the cross dissolve at the end of the storyline back to Mitch on camera.

The transition from the low-pass audio
to the sound bite is off by one second.

The B-roll fades to black
before Mitch suddenly appears.

Slipping to Create Media Handles

When no media handle exists at one edit point for a transition, and you do not want
Final Cut Pro to ripple trim the clip with the potential to affect subsequent clips, you have
another solution: a slip edit. A slip edit allows you to change the visible portion of content
within a clip container. The clip container's duration and position within the Timeline
stays the same, but the start and end points of the content change.

1   Press Command-Z to undo the previous transition that ripple trimmed the project.

    Here is the edit in a different view showing the lack of media handle before the start
    point, as was indicated by the red bracket in the previous images.

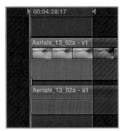

2   From the Tools pop-up menu, choose the Trim tool, or press T.

3   Place the Trim tool in the middle of **Aerials_13_02a**. The slip edit enables.

4   Drag the clip's contents to the left to move content before the start point, thereby creating a media handle.

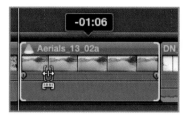

NOTE ▸ The media handle must be at least half the duration of the transition you want to apply.

5   Press A to choose the Select tool.

6   With only the start point of **Aerials_13_02a** selected, press Command-T to apply the default cross dissolve.

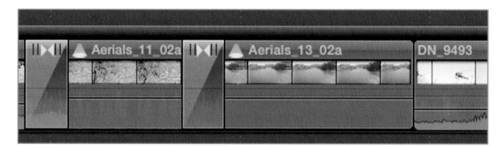

A one-second cross dissolve is applied, but it does not ripple subsequent clips.

When a red bracket encloses an edit point that needs a transition, a transition may be applied at the expense of losing content under the transition. A slip edit allows you to create a media handle while still exercising some content control.

Using the Transitions Browser

The Transitions Browser gives you easy access to organize your transitions, whether they are installed with Final Cut Pro, added from a third-party provider, or saved as one of your customized transitions. In addition to organizing your transitions, the browser also allows you to preview each transition before applying it to a project.

1   In the toolbar, click the Transitions Browser button.

Similar to some of the other browsers, a sidebar to the left displays subcategories of transitions. A search field is present for manually locating transitions.

2   In the Timeline, select the edit point between **Aerials_13_02a** and **DN_9493**. This edit point requires a cross dissolve, but let's first explore some other transitions.

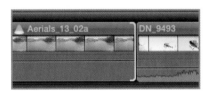

3   In the Transitions Browser, skim over several of the transition thumbnails.

The Viewer and the browser thumbnail demonstrate the effect of each transition by using two template images.

4   While skimming a transition's thumbnail, press the Spacebar to preview the transition in real time.

When you find a transition you will use over and over again in your project, you can set it as the default transition, applied when you press Command-T.

5   Find the Page Curl transition. Control-click it, and from the shortcut menu, choose Make Default.

Page Curl jumps to the top of the Transitions Browser and becomes the default transition. It may now be applied to an edit by pressing Command-T.

6   With the Timeline edit still selected, press Command-T.

The new default, Page Curl, is applied to the selected edit point.

Customizing Transitions

Like clips and effects, when a transition is edited into a project, you gain access to transition parameters you may customize in the Inspector pane.

1   Select the Page Curl transition you just applied in the Timeline, and cue the playhead over the transition.

The Transition inspector appears in the Inspector pane. Any parameters attached to the transition can be modified here. Also, the Page Curl transition has an onscreen control to adjust in the Viewer.

NOTE ▸ Option-clicking a transition or clip both selects the transition and cues the playhead to the selection.

In addition to parameters available in the Transition inspector, in the Timeline, the transition itself has adjustable controls for duration, ripple trim, and roll edit.

A transition has control points as shown in the figure.

Ripple starting of incoming clip

Change transition's duration

Roll underlying edit

Ripple ending of outgoing clip

Change transition's duration

2   Place the mouse pointer over the left or right edge of the transition.

3   Slowly move the pointer toward the top of the transition and back down.

Two different edit tools appear: Ripple Trim and Resize (duration).

4   Position the mouse pointer to enable the Resize tool, and then drag away from the center of the transition.

The transition increases in duration, which slows the rate of transition between the two clips. Because transitions require media handles, the transition may be lengthened only to the duration of the shortest media handle.

Alternatively, you may adjust a selected transition's duration using the Dashboard.

5   With the transition selected, press Control-D to reveal the duration in the Dashboard.

NOTE ▸ The transition, and not its edges, must be selected.

6   With the Dashboard indicating the transition's duration, type *1.* (one, period), and press Return.

The transition returns to a one-second duration.

Before applying more cross dissolves to your project, you should reset the default transition to Cross Dissolve.

7   In the Transitions Browser, Control-click the Cross Dissolve transition, and from the shortcut menu, choose Make Default.

8   To replace the Page Curl with a Cross Dissolve transition (the new default), select the Page Curl transition in the project, and then press Command-T.

Cross Dissolve replaces Page Curl in the Timeline.

NOTE ▶ To delete a selected transition, press Delete.

Adding More Cross Dissolves

After learning more about using transitions, you're ready to resume your Lifted Vignette edit. Using the following list, verify and add a cross dissolve at the following edit points, if necessary. The location is given by the starting clips' start point unless otherwise noted. For example, the second clip listed indicates that a cross dissolve should be applied at the start of **Aerials_11_02a**.

NOTE ▶ For now, leave the **GOPR0009** composite as it is.

- Start of project
- **Aerials_11_02a**
- **Aerials_13_02a**
- **DN_9493**
- **GOPR1857**
- End of **DN_9503**
- **Aerials_11_01a**
- **Aerials_11_03a**
- End of **DN_9420**
- **DN_9424**
- End of **DN_9424**

The majority of the required transitions are now applied to Lifted Vignette. There may be a few, very minor tweaks necessary as you get closer to sharing the project, but overall, the transitions are a great addition to the edit.

Reference 6.4
Compositing Using Spatial Parameters

Final Cut Pro allows you to position an image from any visual clip—video, still, title, or animation—anywhere within the Viewer, and then rotate, scale, crop, and trim that image. This allows you to scale down an image, reframe an image, or place two images side-by-side to create a split screen effect. Combined with the "top-down" compositing behavior, you can create simple to complex composited images within the Timeline.

Here's a quick rundown of the clip parameters you'll encounter when compositing multiple lanes of vertically stacked clips.

▶ Transform, Crop, and Distort: You'll find these parameters in two places for easy adjustment: the Video inspector and the lower-left of the Viewer. A combination of these parameters allows you to place visual images anywhere within the Viewer.

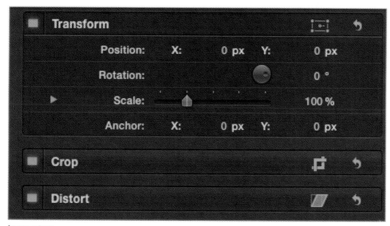

Inspector

Viewer

▶ Opacity: A spatial parameter that may be adjusted in the Video inspector and the Video Animation Editor.

Inspector

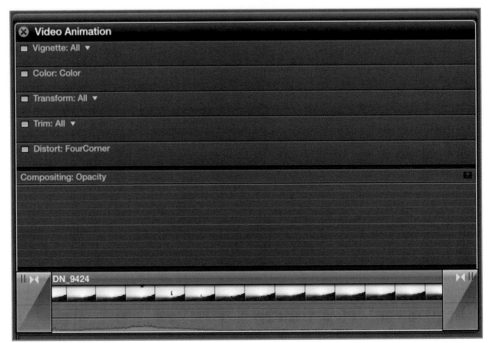

Video Animation Editor

Exercise 6.4.1
Creating a Two-Up Split Screen

In Lifted Vignette, you made an edit, GOPR3310, that shows Mitch flying the helicopter. He leans forward to get a better view. Let's composite two images on the screen at once so the viewer can see what Mitch was looking at.

Performing a Three-Point Edit for the Split Screen

Although the following technique seems complex for a single edit, after you've learned the edit you'll be able to perform it without hesitation.

1   In the project, locate GOPR3310.

You're about to connect a B-roll clip, Aerials_11_04a, at the same Timeline point as GOPR3310, and match its duration. To do so, you will perform a Timeline-based, three-point edit.

In a Browser-based, three-point edit, you specify a duration in the source clip marked by a start and end point. In the Timeline, you may simply cue the playhead as the third point. These are editing steps you've already performed. However, for a Timeline-based, three-point edit, the edit's duration is marked in the Timeline rather than in the Browser. When you mark a start or end point in the Browser, a duration is set. When a duration is marked in the Timeline, its duration overrides the duration set in the Browser (if adequate media is available).

In this exercise, you will set a duration for the edit based on the duration of **GOPR3310**, and then tell Final Cut Pro to use the end point in the source clip for backtime alignment so that the clip backfills the Timeline duration as a connected clip.

2   Select the **GOPR3310** clip, and then press X to mark a range around it.

Selecting the Timeline clip alone does not set the duration for the edit. Pressing X sets start and end points to the duration of the Timeline clip. The visible difference between a selected and marked clip is the appearance of handles at the end of the marked clip.

Selected

Marked

In the clip, Mitch leans forward looking for traffic or hazards several times. You will slip an instance of that action towards the middle of the clip. You will identify an end point of the aerials clip that will align with the marked end point in the Timeline and displays what Mitch is looking at. When you perform the edit, Final Cut Pro will calculate the backfill.

3 In the Timeline, activate the Trim tool by pressing T.

4 With the Trim tool placed in the middle of **GOPR3310**, begin dragging left and then right.

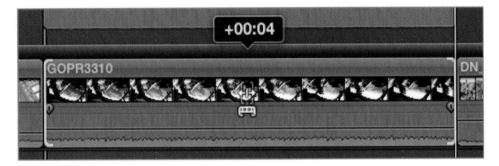

As your drag, the two-up appears in the Viewer showing the clip's start and end points.

5 Continue dragging until you see Mitch sitting back in the chair at the start (left) and slightly leaning forward before he reaches for the sunshade at the end (right). Release the mouse button.

> **NOTE** ▸ Look at the mountains in the background of the previous image for additional help in locating the edit points.

When you release the mouse button, the Timeline clip is already updated with the new points.

6   Press X to again mark the clip.

7   In the Browser, locate **Aerials_11_04a**, cue the playhead or skimmer to around a clip time of 2:30 as the helicopter is rounding the cliff. Set an end point.

You've now set up the edit. The key command to perform this backtimed edit is Shift-Q—that is, the connect edit key command, Q, in combination with Shift.

8   Press Shift-Q to perform the backtimed connect edit.

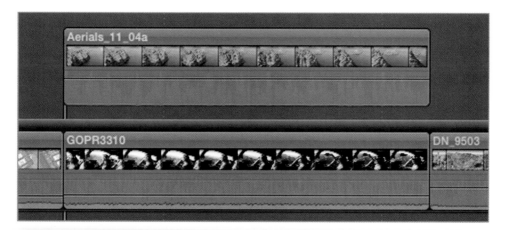

You can't see the result just yet. The aerial clip, layered above the GoPro clip in the project, is blocking the view. The images from the clips may be repositioned to create a composite.

NOTE ► If you received a warning as shown in the following figure, your selection in **Aerials_11_04a** was too short. Click Cancel and then adjust the end point of **Aerials_11_04a** to the right a few frames.

Positioning the Images in the Viewer

Your two B-roll clips are stacked one above the other. Now you will separate them in the Viewer so that both are simultaneously visible within the project.

1   In the Timeline, Option-click **Aerials_11_04a** to select and cue the playhead over the clip.

2   In the Viewer, select the Transform tool.

A wireframe appears around the aerials clip's image, along with control handles indicating that the onscreen transform controls are active. You can scale and rotate the image using the wireframe, and move the image by dragging the center handle. Let's offset the image to make room for the clip of Mitch.

3   In the Viewer, drag the center handle of the cliff/lake clip to the left.

4   Watch the guides to keep the image vertically centered, and continue dragging until the center handle is within the left third of the screen.

The image must be scaled down so that it fits in the Viewer. You can drag a corner control point to do so.

5   Drag the lower-right corner point of the wireframe toward the center of the wireframe. When the leftmost edge of the wireframe appears inside the Viewer, release the mouse button.

You've now positioned and scaled the aerial clip. Now let's bring in Mitch's clip.

6   In the project, select **GOPR3310**.

The clip's wireframe appears in the Viewer. Because the aerials clip is active and on a higher lane than the Mitch clip, the aerials clip is composited as the uppermost level.

7   In the Viewer, drag the lower-left wireframe corner toward the center of the wireframe. Stop dragging when the vertical size of the wireframe matches the vertical size of the aerials clip.

Mitch's clip becomes smaller as you drag. Both clips will not fit side by side in the Viewer, so you will trim the edges of the Mitch clip to fit its image onto the screen.

8   Place the mouse pointer over the image within the wireframe, and drag the Mitch clip to the right, finally aligning Mitch's face with the right third of the Viewer.

A bigger, interview version of Mitch is in the background. But let's wait a moment to address that. First, to fit Mitch in the helicopter on the right side of the Viewer, you will crop the clip.

9   At the lower-left of the Viewer, from the pop-up menu, choose the Crop tool.

The Crop tool has three modes—Trim, Crop, and Ken Burns—that you choose using buttons in the Viewer. Trim allows you to cut off parts of the image. Crop also trims off parts of the image, but then scales up the result to fill the current frame size of the clip. Finally, Ken Burns allows you to animate the visual image using zooms and pans.

10 With the Crop tool's Trim effect chosen, drag the left and right edges of the image toward the center to more tightly frame Mitch.

11 Remember that Mitch is going to lean forward, so leave some room for him.

12 Click Done in the Viewer and review the edit.

Don't forget that you backtime-connected the edit. So, at the end of the composite, the helicopter starts to come around the cliff. Just as that is about to happen, Mitch leans forward, looking for aircraft traffic and any other potential hazards.

Exercise 6.4.2
Exploring the Video Animation Editor

In addition to the parameters available in the Inspector and the presence of some onscreen controls, you have a third way to access and edit parameters in the Video Animation Editor, and see the parameter's settings compared to other parameters of the same clip or other Timeline clips.

1 Control-click the first **MVI_1043** that falls beneath the **GOPR3310** clip, and choose Show Video Animation.

The Video Animation Editor displays the spatial parameters, along with controls for some applied effects that are also accessible in this editor. As you can see, the Compositing Opacity parameter is available along the lower edge of the editor.

When a parameter is accessible, a Maximize button is visible.

2   To view the opacity controls, click the Maximize button.

Three types of controls are available here to alter opacity. The first are fade handles such as those you used with audio clips when softening the edits in Lesson 4. Here, the handles can be used to create a video fade-in or fade-out.

3   Drag the fade-out handle toward the center and review the edit.

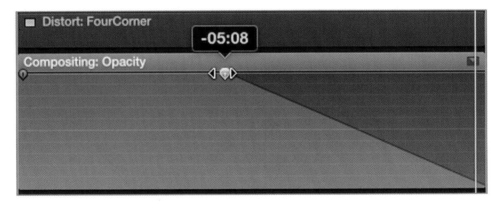

The clip's video fades out to black as if you had applied a transition from a gap clip.

4   Press Command-Z to return the handle to the start point.

The second control type for adjusting opacity is similar to adjusting the audio level.

5   Place the mouse pointer over the opacity control line, and drag the line down to 0%.

The interview of Mitch disappears behind the split screen.

Displayed as a percentage of total opacity, any value less than 100% is translucent until the value reaches 0%, which produces total transparency.

NOTE ▶ The third control type utilizes keyframes, but we'll save that for Lesson 7.

6   Close the Video Animation Editor by clicking the close button, or pressing Control-V.

One down, and one more interview clip to remove visually from the composite.

Copying and Pasting Attributes

For the second MVI_1043 under the split screen, you may use a specialized copy and paste feature called Paste Attributes. You will notice during this exercise that the Paste Attributes feature may be used to speed up the sharing of specific parameter settings amongst many clips.

1   Select the MVI_1043 clip in which you adjusted the opacity, and then press Command-C to copy it.

2   Select the next two MVI_1043 clips to the right, and choose Edit > Paste Attributes, or press Command-Shift-V, to determine which of the copied clip's parameters will be pasted to this clip.

The dialog lists the video and audio attributes available from the copied clip. You can cherry pick the parameters you wish to copy to the second clip. You may have noticed that opacity is not listed. If you'll recall, in the Video Animation Editor, opacity was listed as Compositing: Opacity. Similarly, in the Inspector, Opacity is associated with the Compositing category.

3   Select the checkbox next to Compositing, and click Paste.

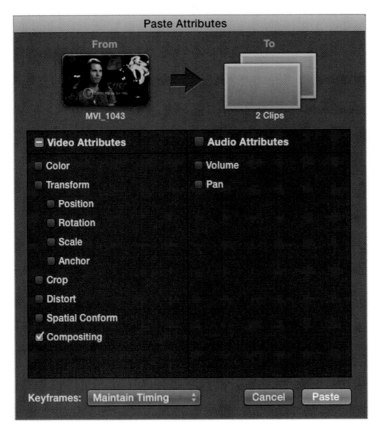

You can verify that the opacity was changed to 0% by reviewing the edit in the project. The full transparency means that you can no longer see the interview with Mitch behind the split screen.

Reference 6.5
Compounding Clips

Everything in Final Cut Pro is a container: clips, the project, events, the library—all containers. Another container in Final Cut Pro, the compound clip, is really the container framework used to create the project and clip media containers. Compound clips, like storylines, are a way to contain media files with similar attributes or purpose within a project.

> **NOTE** ▸ In the Browser, a compound clip is identified by the special icon in the upper left of a clip's thumbnail.

Whether a compound clip is opened from the Browser or the Timeline, the Timeline Navigator displays the compound clip's icon and name in addition to the event.

Compound clips can be placed inside projects and inside other compound clips. A common industry term for this attribute is *nesting*. However, nesting falls short when describing the power of compound clips.

A compound clip can contain one or more clips, storylines, stills, animations, music, sfx, and so on. If something can go into a project, it can go into a compound clip.

Respect the power of compound clips. Compounds are "live" or "hot" clips with contents that remain in sync regardless of where they are used. For example, if Compound A is edited into both Project 1 and Project 2, a change to Compound A in Project 1 is also implemented (hot changes) in the Project 2 Compound A instance. Although you can isolate a compound from its clones, it is not the default behavior. You can find more information about making compound clips into independent clips in the Final Cut Pro X User Guide under the "Reference New Parent Clip" command.

Exercise 6.5.1
Collapsing a Composite into a Compound

One of the best reasons to use a compound clip is to collapse a composite of multiple clips into one easily manageable clip. Collapsing multiple lanes into a single clip tidies up the Timeline, and also allows you to apply an effect to the compound, modifying all of its contained clips.

In the Lifted Vignette project, compounding the wall composite enables you to easily fade in and out of that composite. The compound of those two clips also allows their audio channels to be modified with a single volume control for easier mixing.

1   In the project, scroll to the end, and select the two **GOPR0009** clips you previously composited.

2   With both clips selected, Control-click either one, and from the shortcut menu, choose New Compound Clip, or press Option-G.

A dialog appears requesting a name for the compound and event in which to store it. Similar to a newly created project, a compound is stored within an event.

3   In the Name field of the dialog, enter *Wall Composite*. For the Event, select Primary Media. Click OK.

The two GoPro clips are collapsed into one compound clip stored in the Primary Media event. The compound may be treated like any other clip, like receiving transitions.

4   In the Timeline, select **Wall Composite**, and press Command-T. Lower the audio volume level for now.

The default Cross Dissolve transition is added to both points of the clip.

NOTE ▶ If you need to adjust a clip inside a compound clip or add additional clips to a compound in a project, double-click the compound to open it in its own Timeline, ready for editing.

You've completed the first enhancement pass. As was stated earlier, your project may not require any of these techniques or your project may need all of them. Hopefully, you discovered some Final Cut Pro features that you'll have at the ready for your next editing job.

▶ **Creating Compounds in the Browser**

You can start a blank compound in the Browser and edit within the compound without opening a project. Press Option-G in the Browser and complete the necessary dialog information. When you create a compound in this way, the dialog will look much like a new project dialog asking for video format information. Once created, double-clicking the compound opens it for editing in the Timeline.

NOTE ▶ As you create more compounds, they will add up in the Browser. Don't forget that you can create a Smart Collection to group them in the event using "Type is Compound" from the Add Rule pop-up menu.

Lesson Review

1. Which interface items allow access to the Custom Speed window?

2. What command allows you to experiment with a storyline clip's retiming without creating a rippling effect on later clips in the storyline?

3. You have manually set the retiming rate for a clip; however, at this rate, the clip is too long for the time slot in the project. Which interface item allows you to trim the clip without changing the playback speed?

4. Which command was used to create the retiming effect shown in the following figure?

5. How do you access an effect's parameters to adjust the look (or sound) of that effect?

6. What are the steps to reset an effect's parameters, disable the effect, and delete an effect from a clip?

7. What does the red bracket indicate in the following figure?

8. Referring to the previous figure, describe two ways to create the media handles necessary to apply a one-second transition.

9. Which of the following images displays that you are ready to adjust the transition's
    duration?

A

B

C

10. How do you replace a project transition with a different transition from the Transition
    Browser?

11. Which two interface elements may be used to activate the Viewer's onscreen
    Transform controls?

12. Describe the difference between Paste and Paste Attributes.

13. How do you access the individual components of a compound clip?

Answers

1.

Retime
pop-up menu

Retime Editor

2. Use the Lift from Storyline command to convert the clip to a connected clip. Doing so lets you change the speed and duration of the clip without disturbing later clips.

3.

Ripple trim changes the clip's duration
without changing the set speed rate.

4. The Blade Speed command from the Retime pop-up menu

5. First, the effect must be applied to a project clip. Second, the clip must be selected or the playhead cued over the clip to access the parameters in the Inspector pane.

6.

Reset the parameters by clicking the effect's Reset button (the hooked arrow).

Disable/enable an effect by clicking the effect's checkbox.

With the effect's title bar selected, press the Delete key.

7. The starting clip does not have an adequate media handle to apply a transition.

8. Use the Slip trim tool and drag left on the starting clip; or using the Roll trim tool, drag the edit point right to create a media handle prior to the clip's start point. The use of either method is dependent on available media handles on the opposite point: the end of the starting clip and the end of the ending clip, respectively.

9. C

10. You may drag the new transition to the existing transition similar to performing a replace edit; or with the existing transition selected, double-click the new transition in the Transition Browser.

11.

In the Viewer

In the Inspector

12. Paste applies the copied clip and its attributes, similar to a replace edit. Paste Attributes allows you to select the desired attributes of the copied clip—such as a particular effect, or a specific parameter such as speed—to apply to another clip.

13. Double-click the compound clip.

Finishing the Edit

The finishing stage of the edit workflow is here. During this stage, fun elements such as titles and graphics are added to the project, but you also have some hefty, tedious issues to finally address: The audio levels that are a little too loud, or the B-roll that needs some sound effects. Well, their time has come. This stage is for dotting the i's and crossing the t's.

For Lifted Vignette, it's detail time. A text-based graphic, called a *lower third*, is needed onscreen to identify Mitch as the pilot. Lots of audio details must be fixed to mix the final audio track as a cohesive whole. And then you must perform color correction to resolve white balance issues and realize visual consistency from clip to clip. You have a lot of work to do in this lesson, but the finished result is in sight.

Reference 7.1
Using Titles

Informational graphics answer one or more of the basic questions of who, what, when, where, or why. Whenever a project needs to present information, you have several ways to do so using a title graphic.

A title page at the head of the project may function like a book cover, enticing the audience to sit down and watch, for a few minutes at least. And lower thirds across the bottom of the screen often identify who's who in the project. Finally, your project may need closing credits to recognize its participants. Informational graphics can convey details quickly and concisely.

Final Cut Pro utilizes the real-time, design engine of Motion to add graphics to projects. Motion provides an assortment of high-quality templates inside the Final Cut Pro interface to get you started, even if you don't have Motion installed. If you download Motion from the Mac App Store, you can customize the supplied templates or redesign a new look from scratch. And with a growing user community, a plethora of third-party templates are available for use in Final Cut Pro and Motion.

Exercise 7.1.1
Adding and Modifying a Lower Third

When you started adding B-roll to this project, you held out a window of time for Mitch to appear on-camera. To help the audience identify with Mitch, you can insert a graphic to tell the viewer about him.

1   In Lifted Vignette, cue the playhead to the first frame of Mitch on-camera, at roughly 12 seconds.

2   Click the Titles button to open the Titles Browser.

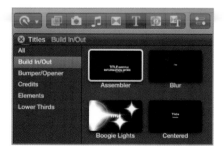

The Titles Browser is similar in layout to the Effects Browser you worked with previously. The title templates are organized by category in the left sidebar. The Titles

Browser also includes subcategories, where applicable, that group titles by theme as assigned by the title's artist.

3   In the sidebar, select the Lower Thirds category; and in the News subcategory, locate the Centered title.

4   Select the Centered lower third, and then press the Spacebar to preview it.

A preview of the lower third plays in the thumbnail and in the Viewer. You'll customize this title with Mitch's name and the company name. To customize a title, you first must add it to a project.

5   With the playhead still cued at the first frame of Mitch on-camera, double-click the Centered title to perform a connect edit.

The title appears as a connected clip at the start of Mitch on-camera. Let's change its text and then format it.

Modifying Title Text

You have two methods of entering text into a title: using the onscreen controls or the Text inspector. You'll start by using the onscreen controls method, which allows you to enter text and also perform some spatial manipulation.

1   In the project, double-click the Centered title clip.

When you double-click, several things happen. The clip is selected, the playhead is cued to the first frame that clearly displays the text, and the first line of text is selected in the onscreen controls.

2   The text in the Viewer is automatically highlighted, so enter, *Mitch Kelldorf H5 Productions*, and then press Esc to exit the text field.

The alternative method of text entry is to use the Text inspector.

3   In the Inspector pane, select the Text inspector.

The Text field already displays the text you entered. Let's make a small change to the title, this time in the Inspector.

4   In the Text field, insert *Pilot,* (with comma) before the "H5 Productions" text.

When working with two text elements on the same line, creating a visual distinction between them improves viewer comprehension. You have a short opportunity in which the viewer will see this lower third.

NOTE ▶ Spell check will underline questionable words and suggest replacement words.

5   In the Viewer, place the mouse pointer over the title.

A bounding box appears around the text, and the Select tool icon changes to a Move tool. Dragging within the bounding box at this point would reposition the title.

6   Leave the title in place for now, but select Mitch's first and last names. Triple-click to select his first name, and then, like a word processor, drag across the text to select both his first and last name.

To visually differentiate his name from his job, let's change the text colors. Two parameters are associated with text color for this title template, and one of them is found in the Text inspector.

7   In the Text inspector, scroll down to the Face section.

By default, the Face parameters are active, but hidden from view.

8   With the mouse pointer on the Face section header, click the Show text button that appears to the right.

The Face parameters controlling the text's font face are displayed.

NOTE ▶ Alternatively, double-clicking an Inspector section's header shows/hides the associated parameters.

For the Color parameter, you'll find two color controls: the color well and the pop-up color palette. You can click the color well to open the OS X Colors window, or click the downward arrow button to open the pop-up color palette.

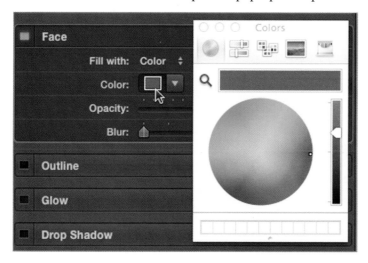

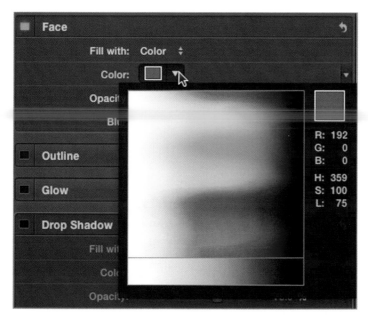

9   Using either the color well or the pop-up color palette, click a black color sample to display Mitch's name in black.

The text color changes to black. It looks good, but let's add some flair by changing its position and the company text font.

10   In the Viewer, select the "Pilot, H5 Productions" text. In the Text inspector, set the Style pop-up menu to Bold Italic. Press Esc.

The title looks great now because we have a difference between the two elements. It adds clarity to the storytelling without getting in the way. There is one technical change to consider, however: how long the title appears onscreen.

One common formula states that if the editor can read a lower third (or any onscreen text) at least twice but no more than three times, that's an appropriate duration to allow a viewer to see, read, and process it. In Lifted Vignette, you already created a short time slot between B-roll clips for this lower third; you should adjust the title's duration to fill that slot.

Extending an Edit

Instead of dragging a clip's start or end point to shorten or lengthen a clip, you can use an extend edit to speed up the process. An extend edit rolls the selected edit point to the playhead or skimmer.

1   Select the end point of the title clip.

By selecting the point, you've identified which edit point to extend edit to the skimmer or playhead. You'll now cue the skimmer to indicate when you want the title clip to end.

2   Skim to somewhere within the title clip.

3   Press Shift-X to extend the selected point to the skimmer's position.

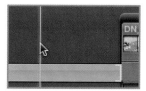

You need to extend the end point of Mitch's title clip to the start of the next B-roll clip.

4   Cue the skimmer to the start of **DN_9455**, and with the title's end point still selected, press Shift-X.

Like the trim start, trim end, and trim selection you learned earlier, the extend edit is another efficiency to speed up the editing process. One bonus, Shift-X, could also be called "retract edit" as it will trim away content.

▶ **Replacing Title Text**

Depending on the number of interviews, locations, or open captions in your project, you may add many titles, and sometimes a spelling error may occur across multiple titles. For example, you may have used lower thirds with the text "Inside the H5 Hangar," "Outside the H5 Hangar," and "Returning to the H5 Hangar," but had misspelled "hangar" as "hanger." The "Find and Replace Title Text" command is your quick-fix solution. Choose Edit > "Find and Replace Title Text," and then use the Find and Replace fields to locate the incorrect text and replace it with the corrected text.

Reference 7.2
Working with Audio

Until now in your workflow, the audio mix hasn't received the full attention it deserves, but for a good reason. Through Lesson 6, the project timing was altered as clips were inserted or removed. Individual clips also changed duration as they were ripple trimmed, speed manipulated, or slipped. And most recently, you composited effects and applied transitions that affected the timing and added elements that still require audio attention. Because of these inevitable duration changes, time spent mixing your audio early in the workflow could be time wasted. By attending to your audio design at this point in the workflow, you can refine some not-so-smooth edits once and for all, and really catapult your project to the next level of excellence.

You should begin working with audio at the clip level. Does every clip have audio? That standard question is often overlooked. If you want to make your sound design very detailed, you may ask an additional question: Is every content element of the image, visible or implied, represented by audio? Take a moment to listen to your current environment. What do you hear? The faint whirring of a computer fan? Cars going by outside the window? A clock ticking nearby? A plane crossing overhead? A conversation in the next room? All of these audio elements define the who, what, where, and even why of your surroundings.

Furthermore, those elements have a pecking order in your consciousness. If the conversation in the next room gets louder, you will conclude that you either moved closer to it; it moved closer to you; or it turned into a full-blown, full-volume argument. If you hear no change in the volume of that conversation, it will recede in your awareness and your attention will turn to other sounds. All of these changes in perception can be reflected in the audio mix to more fully involve your audience in the storytelling.

In Lifted Vignette, you've kept a general lookout for the level and mix. The audio mix favored Mitch's comments throughout the project with the B-roll and music taking a secondary place. Primarily, you kept the audio level below 0 dB, but now your full attention should go to the project's audio on a clip-by-clip, clip-to-clip, and project-wide basis. You'll start with the clip-by-clip focus to ensure that every clip has a source of audio. You will then slide into a clip-to-clip focus of blending the audio of one clip into the next clip—the natural sound of one clip merging into the natural sound of the next clip. This task expands further to blend the clips vertically. Interweaving the music, sound effects (sfx), natural sound, and the sound bites creates the project's audio mix.

Exercise 7.2.1
Adding Sound to a Clip

Sometimes the natural sound recorded with a clip is too low, too noisy, or just not usable. An example of this can be heard in the first clip in the project. The clip was reversed to create the hangar opening shot, which also reversed its audio content. But even if you reverted to normal audio playback, the clip's sound would still need help. Adding a sound effect will greatly improve its impact.

1   In Lifted Vignette, at the start of the Timeline, locate **DN_9488**.

That motor sounds weak because it was recorded on a distant ambient microphone. You need that motor to sound stronger as it opens the hangar doors and your story. Let's search the Music and Sound Browser to find a more powerful sound effect. The Music and Sound Browser gives you centralized access to your iTunes library and playlists, more than 400 iLife sound effects and musical clips (if installed), and over 1300 sound and foley effects that are part of the Final Cut Pro Sound Effects collection.

NOTE ▶ If the Final Cut Pro Sound Effects folder is not available or is empty, choose Final Cut Pro > Download Additional Content to acquire it.

2   In the Final Cut Pro Sound Effects folder, in the search field, enter *motor*.

About 25 results are returned. Most sounds are of motorcycles, but the first four are industrial motors.

3 Double-click various sound effects to preview them.

Motor 4 sounds about the right size to go with the hangar door.

4 Drag **Motor 4** from the Music and Sound Browser to start underneath **DN_9488** at the head of the project.

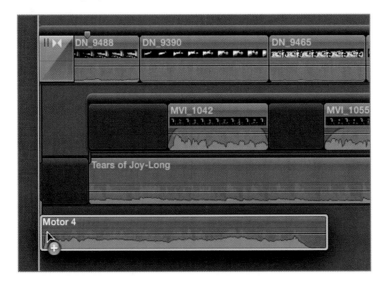

The sound effect is a little too long, but here's the great thing about that: the hangar door continues opening in the second clip, **DN_9390**.

5   Trim the end of **Motor 4** to stop at the end point of **DN_9390**.

You can trim the audio clip using one of the various methods you've learned. Try out each of the following, pressing Command-Z between methods to reset to the sfx's full length:

▶   Using the Select tool, drag the end point of the sfx clip left until the point snaps to the end of **DN_9390**.

▶   With the sfx clip selected, skim to the end of **DN_9390**, then press Option-] (right bracket) to trim the end of the clip to the playhead.

▶   With the end of the sfx clip selected, skim to the end of **DN_9390**, and press Shift-X.

As you've done with the other clips, you need to set the overall volume of **Motor 4** so it sounds as if the viewer is not standing immediately next to the motor.

6   With the Select tool active, move the mouse pointer over the volume control for **Motor 4**.

The control currently reads 0 dB because you just added it to your project. All clips come into Final Cut Pro with a volume level of 0 dB, which indicates that Final Cut Pro will play the clip at the level it was recorded.

7   Using the Select tool, drag the volume control down until the level reading displays −8 dB.

That takes some of the edge off of the motor's initial loudness while maintaining some presence. Speaking of edges, let's take a closer look at that start point of **Motor 4**.

8   Zoom in to the beginning of your project.

There's a four-frame delay here. It's not critical, but we'll take the opportunity to test the difference between trimming with the Select tool and the Trim tool.

9   With the Select tool active, drag **Motor 4**'s start point right while watching the clip's relation to the other clips. You only need to trim four frames; but for now, go beyond that length to see what is happening to the clip.

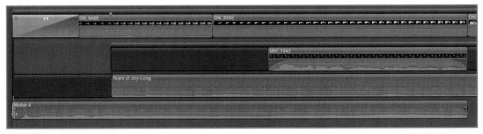

Before trimming

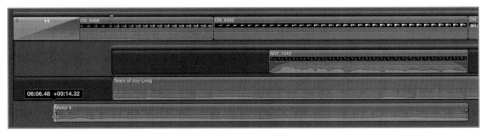

After trimming with the Select tool

The only items changing in this scenario are **Motor 4**'s start point and duration. To complete this edit, you would reposition **Motor 4** at the start of the project. Let's combine all of those actions.

10 Press Command-Z, switch to the Trim tool by pressing T, and repeat the same trim action.

Before trimming

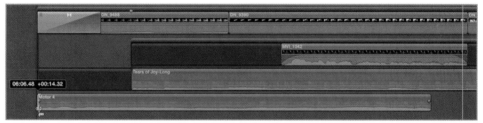

After ripple trimming with the Trim tool

This time you ripple trimmed the start point of **Motor 4**. The start and duration of **Motor 4** changed and the trimmed clip stays in the same position relative to the Timeline at 0:00.

11 Ripple trim **Motor 4** so its start point is on the first sample of sound rather than silence, a change of about four frames.

With either approach, you will need to realign **Motor 4**'s end point with the end of **DN_9390**. Let's move on to another clip that needs audio work.

> ### What Are Those Extra Numbers?
>
> **Motor 4** is a connected audio clip similar to any other connected video clip or connected storyline. It connects to a primary storyline clip and stays in sync according to that connection. You may think of clips staying in sync by video frame, but for audio clips it goes deeper than that. Where standard video is sampled at rates of 24, 30, or 60 frames per second (rounded), most audio for video is sampled at a minimum of 48,000 samples per second. Stand alone audio, whether detached or expanded from video, allows trimming at that subframe level. When trimming audio, those subframes are notated as a 1/80th value after the frame adjustment.
>
>
>
> The audio has been trimmed
> three and 74/80th of a frame.

12 In the Timeline Index and under the Tags pane, click the "Show incomplete to-do items" button.

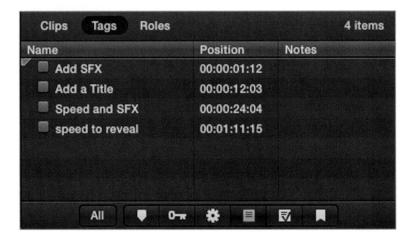

Listed at the top of the Tags pane is the first Add SFX to-do marker you placed to remind you of the audio fix you just performed. That's one to-do down.

13 Select the checkbox for the Add SFX to-do marker to convert it into a Completed marker.

The marker is removed from the to-do list.

14 Because you have also added Mitch's title to the project, you can select the checkbox for the "Add a Title" to-do marker because you completed that task when you added the lower third to identify Mitch.

The next to-do marker is the "Speed and SFX" marker. This clip shows the rotors starting to turn, motivated by a little shot of jet fuel, so you need to add some jet-powered audio to support the visual. Unlike the "motor" scenario you just completed, you already have audio content suitable for the helicopter's engine starting up and running. Rather than getting a helicopter sound effect from the Music and Sound Browser, you will use sound recorded on location.

Retiming Borrowed Audio

For this edit, you will edit only the audio from a clip into the project and time it to match existing video in the project. You could choose from several B-roll shots that contain the sound of the helicopter's rotors turning, but one clip, **DN_9457**, depicts the rotor startup. You will speed up and copy its audio to match the dramatic visual in **DN_9452**.

1 In the Primary Media event, select **DN_9457**.

This is the rooftop clip of the helicopter starting up. The entire clip is 19:16 in length, but you need only a few seconds to cover **DN_9452** in the Timeline. Skimming the rooftop clip, you can simulate the sound of speeding up the audio for this clip.

2 Skim **DN_9457** swiftly but not too quickly.

You'll hear the "meat" of the sfx. Around clip timecode of 2:28:32:00, the turbine's compressor kicks in and accelerates the rotor. Let's use that portion of the audio.

3 Mark a start point at around 2:28:32:00.

4 Leave the end point at its default for a total duration of about 13 seconds.

5   In the Timeline, select **DN_9452** to reveal a duration of approximately two seconds.

NOTE ▶ The duration for a selected Timeline clip appears at the bottom of the window.

That's the two seconds of audio you want to replace with a retimed version of **DN_9457**'s audio. First, you need to make an audio-only edit of **DN_9457** to the Timeline. Next to the three edit command buttons in the toolbar, a Source Media pop-up menu allows you to make standard video+audio edits or to limit an edit to audio or video only.

6   From the Source Media pop-up menu, choose Audio Only.

The edit command buttons include speaker icons to indicate that the next edit is audio only. Now you need to make that audio edit and place the audio clip at the correct location in the Timeline.

7   In the project, cue the playhead to the start of **DN_9452**, and then press Q, or click the Audio-Only Connect button.

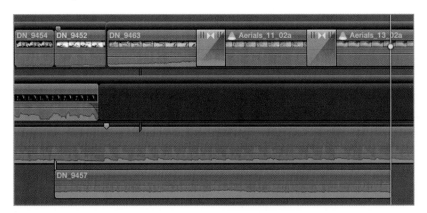

The audio from **DN_9457** aligns to the start of **DN_9452**, but is still about 11 seconds too long. That's OK because you will use that extra content while retiming the clip.

8   Select the audio clip **DN_9457**, and from the Retiming pop-up button, choose Custom.

The Custom Speed window appears above the clip. You know that **DN_9452** is two seconds long. You can use the Custom Speed window's Duration option to retime the audio clip to that desired length. As you did with the motor sfx, you want to extend the audio of the turbine startup into the next clip. You are also going to overlap the preceding clip.

9   In the Custom Speed window, select the Set Speed: Duration option, and in the associated text field, enter 5. (five period).

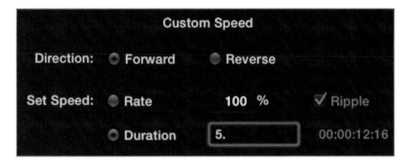

The audio clip shortens, not by trimming, but by increasing playback speed. Although the accelerated audio is shorter, it still overlaps the takeoff clip by three seconds. It would be great to also overlap the previous clip in which Mitch throws the switch.

10   Drag the start point of **DN_9457** left while monitoring the two-up in the Viewer.

The left image in the Viewer displays the video at the point the sound effect would start.

11 Continue dragging left until Mitch presses a toggle switch and the display screens change. The info flag will read approximately five seconds for the clip's new duration.

To refine the effect, smooth the edits into and out of this sound effect using the fade handles.

12 Drag both the start and end fade handles to add *ramps* of just over one second each. You'll add more blending to this sfx in later exercises.

13 Don't forget to select the to-do marker checkbox to confirm that you performed the speed and sfx fix after listening to the resulting edit.

So now you've added sound effects to a couple of clips, and even retimed one, let's see what else needs some audio support.

Splitting Audio with Another Clip

The aerial clips you added did not have audio, which isn't surprising because if a mic had been placed on that camera, it would have recorded pure wind noise. So you're going to need to add some audio to those clips. In the first Takeoff storyline, two aerials are followed by the low-pass clip, **DN_9493**. Rather than borrowing audio, this time you'll share some audio from **DN_9493**. These types of edits are referred to as split edits. Sharing or splitting audio between clips starts with expanding a clip to reveal the video and audio as components of the clip.

1 In the Timeline, double-click the audio waveform of **DN_9493**.

The audio expands away from the video, which allows you to trim the audio and video contents independently while keeping them in sync.

2 Drag the audio start point of **DN_9493**, the low-flying helicopter pass, to the left, just past the start of **Aerials_11_02a**.

Extending the split audio a little into **DN_9463** gives you time to ramp and blend the split audio with the existing audio of the helicopter takeoff.

3 Drag the start fade handle of the split audio right to blend into the audio before the midpoint of the transition.

This split edit arrangement is known as a *J-cut* with the audio leading the video edit from the source clip. The opposite, an *L-cut*, has the audio lagging the video edit point. You'll perform more split edits in later exercises.

Previewing an Audio Blend

You haven't yet mixed these clips, so the blend you performed using the fade handle will not be as smooth as it could be. Let's craft this one quickly so you can hear where we are going by adjusting all these audio details.

You want to realize a progressive, seamless audio transition from the helicopter starting up, taking off down the ramp, and getting airborne in the first aerial clip. This is going to require setting the volume levels of three clips along with some additional adjustments. As you can see in the sound bite storyline, this is the music chorus where you pause Mitch for a moment as the helicopter takes flight. You will not yet adjust the music.

1 The first volume level to set is the retimed startup sound in **DN_9457**. Change the volume level for this clip to –5 dB.

2 The takeoff clip, **DN_9463**, needs about a one-half second ramp in. Drag the clip's fade-in handle right to add the ramp.

3 Boost the volume level of **DN_9463** to –6 dB.

This boost is rather strong to pick up from **DN_9457**. That means you will also have to boost the split audio.

4 Raise the volume level of **DN_9493** to 3 dB and notice that the audio waveform peaks to red toward the end of the clip.

The higher level causes peaked audio waveforms at the end of the split audio. Let's mark that for attention.

5 Cue the playhead to **DN_9493**, and press M twice to set a marker and open the marker window.

6 For the marker name, enter *Fix Audio Peak*, identify this as a to-do marker, and click Done.

7   Review the project from the startup clip to before **DN_9493**.

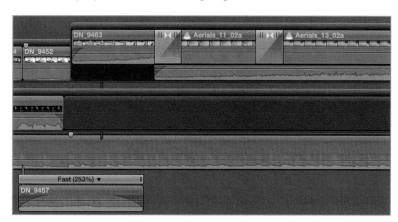

That's a nice audio transition from the ground into the air. You'll fix the peaked audio later when you complete the audio mix. For now, there are more clips that need additional audio before they can be mixed.

Adding, Borrowing, and Splitting Audio

You don't need to look far to find the next split audio opportunity. **GOPR1857** has a nice, consistent cabin rumble sound. The next three clips, which were also shot inside the cabin, would sound more authentic with the GoPro's continuous audio underneath them. Audio continuity from clip to clip would also lessen distractions during Mitch's sound bites.

1   As an alternative to double-clicking the audio waveforms, Control-click **GOPR1857**, and from the shortcut menu, choose Expand Audio/Video, or press Control-S.

2 With the GoPro's audio expanded, drag the end point right to just over one second into the last, low-pass clip in this storyline. Then add a ramp out to the end of the split audio.

That rumble gives you a foundation of consistent cabin audio. This edit arrangement is an L-cut with the audio lagging the video edit.

Moving on to the Triple Aerial/Sunlight storyline, the silent aerial clips need sound because you have no usable audio in them. Unfortunately, the audio on **DN_9420** isn't long enough for a split audio edit. You're going to have to track down some audio, but fortunately some is available. You could use the audio from **GOPR0009** or from two helicopter sound effects in the Music and Sound Browser's iLife collection.

3 Edit in your choice of sfx for at least the three aerial clips in the Triple Aerial/Sunlight storyline. Adjust the volume level and fade handles, as necessary. Refer to the following figure to see one approach to completing this edit.

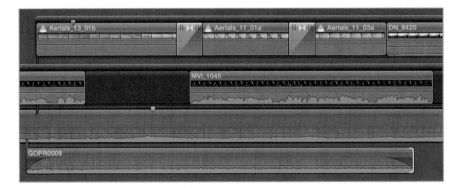

Some clips at the beginning of the project have too much audio. **DN_9454** has some off-camera chatter that should be removed.

4 With View > Clip Skimming enabled, skim **DN_9454** to hear the off-camera audio.

5   Expand and extend **DN_9453**'s audio under **DN_9454** creating an L-cut.

6   Lower **DN_9454**'s audio volume level to −∞ dB to remove it from the mix.

The same off-camera chatter mars **DN_9465**. You may borrow the audio from **DN_9470** by creating another split edit.

7   In the hangar storyline, create a J-cut of **DN_9470**'s audio underneath **DN_9465**.

8   Lower **DN_9465**'s audio to −∞ dB to remove it from the mix.

You've now performed a clip-by-clip pass and started a clip-to-clip pass at the audio for Lifted Vignette. Every clip has audio content, whether it is native to the clip or added from another source. And some of that B-roll audio was achieved using split edits, sharing the audio from one clip to one or more clips.

Exercise 7.2.2
Adjusting Volume Levels over Time

So far, you've adjusted audio clip volume at a constant level. You lowered (attenuated) or raised (boosted) the volume level for an entire clip. However, using only this constant level adjustment has created a problem in the Takeoff storyline where you split the audio from **DN_9493** using a J-cut to the prior two aerials.

Take a look at the audio waveforms for **DN_9493**. They indicate that the audio is too loud. A good level should not have red peaks. This enhanced visual indicator is a great feature of the "live" audio waveforms for each clip. Without playing the clip, they help you identify clips with volume levels that are too high or too low. For **DN_9493**, the volume level needs to be higher to have the *nats* blend from the earlier nats of **DN_9463**, but the volume level should be significantly lowered later in the clip to address the peaks occurring during the middle of **DN_9493**'s video.

Varying volume levels within a clip involves setting *keyframes*. Keyframes are created using the Select tool and the Option key.

1   Visually scan the audio waveform of **DN_9493**'s J-cut.

    You can see the helicopter approaching the microphone as the audio waveform creeps higher and higher. You can literally see the volume ramp up!

    You can use keyframes to flatten that ramp up and tame the loud helicopter at the end of the clip.

2   In the audio waveforms of **Aerials_11_02a**, place the Select tool over the volume control at the midpoint of the start transition

A level reading of about 3 dB appears, and the mouse pointer changes to two arrow-heads arranged vertically. This is where you will set the first keyframe so the level is locked-in-time at or before the fade handle completes the fade-in.

3   With the Select tool located over the level control at the midpoint of the transition, Option-click the level control.

Your first keyframe is created, locking the volume control's setting at that frame. It takes a minimum of two keyframes to animate a volume control. Your single keyframe needs a second keyframe to determine whether the animation will raise or lower the audio level.

4   To set a second keyframe, position the Select tool over the volume control at the midpoint of the transition between **Aerials_11_02a** and **Aerials_13_02a**. Option-click the volume control to create a second keyframe.

Keyframes may be adjusted after they are created. You may move keyframes laterally to change their timing within a clip and/or vertically to change the volume level at the keyframe. You are attempting to adjust the helicopter sound to set a consistent level between the keyframes for this clip.

5   If you set the first keyframe at 3 dB, set this second keyframe to about −5 dB.

This clip needs a third keyframe at the midpoint of the third transition to further tame the audio of the approaching helicopter.

6   Create the third keyframe at the midpoint of the third transition, and adjust it to flatten the waveforms for the second clip.

The third keyframe should be around –10 dB. The end of **DN_9493** will be louder to emphasize the low pass of the helicopter before the start of Mitch's next sound bite. The available time after the apex of the helicopter passes, but before the sound bite starts, will determine the timing you assign to the next two keyframes. The goal is to duck the helicopter sound under the sound bite rapidly, but smoothly enough so that it doesn't stand out. Also, the level needs to blend into the audio of the next clip in the helicopter cabin.

7   Start by applying two keyframes to the end of **DN_9493**: one at the apex of the helicopter sound, and the second immediately after the sound bite starts.

Play the clip, listening to the presence of the helicopter over the music, but more importantly, to the helicopter ducking under Mitch's audio.

The helicopter sound has a natural *Doppler effect* that drops the passing sound's pitch as the helicopter flies by. You can exploit that effect to quickly lower the sound.

8   Place the two keyframes at around –10 dB and –25 dB as the pitch reverses on the backside of the Doppler effect.

9   Now apply a quick ramp-up by dragging the sound bite's fade handle, if one does not exist.

You are now really taking control of your audio. Keyframes allow you to shape the audio within a clip, from clip-to-clip horizontally, and from clip-to-clip vertically. That's a lot of audio manipulation occurring within about 12 seconds. The range of time within which these three techniques shape the audio will become even shorter and more granular the deeper you get into sound design. You may be working with 6 or 10 clips vertically within a four-second span, for example, as you enrich and refine a project's soundtrack.

Reading the Audio Meters

As you move into mixing clip-to-clip vertically, you'll want to hear the audio subjectively while viewing the audio levels objectively. As you listen to your project over and over, you will develop a perception of how loud those clips are within the mix. The Audio meters provide a visual confirmation, or reality check, of your perceptions.

1   If necessary, show the larger Audio meters in the Timeline by clicking the smaller Audio Meter button in the Dashboard.

The Audio meters appear on the right end of the Timeline. You may want to increase their size.

2   Drag the left divider of the Audio meters to the left to enlarge the meters.

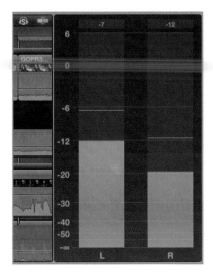

You already used the Audio meters to measure the peaks in the audio mix. The goal was to keep the audio from peaking at or above 0 dB. At this point in your workflow, however, you're focused on creating a dynamic mix in which the audio ebbs and flows with the sound effects, music, natural sounds, and the sound bites. These items must be mixed so they do not peak the meters, and remain within a *dynamic range*, the distance between the lowest and highest levels of the audio mix. The width of that range should be guided by the quality of your target audience's audio system.

In a movie theater, the speaker system is tuned to deliver very quiet sounds at pin-drop levels, followed by percussive, loud thunder as a storm overhead shatters the silence. To ensure that the audience feels the difference in volume, the mix is created with about 36 dB of dynamic range; that is, if the loudest sound is just shy of 0 dB, the quietest sound has a level of –36 dB on the meters. That is a very wide range and sounds awesome on a speaker system that can support such a dynamic range.

While that wide range works in a theater, the same dynamic sound is not possible, for example, on a smartphone. Delivering the same 36-dB dynamic-range mix to a mobile device will motivate the viewer to constantly adjust the volume level. An acceptable dynamic range for mobile devices and computers is 12 dB, so the average or nominal value of that dynamic range may be set to –6 dB. An average of –6 dB with 12 dB of range allows the loudest value to get close to 0 dB and places the softest sounds at –12 dB. That average value may be even lower for specific facilities or networks. Some facilities require a –12 dB average level, resulting in the loudest sounds at –6 dB and the softest at –18 dB. To test your mix, you can play a sample mix through a typical target platform to decide what average level and spread of dynamic range will be most enjoyable for your audience.

Changing Channel Configuration

As you prepare to put the mix together, one more audio issue needs to be resolved. Mitch's sound bite audio was recorded split level, that is, with one channel louder, or "hot," and the other channel set to record the same microphone at a softer, or "cold," level. This is a common practice when recording with a crew of one (or no) dedicated audio engineer. The practice is to use the "hotter" channel for editing unless the source gets "too hot." Then, the editor can switch to the "cold" channel momentarily to avoid overmodulation. The "hot" signal is more desirable to use because it records at a better signal-to-noise ratio than the "cold" signal (barring any other technical issue such as AC hum or background noise.) Because Mitch's audio level does not overmodulate, you will disable the second channel while redirecting the first channel to both left and right outputs. You'll start by selecting all of Mitch's sound bites.

In the Timeline Index, you have several ways to select just the sound bites (depending on the accuracy and depth in applying metadata to the clips):

▶ Using the Tags Index, search for clips with, at minimum, the interview keyword, and then select all clips in the listed results.

▶ Using the Clips Index, search for clips with the letters "MVI" in their name, and then select all clips in the listed results.

> **NOTE** ▶ A third method is to Shift-click the sound bites directly in the Timeline. However, if your project was, for example, a two-hour documentary with many "slivers" of sound bites, selecting the sound bites by metadata could be safer.

1   Using the method you prefer, select all of Mitch's sound bites in the project.

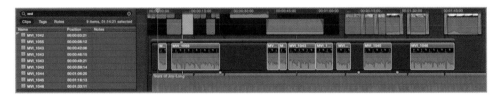

2   In the Audio inspector, scroll down to the Channel Configuration section. Double-click the Channel Configuration header to reveal the current setup, if necessary.

3   Next to the channel checkbox, click the disclosure triangle.

With the current configuration set to stereo, the channel 1 and channel 2 signals are treated as a stereo pair and linked together.

4   From the configuration pop-up menu, currently set to Stereo, choose Dual Mono.

The individual channels or components are displayed.

5   Deselect the mono 2 component to mute the channel, leaving mono 1 as the only audio source for the sound bites.

6   Play the Timeline and notice that Mitch's voice is played in both speakers equally.

With Mitch's sound bites set to one balanced source, you can move on to the audio mix.

Setting Volume Level by Role

Now that you have an understanding of the Audio meters, the average or nominal value of a dynamic range, and the dynamic range itself, look at the clip groups that make up the mix. In Lifted Vignette, you have four audio group clips: dialogue, music, effects, and natural sound. Earlier, you categorized these clips into roles. You may use these roles to solo a group using the Timeline Index. Soloing by role allows you to identify any errant clip within the role and to set consistency for a role's clips.

1   If necessary, open the Timeline Index, and click the Roles button.

The Roles Index lists the roles set for Timeline clips. You can mute multiple roles by deselecting a role in the index.

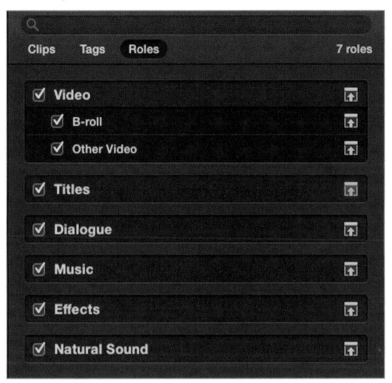

2   To hear only the dialogue, disable all the audio roles except Dialogue by deselecting each role's checkbox.

You may find a few clips, probably natural sound clips, that have not had their roles reassigned.

3   If necessary, select any unassigned or mis-assigned clip roles in the Timeline, and in the Info inspector, reassign their audio and video to the correct roles.

With the Roles Index set to play only dialogue clips, you may focus on setting the dialogue levels using the Audio meters. Those clips should already be close to the desired audio level for this project. The dialogue clips have an average peaking of –12 dB with a top peak of –6 dB. You will need to have that 6 db of headroom available when you later add music and sound effects to the mix.

4   Play the project, attenuating any sound bite that exceeds –6 dB or boosting any clip that is not reaching –12 dB in the Audio meters.

Almost every sound bite could be boosted by up to 4 dB. With the sound bites playing at a consistent, strong level, you'll re-enable all roles.

5   Return all roles in the index to enabled status.

You've set the volume level for the sound bites. Now you'll weave them together with the sound effects, natural sound, and music.

Ducking and Swelling the Sound Effects and the Music

The music clip drove the addition of a couple sound bite and B-roll edits in your project. For several of those edits, the music should be boosted to emphasize its importance. The music and sound bites should work together to maintain the forward momentum of the project, and to avoid leaving "holes" in the audio mix. In this exercise, you will use key-frames and the Range Selection tool to define when an audio element such as the music should *duck* under the sound bites or when the music should *swell* to drive the edit.

1   If necessary, adjust your view of the Timeline to focus on the beginning of the project.

Because you are focusing on audio editing, let's go to an audio waveform-only view of the Timeline.

2   Click the Clip Appearance button and select the first display option.

NOTE ▸ The keyboard shortcut Control-Option-1 selects this appearance option. Control-Option-Down Arrow moves to the right through the options, decreasing the waveform size. Control-Option-Up Arrow goes right to left, increasing the waveform size.

Start with **Motor 4**. The sound effect should be strong at the start, and then get softer as the music and sound bites enter. You will duck the sound effect under the music.

3   In **Motor 4**, create two keyframes: the first about one half-second before the music starts, and the second where **DN_9390** starts.

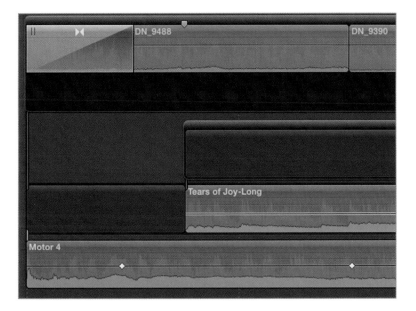

4   If necessary, adjust the first keyframe to –8 dB.

The second keyframe's level is dependent on the music clip's level. That level should currently be around –11 dB, although you will change that in a moment.

5   Set the second keyframe of **Motor 4** to –21 dB or lower.

Motor 4's audio will duck under the music's entry. The motor sound effect literally cuts out at the end of the sound effect. You can smooth out the sfx's exit so its currently abrupt ending doesn't jar the audience.

6   Drag the fade-out handle left to align with the start of the sound bite.

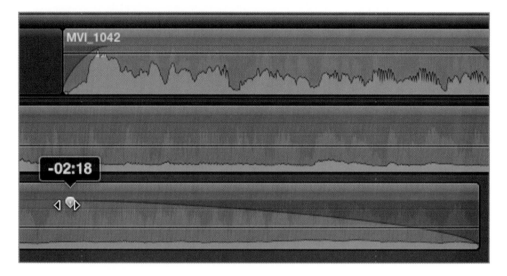

The sfx quietly leaves rather than abruptly ending while Mitch is talking. The start of the music clip is weak in the mix. The music should make a stronger entrance, and then duck under as Mitch's sound bite plays.

7   In the music clip, set two keyframes: one before the first sound bite starts, and one about one half-second after the first sound bite starts. Adjust the two keyframe's values to –4 dB and –10 dB, respectively, so the music ducks as Mitch starts talking.

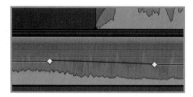

Setting keyframes is not always about ducking, or lowering the volume as another clip starts. At times, keyframes are needed to raise the audio level as the clip progresses. In Mitch's first soundbite, he starts strong, but then tapers off. The clip waveform shows his volume decreasing. You'll need to add keyframes to bump up his volume.

8   Set a first keyframe in **MVI_1042** when Mitch says, "something." Set the second key-
    frame about mid-clip.

9   Using the waveforms as a guide, drag the second keyframe upward to align the audio
    waveform peaks to almost the same height, approximately 9 dB.

This will keep Mitch's voice strong while still exhibiting some fall-off.

As you review those changes, listen for the interweaving as the sound effect starts
strongly but is pushed to the background when the music starts. That change in audio
focus should neither be too sudden nor too drawn out. It will take practice adjusting
the keyframes vertically and horizontally to find the right balance of levels and
timing.

Using Range Selection for Keyframing

A little farther down the Timeline, the audio focus should return to the music when the
helicopter takes off, the music goes to its chorus, and we hear the sound effect you added
using **DN_9457**. To do so, you must swell the music, and if necessary, adjust the sound
effects and natural sound clips' levels to suit the new mix.

Before setting the next two keyframes on the music clip, look down the Timeline to
examine the upcoming sound bites. Rather than setting two keyframes at the start of the
chorus and later setting two more keyframes to duck the music, you may use the Range
Selection tool to set all four keyframes at once.

1   From the Tools pop-up menu, choose the Range Selection tool, or press R.

2   Using the Range Selection tool, drag a range within the music from before the sound bite **MVI_1055** ends to after the next sound bite, **MVI_1043**, starts.

Using range selection, you've defined a range where the volume control should swell and where the music should duck under.

3   To set the keyframes for this range, drag the volume control within the range to raise the level to +2 dB.

The marked range will set the four keyframes you will need to swell and duck the music as you raise the level within the range.

4   Click in a gray area of the Timeline to clear the selection, and press A to return to the Select tool.

You'll need to adjust the four keyframes for volume level (vertical) and timing (horizontal). A big advantage in making these changes is that at the start of **MVI_1043** the helicopter makes a low overhead pass. You'll be able to duck the music under the helicopter sound to make another smooth change in audio focus.

5   Adjust both pairs of keyframes, as necessary, and ask the following questions about the results:

▶   When the chorus starts at about 00:28 in the Timeline, do your music keyframes complete the music swell so the chorus is strong on its first beat?

▶   Does the music volume setting for the swell keep the audio mix below –6 dB when the helicopter does its low-pass fly-by?

▶   Are you taking advantage of the fly-by at the end of the swell section to conceal the music ducking?

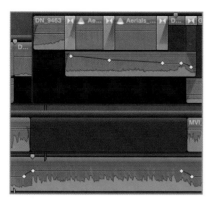

6   You still need to complete four major edits to the music. Here are the first three:

▶   Swell the music during the "race to the lake" clip, and then duck under **MVI_1045**. Use the Range Selection tool.

▶   Swell and duck the music at the "sunlight through the windows" clip.

▶   Using the Select tool, at the end of the music clip, perform a brief swell and fade-out.

The last of these edits is needed under the **MVI_1044** clip. The instrumentation in the music clip naturally crescendos during the **MVI_1044** sound bite. It reaches a climax well into the "sunlight through the windows" clip. During its crescendo, Mitch and the rest of the audio gets drowned out.

7   With clip skimming enabled (choose View > Clip Skimming), skim the music clip, and create keyframes at music timecodes 1:01 and 1:05.

This is where the instrumentation changes slightly to a brighter- and louder-sounding passage. To ensure that Mitch is still clearly intelligible, you'll lower the music's volume slightly before the swell.

8   Using the Select tool, lower the Volume control by –4 dB for the segment after the 1:05 keyframe.

The brighter section is toned down and then swells to the "race to the lake reveal" keyframes you created earlier in this lesson.

9   If necessary, you may tweak the volume of the helicopter low-pass, **DN_9503**, to mask the music volume ducking.

You've done quite a bit of editing while working on this audio mix. Take another two or three passes at playing the Timeline, while listening to the mix and timing of the sound bites in relation to the music, and the sound bites compared to the natural sound and sound effects. Evaluate whether they compete against one another, and then listen to the ways in which they work together, interwoven to carry your story forward. Animating the volume control requires a minimum of two keyframes. You can and should use more.

Always remember that you should spend as much, if not more, time on the audio edit as on the video edit. And be aware that your audio edit did not start in this lesson. Your audio edit actually began when you first selected sound bites in Lesson 3. Although beautiful visuals are important, audio refinement makes the difference between competence and excellence.

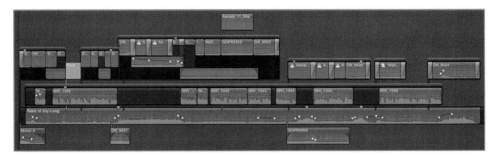

Reference 7.3
Understanding Audio Enhancements

Final Cut Pro includes audio enhancement features you can use to repair errors in recorded audio. Acquiring the audio correctly the first time makes these features unnecessary, but correctly acquired audio is not always available. These analysis and correction features are found in the Audio inspector. Here are the three areas of analysis and correction:

▶ Loudness: This analysis evaluates if a clip's volume is too low. The correction it offers is to boost the volume without over-modulating or peaking. The Amount parameter controls how much gain to boost the signal while Uniformity compresses the range of loudness between the softest audio and the loudest audio.

▶ Background Noise Removal: Identifies and removes a constant noise within a clip (such as an air conditioner or the rumble of traffic).

▶ Hum Removal: Identifies electrical noise present in the audio signal. Select the appropriate AC Ground Loop frequency and Final Cut Pro will remove the hum. In the U.S., the AC frequency of a standard 110v outlet is 60 Hz.

When the Audio Enhancements pane is open, every selected clip or cued clip under the playhead is automatically analyzed. If a serious problem is detected, the respective repair is flagged as shown in the previous Background Noise Removal image. You may alter or disable each repair by selecting or deselecting the feature's checkbox and adjusting the parameters associated with repairing the detected issue.

If a slight to moderate problem is detected, the analysis feature is flagged in the Audio Enhancements pane. The repair parameters are not enabled allowing you to decide the severity of the issue.

Reference 7.4
Correcting the Image

An editor's dream is to always have clips that are perfectly white balanced and ready for editing, but that isn't always what's recorded in the field. That's when the Final Cut Pro Color Correction tools earn their keep. A wide range of scenarios lead to an editor needing to know something about color correction. The deluge of raw material—from easy-to-use HD sources such as GoPros and iPhones edited alongside DSLR, ARRI, and RED material—can be overwhelming. The task of trying to give a scene a consistent look with that diversity of source material is not an easy one.

And the most common color correction scenario? The camera had been white balanced at the start of the recording day, but due to shifts in the lighting temperature or setups during the day, clips created later in the day have a color cast or unwanted color tint. The correction tools include an auto balance feature that instructs Final Cut Pro to neutralize the color and brightness of an image.

The balance feature neutralizes any detected color cast within an image to create a color-balanced image. Final Cut Pro attempts to create a clean image in which shadows are clean blacks and highlights are clean whites with no color casts. The balance feature also works to maximize the **contrast** of the image. There are two sub-states to the Balance feature: Not Analyzed and Analyzed.

▶ Not Analyzed: An auto color balance is performed based on the frame under the playhead.

▶ Analyzed: An auto color balance is performed based on an average color balance correction for the entire clip.

A clip or clips may be analyzed for color balance during import, but also later in the editing or finishing stages. In the next exercise, you'll enable the automatic balance feature, but you will spend more time learning how to manually adjust an image for a deeper understanding of the correction tool set.

Exercise 7.4.1
Neutralizing a Clip

Your current project is typical. Some shots look great, while others need a little visual repair or flair. The clip you'll correct first is **DN_9287**. While white balancing this clip, you'll learn the difference between the color balancing (automatic) and color correction (manual) controls.

Balancing Color Automatically

Let's first explore the automatic balancing feature for white balancing.

1 In the Primary Media event, select **DN_9287**, and if necessary, open the Video inspector.

When a Browser clip is selected, the Video inspector displays a reduced list of adjustable parameters. One of those parameters, Balance, is in the Color section. At this point, the Balance status is Not Analyzed because you did not analyze the clip during import. That's OK because an unanalyzed clip may still be color balanced.

NOTE ▸ You may analyze a selected Browser clip by choosing Modify > Analyze and Fix.

2   With the playhead cued over the clip, in the Color section of the Video inspector, select the Balance checkbox.

Final Cut Pro analyzes the frame and then applies a color correction to adjust the contrast and remove any detected color cast. The balance results will be based on the cued frame in the clip because this entire clip was not analyzed. This could be a great start for further manual correction. For training purposes, let's deactivate the automatic correction and learn the manual method.

3   Deselect the Balance checkbox to return the clip to its original state.

Correcting a Clip's Exposure Manually

To access the color correction parameters, the clip must be edited into a project. To avoid distractions, you'll create a new project for experimentation with **DN_9287**.

1   In the Lifted library, Control-click Primary Media, and from the shortcut menu, choose New Project.

2   Name the project *Color Test* using the automatic settings. Append edit **DN_9287** into the Color Test project. Cue the playhead over the clip.

Now that the clip is in a project, you can apply a manual correction to adjust the image's contrast and color balance. Each video clip has a Correction 1 enabled in the Color section of the Video inspector, by default.

3   In the Video inspector, to the right of Correction 1, click the Show Correction chevron to open the Color Adjustment pane.

Before you dive into the correction, you should know that your eyes and brain will fool you when performing color correction. Unless you're trained as a colorist, your eyes and mind will tend to lead you to make more corrections than necessary. To supplement your subjective perceptions, color correction has *video scopes* that present an objective representation of the values you are adjusting.

4   In the Viewer, click the Viewer Display Options button, and from the pop-up menu, choose Show Video Scopes, or press Command-7.

The Video Scopes pane appears to the left of the Viewer. Let's reconfigure the upper-half of the interface to help specifically focus on the tasks at hand.

5   Choose Window > Hide Browser.

The Libraries and Browser panes are hidden from view. The first video scope, Histogram, is now on the left; the Viewer in the middle; and the Video Inspector is to the right. When you perform color correction or grading, you should start by adjusting contrast. Contrast may be monitored in the waveform.

6   From the Settings pop-up menu, choose Waveform. Also, from the Settings pop-up menu, choose RGB Parade.

The Waveform scope now displays the measurement of pixel brightness within each of the Red, Green, and Blue channels that comprise color video. Although you are seeing "colors" in the RGB Parade mode, the Waveform is measuring only the brightness levels of gray within these three channels. The Waveform scope and its RGB Parade mode aids in identifying needed adjustments to maximize contrast and any color cast localized to the brightest or darkest pixels for removal. To start with contrast, you need to reveal the correction's Exposure controls in the Inspector pane.

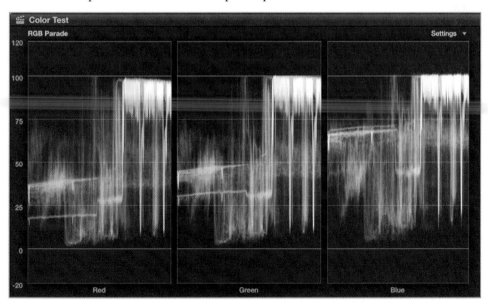

7   Click the Exposure button to open the Exposure pane.

The Exposure pane controls only the **luminance** of the image's pixels. The Exposure pane includes controls to adjust the grayscale luminance of each pixel according to four parameters.

Exposure Controls of Pixel Grayscale Luminance

Control	0–100	0–70	30–70	30–100
Global	X			
Shadows		X		
Midtones			X	
Highlights				X

All the controls, called *pucks*, overlap the grayscale values of other pucks. This results in smooth blending across the image (unless extreme adjustments are set). This broad coverage also means adjusting one puck may require the tweaking of another puck to remove the correction from a different part of the image grayscale-wise.

 For example, the Global puck alters the luminance of all pixels in the image. If you need to raise the brightness of a generally dark image, you would drag up the Global puck. But raising the Global control may send the brightest pixels, the highlights, over 100. You would fix that problem by dragging down the Highlights puck to reduce only the brightest pixels below 100 on the Waveform scope.

Looking at the Waveform's RGB Parade, you'll notice that the lowest *traces* don't extend down to 0. The Red and Green are closer than the Blue. When a black object is onscreen, such as the helicopter, all three channels should have pixels down to 0 on the Waveform.

8   With the playhead cued to a point where the helicopter is still on the ground, drag down the Shadows puck as you watch the Waveform's lowest traces drop towards 0.

The Blue traces are still above 0. Glancing at the Viewer, the black of the helicopter has a blue tint to it. That's what the scope is telling you. Adjusting the Exposure controls is not removing the color cast, it's just making the pixels darker (or brighter). That makes Exposure controls the best to set contrast. Let's set this image up for contrast with 0 brightness for the black pixels of the helicopter.

9   In the Exposure pane, drag the Shadows puck down (or back up) to –2%.

NOTE ▶ The puck values are displayed beneath the pucks in the table.

10 To remove the blue cast from the darkest pixels, switch to the Color pane or Color Board at the top of the Inspector pane.

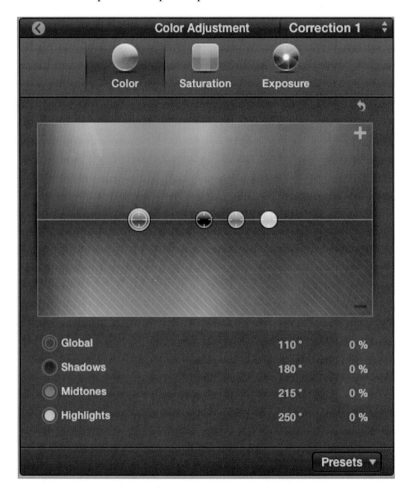

The Color Board has the same Global, Shadows, Midtones, and Highlights pucks as in the Exposure pane. However, these pucks are on a board of color that represents the color spectrum using positive values in its upper half and negative values in its lower half. To subtract blue from the darkest pixels in the image, you drag the Shadows puck downward in the blue portion of the board.

The useful video scope when dealing with color, or chroma, is the Vectorscope, which measures only the color values in an image.

11 In the Settings pop-up menu, choose Vectorscope.

When an image does not have a color cast, the traces typically pass through the center point of the Vectorscope, which represents white. Video is an additive color system. Add all the video colors together at their maximum chroma values and you get white, whereas the absence of all chroma values results in black.

The Vectorscope represents the hues of color in the 360-degree scope display. A hue's saturation is represented by a trace for that color extending from the center to a target point. The farther the target point is from the center, the more saturated the hue.

Why Is the Color Board a Board and Not a Wheel?

The Color Board represents a color wheel, much like a 2D world map represents a globe. The Color Board presents the 360 degrees of the wheel's hues as left to right and the saturation of a hue as upward from the center. So, without having to know color theory, one can look at the Color Board and correctly guess that dragging a puck upward in the +Blue area would add blue, whereas dragging downward in the −Blue area would subtract blue from the image. That is, Final Cut Pro will add yellow (the complementary hue to blue) to reduce a blue cast in the image.

Correcting a Clip's Color Manually

With the interface and clip prepared, you'll now adjust the Color Board for **DN_9287**. What follows are some general guidelines.

> **NOTE** ▶ At the professional level, color grading is a meticulous art that requires a properly calibrated environment (wall color and lighting), specifically configured hardware (displays, Color Sync profiles, and external monitors), and eyes trained for the task. Your results may differ from those presented here due to any of those elements missing from your workflow.

1　Looking at the Vectorscope for **DN_9287**, notice that the majority of the traces point to the Blue target on the right side of the scope.

If you subjectively perceived a blue cast in parts of the image, the Vectorscope just confirmed it.

2   To remove the blue cast, drag the Global control to –Blue. Starting at the center line, drag the Global control downward in the blue area and observe the results in the Viewer and Vectorscope.

Yellow was added to the image as the traces shifted away from blue. Changing the entire image with one control is too much for this clip. Let's try that again but this time using the three separate pucks.

3   In the Color Board, click the hooked-arrow Reset button.

4   First drag the Shadows puck to –Blue to remove the blue cast from the black areas of the helicopter. Be careful that you don't add too much yellow.

5   Continue fine-tuning by dragging the Midtones and Highlights pucks. Because of the overlapping and interactive nature of these controls, you may find that some controls will extend over into other hues. In some cases, you may be adding versus subtracting. Changing one will most likely require a change in at least one other control.

Color correction is an art. Different mixes of different colors may achieve the result you are looking for. Experiment with color...you can always use the Reset button to start over. Try one way of adjusting the pucks, reset, and then try a different combination of puck settings. Experiment and reset, experiment and reset.

Exercise 7.4.2
Matching Color

Sharing a consistent appearance from one clip to another establishes continuity of time and space among clips. Final Cut Pro helps you realize that visual consistency using Match Color. It allows you to copy the visual parameters of another Timeline clip, a Browser clip, or a still image to one or more clips to achieve a consistent appearance. In Lifted Vignette, you will copy the look from one clip to another using the Match Color feature.

1   If necessary, click the left "less than" chevron to exit the Color Adjustment pane.

You'll first select a destination clip you want to modify.

2   Option-click the **Wall Composite** compound clip to select the clip and cue the play-head over it.

3   In the Video inspector, to match color, click the Choose button.

The Viewer becomes a two-up display that shows a selected source clip on the left and a destination clip on the right. Using the two-up Viewer, you can skim over a Browser clip or another Timeline clip to preview a source clip. You then click to identify the clip with the "look" you want the destination clip to receive.

4   Skim over the "sunset through the windows" clip to preview it. Click to set the source frame.

In the Viewer two-up display, the destination Wall Composite compound clip updates with its new "look."

5   If you want to try using another frame of the source clip or a completely different clip as the source, you can skim to and click the new source clip to see the results in the Viewer. When you have a look you like, click the Apply Match button.

6   Review the updated Wall Composite compound clip in the Timeline to evaluate its appearance.

7 Try applying the same look to the last clip, DN_9424.

In just a few clicks, you can unify and bring visual continuity to several clips.

You've achieved a lot in this lesson. You started by adding and customizing a lower third. You then moved into detailed audio design exercises to create and enrich the audio mix. And lastly, you applied some of the color correction features to color balance and color enhance the visuals. In the next lesson, you'll share your work with the world.

Lesson Review

1. What happens when you double-click a title in a project?
2. What key should be pressed to exit text entry in the Viewer?
3. What type of audio clip may be trimmed at the subframe level?
4. What modifier key used with the Select tool will create audio keyframes?
5. What command creates a split edit without creating an accidental sync offset in the Timeline?
6. What function turns the skimmer into an "audio solo" skimmer?
7. Where can you switch a clip's audio channels from stereo to dual mono?

8. Your Timeline looks like the following figure and not all of the audio clips are audible. What should you do to hear and "see" all of the clips?

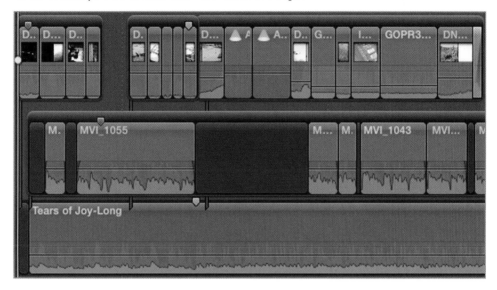

9. What tool prepares a section of an audio clip to receive four keyframes?

10. Compare the difference between a color balance based on Not Analyzed and Analyzed status.

11. Which video scope measures brightness (luma) based on the grayscale of the entire image?

12. Looking at a clip's image in the Viewer, the brightest parts of the image have a slight blue tint. How do you remove the tint?

Answers

1. The title is selected, the playhead cues to a frame where the text elements are visible, and the first line of text is automatically selected, ready for text entry.

2. Press the Escape key to exit text entry.

3. An audio-only, connected clip or an audio/video expanded clip may be trimmed at the subframe level.

4. Option

5. Expand Audio/Video

6. Clip Skimming

7. With the clip selected, the Channel Configuration section of the Audio inspector

8. Look in the Timeline Index for roles that have been minimized and deselected (disabled).

9. Range Selection

10. Color balancing a Not Analyzed clip will create the color balance calculation based on the frame under the playhead. With an Analyzed clip, the color balance correction is based on the average color cast in the entire clip.

11. Waveform

12. In the Color Board, drag the Highlights puck toward positive yellow, or drag the Highlights puck down toward negative blue.

Lesson 8
Sharing a Project

The two previous phases of the Final Cut Pro work-flow—import and edit—led to this concluding phase: sharing. All your editing goes unrecognized if your project isn't made available to an audience, whether it is one person, a few hundred viewers, or millions. Craft doesn't become art until it is seen.

In Lesson 4, you exported an iOS-compatible file that would play in any recent OS and on most hosting platforms. In this lesson, you'll explore a few more export options. You will work briefly with Compressor, the Apple batch-transcoding application available in the App Store. We'll also discuss the powerful options available for exchanging a project with collaborators using third-party applications.

GOALS

- ▶ Export to a media file
- ▶ Post media to an online host
- ▶ Create a bundle for multiple platforms
- ▶ Understand the XML workflow
- ▶ Identify and distinguish the two Compressor export options

Reference 8.1
Creating a Viewable File

Sharing media from Final Cut Pro, also known as exporting, is a simple process, especially when sharing media in a commonly used format. The presets, called *destinations*, are named according to the target delivery platform. For example, if you needed to deliver a project to YouTube, you would select the YouTube destination. Or, if you needed to deliver a sequence of JPEG or PNG images to a collaborator or archivist, you would add an Image Sequence destination.

The default share destinations

No matter which platform you select, a compatibility checker confirms which devices will be capable of playing the shared file.

If the available destinations do not fit your needs, you can create custom destinations in the integrated Compressor app.

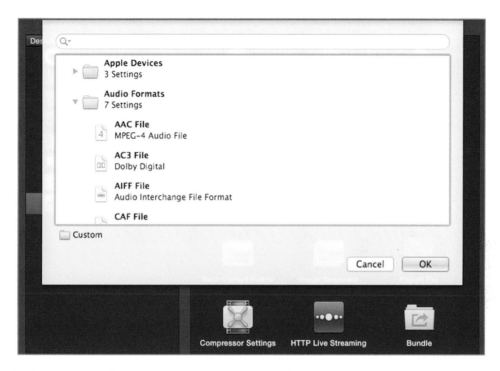

In this lesson, you will turn your attention to direct online hosting delivery and also learn how to create a high-quality archival master.

Exercise 8.1.1
Sharing to an Online Host

Final Cut Pro includes preset destinations for several online hosting services, including CNN iReport, Facebook, Tudou, Vimeo, Youku, and YouTube. Each of these destinations require that you enter your login credentials into Final Cut Pro, after which you can automatically upload files to the desired service following transcoding and the addition of metadata. Because all destination presets share similar options, you'll learn the sharing process in the course of preparing your media for one platform, Vimeo.

1   With the Lifted Vignette project open, press Command-Shift-A to deselect all selected items and clear all marked ranges.

  This keyboard shortcut is important to use because when a range is selected, Final Cut Pro shares only the range rather than the entire Timeline.

2   In the toolbar, click the Share button.

The preset destinations list appears.

NOTE ▶ The name of the destinations list is either Share Project to indicate that you are sharing a project, or Share Clip Selection to indicate that you are sharing a clip or range.

3   From the list of destinations, choose Vimeo.

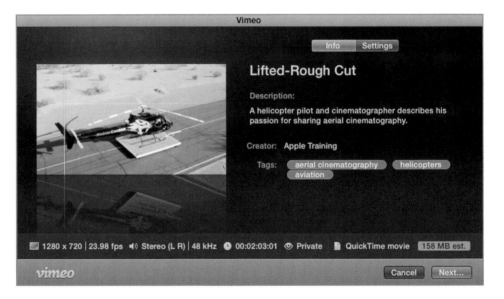

The Share window appears with four main elements: a skimmable preview area to verify the content to be exported, Info and Settings panes, and a File inspector that summarizes the shared file's settings.

The Info pane displays the metadata to be embedded into the file. This metadata will flow into corresponding fields in the Vimeo file, if applicable.

4   To share the Lifted Vignette project, set the following metadata information:

▶   Title: *Lifted Vignette*

▶   Description: *A helicopter pilot and cinematographer describes his passion for sharing aerial cinematography.*

► Creator: [Your name]

► Tags: *aerial cinematography, helicopters, aviation*

NOTE ► To enter the tag "tokens," type the tag's text followed by a comma to close each tag.

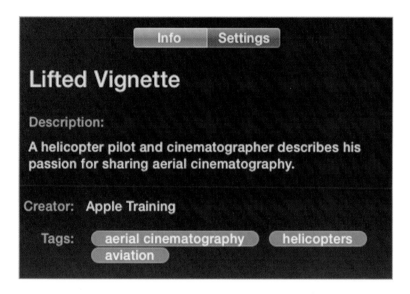

5   After entering the metadata, click the Settings tab to modify the file's delivery options.

If you have not yet provided your online account's credentials, you may click the Sign In button to do so.

NOTE ▶ To maintain the security of your login information, do not enter your credentials on a public use computer.

6   Enter your credentials, if applicable.

The preset options work perfectly for most initial uploads, but you should adjust them as needed. Also, you should always review the summary strip to perform a final check of what you will be uploading.

7   Because you will not be uploading this project, you should now click Cancel. If you intended to upload the project, you would click Next.

NOTE ▶ When uploading, a Terms of Service statement from the respective online platform appears. To continue, click Publish.

During the sharing process, the Background Tasks button lights up with a progress indicator. Clicking the button opens the Background Tasks window for more details on the sharing task.

When sharing is completed (and your file is fully uploaded to the destination), a notification alert appears. The alert has a Visit button you can click to go directly to the video online.

However, you have another way to see the video and determine where and when a video was shared to an online hosting service: You can select the project in the Browser. A simple way to do so is by using a keyboard shortcut.

8   With the project active in the Timeline, choose File > Reveal Project in Browser, or press Option-Shift-F.

The event containing the project is selected, along with the project, itself. Information about the selected project appears in the Inspector pane.

The Inspector pane for a selected project includes two inspectors, Info and Share. The Info inspector displays project metadata, such as when you created the project, the project's location, and the containing library and event. The Share inspector allows editing the Info pane's attributes that appear during the share process, and includes a log of shared instances.

9 Click the Share tab to open the Share inspector.

In this Inspector pane, when the project is published, an entry appears below the attributes. Click the pop-up menu to the right to view the options for the destination hosting service.

It's just that easy to post projects online. If you want to share to a hosting service not preset in Final Cut Pro, as long as the site accepts H.264 (AVCHD) format files, you should be able to post video files created with the Apple 720p or 1080p presets.

Exercise 8.1.2
Sharing to a Bundle

When you have projects to deliver to a corporate client who understands social media (which includes most of them these days), you may need to post those finished projects to more than one site. The bundling function available as a preset destination reduces this "distribute many" task to a one-click operation.

1   From the Final Cut Pro menu, choose Preferences.

2   In Preferences, select the Destinations pane.

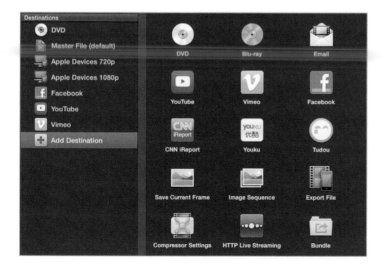

You should start by creating customized destinations, if necessary. This involves dragging additional destinations to the Destinations list, selecting each one, and adjusting its preset's parameters.

You may reorder destinations in the list, and rename destinations to your liking. Once all the destinations to be bundled are placed and configured in the list, you can create the bundle.

3   Drag the Bundle preset to the left list, and position it as you choose.

4   Drag the desired presets from the Destinations list to the Bundle folder.

5   Click the disclosure triangle to display the bundle's contents.

Because you may create multiple bundles, you might want to give it a descriptive name for future reference.

6   Click the bundle's name, and enter *Social Sites for Lifted*.

7   Close the Preferences window.

Let's select the "Social Sites for Lifted" bundle to see the options available in the Share window.

8   With the project active in the Timeline, from the Share pop-up menu button, choose the "Social Sites for Lifted" bundle.

The Share window opens as it did previously with one exception. To the left, the name of the first social media site is displayed with a pair of navigation buttons.

9   Click the forward navigation button to review each website's video. This is your last chance to verify the general description and tags for all sites and the privacy and category settings for each destination site.

10 Click Cancel.

Edit once, distribute many. The Share command and customized destinations makes it fast and convenient to do so.

Exercise 8.1.3
Sharing a Master File

After making the distribution files, or even before, you should make a master file of your project. This is a high-quality media file of the final, edited project used for backup/archival purposes. You can't share a higher-quality file than this. Not only is the master ideal for your archivist, but it is also useful for sharing quick-turn transcodes in the future. Currently, H.264 is the preferred format for web delivery. Whatever future format may be required, however, if Compressor supports it, you may simply send this master file straight to Compressor to create a transcode, bypassing Final Cut Pro entirely.

1   With the Lifted Vignette project open, ensure that no clip or range is selected in the project by pressing Command-Shift-A.

2   In the toolbar, click the Share button.

3   From the list of destinations, choose Master File.

> **NOTE ▶** If you placed the Master File destination into the bundle earlier, use Final Cut Pro > Preferences to re-access the Destinations preference. Control-click in the sidebar and choose Restore Default Destinations.

The Share window appears with the Info and Settings panes plus the summary data along the lower edge.

4   Set the following metadata information:

▶   Title: *Lifted Vignette*

▶   Description: *A helicopter pilot and cinematographer describes his passion for sharing aerial cinematography.*

▶   Creator: [Your name]

▶   Tags: *aerial cinematography, helicopters, aviation*

5   After entering metadata, click the Settings tab to view the file's delivery options.

The defaults produce a high-quality QuickTime movie file encoded in Apple ProRes 422 format. Because Apple ProRes 422 is the default render format and because it produces higher quality than most HD codecs, you should accept "Video codec: Source - Apple ProRes 422" as your preferred option. If you need a less compressed video codec because you acquired with a higher-quality codec, you could consider choosing a codec such as Apple ProRes 422 (HQ), Apple ProRes 4444, or Uncompressed with the knowledge that these codecs will produce a larger master file.

When working with a third-party audio engineer or archivist, you will probably be asked to export *stems*, a submix of one group of elements, such as the sound bites or the B-roll's natural sound. These submixes may be set up for easy enabling/disabling using roles.

6   Click the "Roles as" pop-up menu.

When delivering stems, you may choose to output them as a multitrack QuickTime movie or separate files. The multitrack and separate files options deliver practically the same thing. The difference is whether the audio is embedded in a QuickTime file or is bundled with, but external to, the QuickTime file.

7   From the "Roles as" pop-up menu, choose Multitrack QuickTime Movie.

All the active roles and subroles are listed.

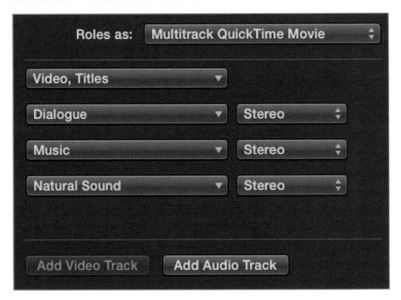

8   Click the "Video, Titles" pop-up menu to view the available subroles.

9   Move the mouse pointer over the Dialogue role to display the Remove (–) button.

You can insert or remove roles to change the number of tracks included in the
QuickTime file.

10 Click one of the Stereo pop-up menus.

Each of the audio roles may be set to Mono, Stereo, or Surround.

11 From the "Roles as" pop-up menu, choose QuickTime Movie to reset to the default format.

12 With the settings set for mastering, click Next.

13 In the navigation dialog that appears, set the Save As name to *Lifted Vignette*, if necessary. Press Command-D to set the Desktop as the destination, and click Save.

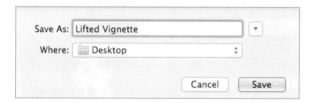

When the Share is completed, the file opens in QuickTime Player according to the default value chosen in the "Open with" pop-up menu in the Share Settings pane.

You now have a large, but very high-quality file for your archives or future transcodes.

Reference 8.2
Creating an Exchangeable File

Several third-party applications take advantage of the robust, interchange file format included with Final Cut Pro. Known as XML (eXtensible Markup Language), this file allows other applications to read and write Final Cut Pro data related to an event or a project. This info can include which clips are in your event and which clips you used in the project, along with metadata about them. XML allows you to use third-party applications that read/write Final Cut Pro XML data such as Blackmagic Design's DaVinci Resolve, the various applications from Intelligent Assistance, and Marquis Broadcast's X2Pro.

> **NOTE ▸** Check with each software vendor to identify software requirements and any file preparation required within Final Cut Pro before exporting or importing an XML file to its product.

▸ To export an event XML file: With the event selected, choose File > Export Event XML.

▸ To export a project XML file: With the project selected, choose File > Export Project XML.

   When exporting, you may select how much metadata, if any, to include with the XML file.

▸ To import an XML file, choose File > Import > XML.

   When importing, you must identify which library will receive the imported data.

Reference 8.3
Utilizing Compressor

If you've created a customized preset in Compressor, you have two ways to access the preset when transcoding a project.

Adding a Compressor Setting to the Share Destinations

You may access a customized Compressor setting within Final Cut Pro. As with other Share commands, when you start a share operation, it becomes a background process that allows you to continue editing, even including the project you are sharing.

1   In Final Cut Pro > Preferences, access the Destinations pane.

2   Drag the Compressor Settings preset to the Destinations list.

A Settings dialog appears listing the preset and custom settings from Compressor.

3   In the list, select your custom setting, and click OK.

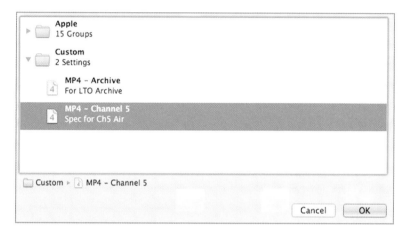

The Compressor Setting preset will take the name of the setting; however, you may rename it if you choose.

Sending to Compressor

You can also take advantage of Compressor's distributed processing by choosing to "Send to Compressor" within Final Cut Pro.

1   With your project open and ready for sharing, choose File > Send to Compressor.

Compressor opens, and the project becomes a job in the center batch.

2   Click the Show button to display the Settings options.

3   Drag the desired setting or settings to the job (your project) where it says "Add Outputs."

You may customize the Location and Filename targets for the jobs output file.

4   Control-click the Location in the target, and from the shortcut menu, choose a new location, such as Desktop.

5   Double-click the filename, and rename the file *Archive- Lifted Vignette*.

6   To start the export, click Start Batch.

The Compressor interface switches to the Active panel. Here you may monitor the progress of the export.

NOTE ▸ Click the Elapsed Time column header to display a time remaining column.

7   When the export is complete, close Compressor.

Compressor is not mandatory when using the Share Destination presets. But when you want to create custom destinations or take advantage of distributed processing with built-in Final Cut Pro integration, Compressor is just a click away in the App Store.

Congratulations, you have taken your raw video to a distributed, finished project with Final Cut Pro. As you have learned, Final Cut Pro provides a flexible approach to video post-production workflow. The magnetic timeline encourages experimentation, freeing you to audition different arrangements of your story by removing technical barriers and editorial apprehension. Although you can stay on the surface level of editing as the job allows, Final Cut Pro quickly lets you go deeper into your workflow when necessary.

If you are not a daily video editor, you are encouraged to find a small story to shoot and edit at least once a month. Even if your subject is your dog playing fetch as recorded on your iPhone, get in the art and stay in the art. The more time you spend with its tools, the more Final Cut Pro will work for you to tell your story.

Lesson Review

1. Which Share window button do you click to display the compatible platforms for the current export settings?

2. When sharing to an online host, which interface item displays details about the upload's progress?

3. Where can you find a history of a project's shared instances?

4. Which destination preset allows you to distribute to multiple platforms in a single share session?

5. Which Master File Settings parameter allows you to export audio stems from inside a QuickTime movie?

6. What export command outputs your project to a file format readable by several third-party applications?

7. Name two export methods that utilize Compressor custom settings.

8. Of the two export methods in the previous answer, which one uses Compressor's distribute processing capabilities?

Answers

1.

The Share window's compatibility checker

2. Click the Background Tasks button in the Dashboard to see details of the upload's progress.

3. With the project selected in the Browser, look in the Share Inspector.

4. The Bundle destination preset

5. Roles as: Multitrack QuickTime Movie

6.   File > Export Project XML

7.   The Compressor Settings destination preset in the Share pop-up menu, and the File > Send to Compressor command

8.   File > Send to Compressor

Managing Libraries

Libraries provide a convenient way to manage, store, share, and archive one or more events and projects. In Lessons 1 through 8, you created a new library and imported files as referenced external media or as copied managed media into the library's events. This process of working within libraries and events occurs every time you start an editing job in Final Cut Pro. In this lesson, you'll experiment with managing the events, associated media files and projects, and archiving.

GOALS

► Differentiate external and managed media

► Import as managed and external media

► Move and copy clips within and between libraries

Reference 9.1
Storing the Imported Media

Editors are creative control freaks. For a couple of decades, our workflows required us to cram information about a clip into its name and to create a precise, descriptive folder structure to store the clip's source media. The alternative was to bow to the demands of an editing application's rigid file structure. The external media management features of Final Cut Pro allow you to keep these habits (or scars), but apply an organizational structure in advantageous ways not currently available in other editing systems.

However, a few editors work a little differently. They are slightly (if not completely) disorganized when it comes to media management. Naming source media files is an afterthought, and storing source media files on the desktop is a standard procedure in their workflows. The managed media solution within Final Cut Pro can change these editors' habits in a positive yet not painful way. Let's look at how Final Cut Pro addresses each approach.

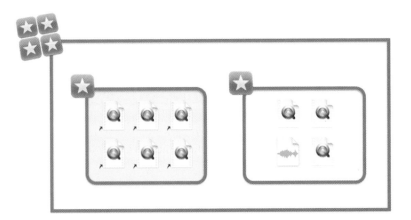

The key to library management in Final Cut Pro is the media management of its contained events. Because the events inside a library may include both external and managed media, the choices you make for managing source media files will result in *media empty* or *media full* events/libraries, or something in between.

When a library is media empty, the media files for the events are *symlinks* to the external, referenced media files. The empty library has a small file size compared to its counterpart, the media full library.

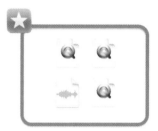

The full library contains all the source media files for all events and projects within the library. However, with all the source media files stored inside the library, this file may use a great deal of storage space.

Utilizing external media is a best practice for media storage in Final Cut Pro. Keeping the library media empty helps minimize the library file size, which allows you to easily pass a library to collaborators during the run of a job. The source media files may be stored in one centrally accessible location where they are available to multiple users. Sharing a media empty library file that references only externally managed media enables efficient and cost-effective collaboration using just one set of source media files on a server. Furthermore, that one set of external files may be accessed by other applications such as Motion or Logic Pro X, so compositors and audio engineers may also collaborate seamlessly with the editorial team.

The media full managed solution works well for an editor who is working solo and/or prefers to have Final Cut Pro manage the media. Every imported source media file is copied into the library file. This may result in duplicate media files on the volume, but that's not necessarily a bad thing unless you are running out of available storage space.

> **NOTE** ▶ Technically, the library file is a collection of files. Therefore, you should modify the contents of the library only within Final Cut Pro, and not change them directly in the Finder.

Exercise 9.1.1
Importing as "Leave Files in Place"

The ultimate external media import option for the obsessive-compulsive editor is "Leave files in place" (the opposite import option of "Copy files into"). "Leave files in place" references these external files with no moving or copying of the imported source media files. Symlinks are created within the receiving event that point to the external files, wherever those files may be.

> **NOTE ▶** Camera source media files stored on flash media are copied to a library or may be directed to an accessible location on any available volume.

"Leave files in place" is the ideal choice when you need to share source media files in a collaborative environment, such as a high-bandwidth, low-latency network. Even if such a network is unavailable to you at the moment, you may still practice importing a clip with this option.

> **NOTE ▶** Choosing to "Leave files in place" virtually mandates that you organize your source media files before importing them into an event because moving, renaming, or deleting a source media file causes the referenced clip to go offline in Final Cut Pro. When you decide that you will manage external media, then you are directly responsible for keeping Final Cut Pro abreast of any media management you perform outside of the application. See "Relinking Offline Clips to Source Media" in this lesson.

1   From the menu bar, choose File > New > Library.

2   In the dialog that appears, name the library *External vs Managed*, and for the purpose of this exercise, set the location to the FCPX Media folder.

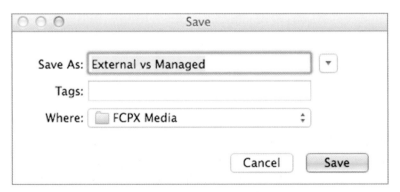

NOTE ▸ Outside of this lesson, you may set the location to any accessible location on an available volume.

3   In the Libraries pane, rename the "External vs Managed" default event to *External*.

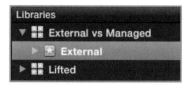

For this event, you will import two of the aerial clips with "Leave files in place" chosen.

4   Press Command-I to open the Media Import window.

5   In the Media Import window, navigate to the FCPX Media/LV2/LV Aerials folder, select **Aerials_11_03a** and **Aerials_11_04a**, and click Import Selected.

6   In the Media Import Options window, ensure that "Add to existing event" is selected and the External event is chosen in the pop-up menu.

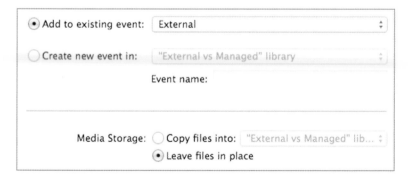

Choosing the External event here does not determine the external or managed state of a source media file. To be available for editing, every clip must be in an event. However, the actual media file does not have to be stored within that event. A symlink can stand in for the clip's source media file within the event. The choice of event within the pop-up menu defines only where the clip will appear in the Libraries pane. The physical location is controlled in the Media Storage section of the Media Import window. The "Leave files in place" option is literally an "edit in place" command. It produces no copies, and it does not move media. It just creates a reference to the source media file and adds it to the chosen event.

7   With "Leave files in place" chosen, deselect any other import and analysis options, and click Import.

The two aerial clips appear in the External event's Browser and appear to be normal clips. When you look at the clips in filmstrip view, you'll see no indication that these clips are externally referenced. Let's continue importing managed clips, and then compare their storage locations.

▶ Relinking Offline Clips to Source Media

If you open a library, and instead of video thumbnails, discover red thumbnails with the very humbling text, "Missing File," take a breath for a moment. The files go missing and the clips go "offline" when Final Cut Pro is unable to find the clips' source media files. In a worst-case scenario, the source media files were deleted, and the deleted files must be reimported. In a not-so-bad scenario where the source media files were renamed or moved, you may be able to point the offline clips toward the alternative source media files.

1   Select the event in the Library containing offline clips.

2   Choose File > Relink Files.

3   Choose to relink only missing clips or all clips.

Continues on next page

▶ **Relinking Offline Clips to Source Media** *(continued)*

4   Click Locate All.

5   Navigate to the listed file's location. Select the file and click the confirmation.

6   In the Relink Files window, choose whether you want to copy files to the event
you select in the next pop-up menu, or leave them in place as reference source
media files.

7   Click Relink Files.

Exercise 9.1.2
Importing as Managed Clips

For the editor who struggles with media management, handing the media management
duties over to Final Cut Pro may save hours (or days) of frustration. A simple selection in
the Media Import Options window creates managed media within an event. By allowing
Final Cut Pro to take command, struggles with media management are instantly diminished.

1   Reopen the Media Import window by pressing Command-I.

2   From the LV Aerials folder, select **Aerials_13_01b** and **Aerials_13_02a**, and then click
Import Selected.

You want to clearly identify these two clips as externally managed, so you will create a
new event for them in the Import Options window.

3   Select the "Create new event in" option, and from the pop-up menu of all open libraries, choose the "External vs Managed" library.

4   For the event name, enter *Managed*.

5   In the Media Storage section, select the "Copy files into" option.

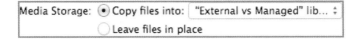

Choosing this option identifies the incoming clips as managed media. The destination pop-up menu for the option lists the library containing the event you previously selected. Although you could copy the file to an external location, in this exercise you want Final Cut Pro to completely manage the clip, so you should choose the listed library rather than an external location.

NOTE ▸ The "Copy files into" pop-up menu allows you to redirect imported media to an external location. This functionality is available regardless of whether the source media files are located on a camera card or a local/network volume.

6   From the Copy destination pop-up menu, choose "'External vs Managed' library," and click Import.

Now that you have a library of events containing both managed and external media, let's see how you can tell the difference between them in the Info inspector.

7   Select the "'External vs Managed' library" to display all clips in the Browser.

8   In the Browser, switch to list view, and then select **Aerials_11_03a**.

9 With the clip selected, look at the lower portion of the Info inspector to find the File Information section.

This section lists the containing event for the selected clip. In this instance, Aerials_11_03a is stored in the External event. Looking at the next info item, you'll find that the location is the volume where you placed the FCPX Media folder. If your FCPX Media folder is stored on your desktop, for example, then Location will display the volume's name.

10 In the Browser, select Aerials_13_01b.

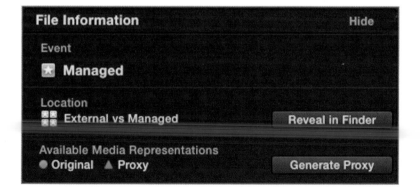

The Info inspector's File Information displays the location of this file as the "External vs Managed" library. This is a managed media file as it is stored in the library.

By making some simple choices during import, you are setting some important properties for your imported clips. These choices are not irreversible, but if you choose wisely during the first and subsequent imports, your workflow will move more smoothly.

Importing by Dragging from the Finder

You may import source media files directly into an event in the Libraries pane by dragging them from the Finder or a supported application. While dragging, the pointer will indicate whether you are importing the files as external or managed media.

▶ A hooked arrow indicates that the file is imported as an external media file.

▶ An arrow with a circled plus sign indicates that the file will be copied into the event as managed media.

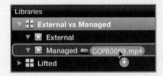

If you do not see the pointer you want, try a holding down the Option key, Command key, or the Command-Option keys as you drag.

No Duplicates

A Library's database efficiently manages media in several ways. One efficiency activates when importing the same source media file...again. If the source media file **SMF1** exists (external or managed) in Event A of Library X, and you re-import **SMF1** to Event A or B, no duplicate source media file is created. **SMF1** is used as the source media file for the clip in Event A and Event B—two clips referring to a single source media file.

Exercise 9.1.3
Moving and Copying Clips Within a Library

Perhaps you selected the wrong event in which to import a source media file. To fix this, the Libraries pane allows you to drag a clip from one event to another event in the same library. What you may not be aware of while dragging is the complex media management Final Cut Pro performs for you in the background.

NOTE ▶ Media management is best (and most safely) performed inside Final Cut Pro, not in the Finder.

1   In the External event, locate the **Aerials_11_03a** clip, and verify its referenced media status in the Info inspector's File Information.

This file is an external source media file. The Location field displays the volume from which you imported it.

2   Drag **Aerials_11_03a** from the External event to the Managed event.

Notice that the pointer remains an arrow and does not change to a circled plus sign. This indicates a simple clip move, the default behavior of dragging clips between events within a library.

3   In the Managed event, select the added Aerials_11_03a.

The Info inspector displays the external volume where the file is stored, which indicates that it remains an external source media file. If this were a managed file, the Location field would display the library that contains the managed media.

An external file remains an external media file even when you copy it to another event. Let's try dragging Aerials_11_04a to verify this behavior.

4   Option-drag Aerials_11_04a from the External event to the Managed event.
The Option key instructs Final Cut Pro to copy the clip to the second event. When the plus sign appears over the destination event, release the mouse button.

5   In the Managed event, select Aerials_11_04a, and verify its location in the Info inspector.

The location still appears as the volume storing the external media file. This management behavior allows you to drag virtual copies of clips into multiple events within a library without creating multiple copies of the source media file (and thereby enlarging the library).

When you copy managed media, the library database keeps only one copy of the source media file. Additional instances of the clip in any event in the same library will reference the original source media file. Whether managed or external, Final Cut Pro strives to avoid storing duplicate source media files in your libraries.

▶ **Using Clips Between Libraries**

You may not only drag clips between events within the same library, but also between events in different libraries. This is handy when you've created a library that contains stock footage because you may often add and copy clips from that stock footage library. Whenever you copy or move a clip between libraries, a dialog reminds you that external files remain external. You are also offered the option to copy any applicable optimized and proxy files with the copied source media files. As you've learned, using externally referenced media is a best practice, but you can still switch to a managed media library at any time, as you'll discover in the next exercise.

Exercise 9.1.4
Making a Library Portable

With a MacBook Pro and a Thunderbolt or USB 3 hard drive, an editor has a lightweight, HD-capable edit system to take on the road. In this exercise, we'll assume that you have a Mac Pro in the office where you usually edit; but for this client's job, you have to finish editing your project on-site. Final Cut Pro provides a built-in, two-step process that allows you to copy a library to wherever you have access.

> **NOTE** ▶ This exercise copies a project to a new library. Alternatively, you may copy a project and all its media to a portable volume, or copy individual events to an external hard disk.

1   In the Libraries pane, select the "External vs Managed" library.

This is the library you want to use when remote editing. You want to leave everything on the Mac Pro system as it is, and just copy this library to your portable volume.

2 From the menu bar, choose File > New > Library. In the Save dialog, enter *On the Go*. Select the desktop, and click Save.

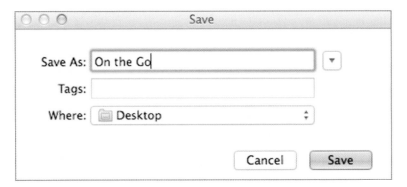

The new library appears in the Libraries pane with an empty, default event. Leave the event's default name because you will delete it in a moment. With the library created, you're ready to copy the events.

3 In the Libraries pane, select the External and Managed events, and then choose File > Copy Events to Library > On the Go.

A dialog notifies you that external media will be referenced whereas managed media will be copied. Because you need to take a self-contained version of your project on-site, you need to copy all source media files to the "On the Go" library. Let's see how to do it.

NOTE ▶ Ensure that you have selected the two events, and not the library.

4   Deselect the Optimized Media and Proxy Media options, and click OK.

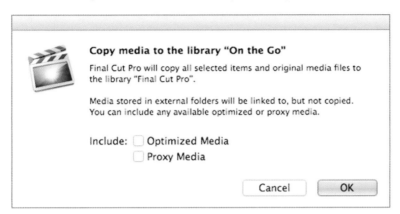

If you were able to see it, the background tasks button indicated for just a moment that some background task was activated, but it was not activated long enough to copy all the source media files. Let's verify that not everything was copied.

5   In the Libraries pane, locate the "On the Go" library, and select its External event. Select **Aerials_11_04a**.

6   In the Info inspector, verify in the File Information section that the event is External and a volume (such as Macintosh HD) is listed.

7   Select a couple more files, and note their individual file information details.

A few files are different as regards their storage location. Because you want everything packaged up for this on-site edit, you need to apply one command to this library to copy all the source media files.

8   With the "On the Go" library selected, choose File > Consolidate Library Files.

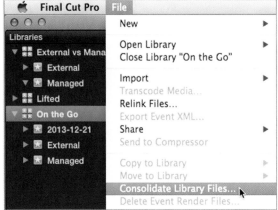

A dialog asks where you would like to collect the source media files. You have the option to create a new external folder and copy all the source media files to it. You also have the option to consolidate the source media files into a managed library. Let's choose the managed option to see it in action.

9   From the dialog's pop-up menu, choose the "On the Go" library, and click OK.

The background tasks progress indicator takes a few moments longer this time. Let's verify that the source files are now in the library.

10   In the "On the Go" library Browser, select each clip and verify its file information.

All the clips are now located in the "On the Go" library with some clips in the Managed event and others in the External event. You are ready to close the library to remove it from the Libraries pane.

11 Control-click the "On the Go" library and from the shortcut menu, choose Close Library "On the Go."

By choosing to consolidate the media, your source files are packaged as managed media within the library or as externally referenced media in the location of your choice. This one Final Cut Pro feature avoids many frustrating hours of hunting down stray media files to package up a complete project.

NOTE ▶ To open an existing library, choose File > Open Library and select from the list of recently opened libraries, or select Other to select an unlisted library.

▶ **Archiving a Library**

Archiving a library basically follows the "portable library" creation process you just completed. When archiving, as when preparing a project "to go," you want to consolidate media after making the copy. If you don't, your archive library may be missing some crucial source media files required to play back the library's projects. Also, some items that don't need archiving—such as render files, proxies, or optimized media—should be deleted to conserve volume space. Here are a few steps and tips to follow when archiving:

▶ With the library's events for archiving selected, choose File > Delete Event Render Files. Choose All in the dialog that appears, and click OK to delete all the events' render files.

▶ As you did in the previous exercise, you should make the archive library a managed media library to simplify the final archived item to a single library file.

▶ Do not archive optimized or proxy media if you retained all the original source media files or their camera archive sources.

▶ In the Libraries pane, delete extraneous events. After quitting the application, you may delete the library from which you made the archive. You may also then move the archived library to a different location, if desired.

Continues on next page

▶ **Archiving a Library** *(continued)*

▶ Don't forget to empty the Final Cut Pro internal trash can by quitting and relaunching the application.

▶ In the Finder, locate the camera archives separately, and store them in the same location as the archived library file.

▶ **Other Library Features**

The robust library architecture of Final Cut Pro allows for performing powerful media management functions in just a few clicks. Here are a few additional notes on libraries and events:

▶ Automatic backups of the library's metadata are made every 20 minutes. If you need to revert a library, select the library in the Libraries pane, then select File > Open Library > From Backup. A dialog appears with the date/time stamp list of available backups.

▶ Rather than watching the mouse pointer to indicate a move or copy function, you may move or copy events between libraries with the explicit Copy Events to Library and Move Events to Library commands in the File menu.

▶ You may combine events to reorganize your library using the File > Merge Events command.

▶ If your original source media files were deleted for some reason, you may recover any camera source media files of which you still have the camera media (SD card, magazine, and so on) or that you chose to make a camera archive during import. Select the offline clips in the event, then choose File > Import > Reimport from Camera/Archive.

Lesson Review

1. Define and compare managed media and external media.

2. How is external media referenced in a project event?

3. What media storage selection do you choose to define media as external?

4. How can you find the File Information section shown in the following figure?

5. When archiving or preparing a library for transport, describe a few tasks you should complete.

Answers

1. Managed media files gives Final Cut Pro the responsibility of storing your source media files inside the library you designate. Storing media externally saddles you with the responsibility of watching over the source media files. In either case, you determine where the media files are physically stored. The difference is who is responsible for tracking that media: Final Cut Pro or you.

2. External media is referenced inside an event through the use of symlinks.

3. The first answer is "Leave files in place"; however, "Copy files into" can designate an external folder outside a library, which would also result in external media.

4. With the event selected in the Libraries pane, you will find File Information in the Info inspector.

5. Consolidate the library as a managed library, delete render files, and do not include optimized or proxy media.

Advancing Your Workflow

Regardless of the project, every editor follows the same general workflow: import, edit, and share. Source media files are ingested into Final Cut Pro, the edit is made, and the final video is exported. The individual work-flow tasks or *sub-workflow* during each phase may vary depending on the project and the client. Furthermore, those three "big picture" workflow phases may be assigned across a team of 20 collaborators, or fully completed by only one person.

The sub-workflows described in this lesson provide you with additional information and steps you can apply to enhance the workflow you've followed throughout this book. These are some specific workflow items you may think you'll never need; however, these exercises may contain some knowledge nuggets you can use in your workflow.

GOALS

- ► Identify manual options for new projects
- ► Synchronize dual system recordings
- ► Create a chroma key
- ► Understand the multicam workflow

Sub-workflow 10.1
Using Manual Settings for a New Project

Every project is defined by frame size (resolution) and frame rate. These two items are set in one of two ways when starting a new project:

▶ Automatically, by conforming to the first edit; the default setting

▶ Manually, by selecting "Use Custom Settings" in the Project Settings window

The Automatic setting is recommended for most projects and editors. Using the custom settings to manually set resolution and rate is required when one of the following is true:

▶ The delivery resolution and rate are known and differ from the source media files.

▶ A video clip of non-native resolution is used as the first edit.

▶ A nonvideo clip (audio only or still image) is used as the first edit.

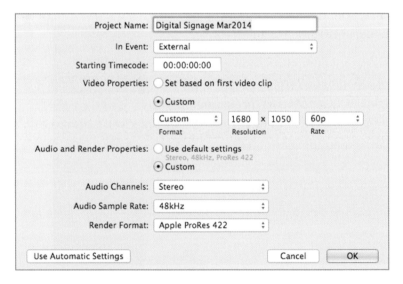

"Non-native resolutions" refers to a frame size not common to video formats. This resolution requirement has become more common with the growing use of video in nontraditional venues. Digital signage video is growing as businesses and advertisers compete to attract more eyeballs (compared to traditional static billboards, business advertising banners, and menu boards). These displays require non-native resolutions because many are "banner" layouts on custom displays or vertical "portrait" orientation. Other industries now exploring creative video display installations include museums and trade-show venues.

NOTE ▸ Although a project's resolution may be changed at any time, the frame rate locks after the first edit in the project.

This sub-workflow exercise exposes you to a project's manual settings. You will create a new project for this exercise that may be discarded later.

1 In the Libraries pane, Control-click the Lifted library, and from the shortcut menu, choose New Project.

The New Project window appears in which you can enter a project name and configure custom settings.

2 For Project Name, enter *Custom Project*. Set the In Event pop-up menu to Primary Media, and click the Use Custom Settings button.

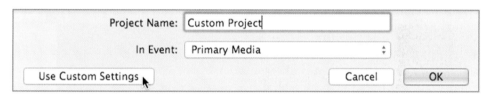

The custom settings controls appear as the window expands. Here you'll find options with which you can manually configure the project.

3 Select the two Custom buttons in the Video Properties and "Audio and Render Properties" categories.

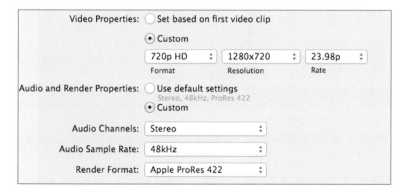

In the Video Properties custom settings, you can set the frame size (resolution) and frame rate. The Format pop-up menu filters the Resolution and Rate pop-up menus to the native, supported settings. However, at times you may need to set an uncommon frame size for a project.

4   To manually enter a resolution, from the Format pop-up menu, choose Custom.

The Resolution pop-up menu becomes two numeric fields in which you can enter a custom frame size. The Rate pop-up menu also changes to display an expanded list of supported frame rates.

5   For this sub-workflow exercise only, set the following values:

▶   Format: Custom

▶   Resolution: 1080 × 1920

▶   Frame Rate: 29.97

With the video parameters set, let's look at the "Audio and Render Properties" options.

6   Click the Audio Channels pop-up menu to see its two options: Stereo and Surround.

This control sets the number of audio channels you'll be working with in the project: two-channel stereo or six-channel surround.

7   Set the Audio Channels pop-up menu to Surround.

8   Click the Audio Sample Rate pop-up menu to view its choices.

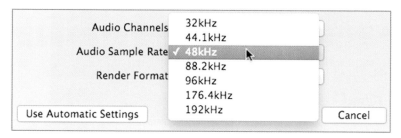

Final Cut Pro supports a wide range of audio sample rates that determine how many times per second an audio signal is measured and recorded (sampled). The common sample rate for video production (and the default value here) is 48kHz, which means that the audio is sampled 48000 times per second. The higher the sample rate, the more accurately the sample will represent the original source.

9   Leave the sample rate set to 48kHz, and then click the Render Format pop-up menu.

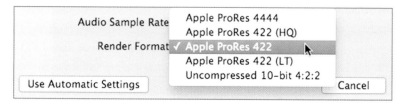

When you added transitions, effects, and the title in previous lessons, a render bar temporarily appeared in the Timeline.

A render bar indicates the application will generate a media file to increase performance for that timeline section. You may not have noticed the render bar because the project played without rendering. When the application renders an element, the Render Format pop-up menu determines the *codec* used to generate the rendered media file. When you are rendering HD video, stills, and graphics for your projects, the default Apple ProRes 422 is an excellent codec choice because it produces small media files of near-lossless quality.

NOTE ▶ Because Apple ProRes 422 produces higher quality than most HD codecs, you should utilize Apple ProRes 422 as your preferred option. If you need a less compressed video codec because you acquired with a higher-quality codec, you could consider choosing a codec such as Apple ProRes 422 (HQ), Apple ProRes 4444, or Uncompressed with the knowledge that these codecs will produce larger-sized render files.

10 With Render Format set to Apple ProRes 422, click OK.

Your project is created and opened into the Timeline. At the lower part of the Timeline window, you can verify that the project's settings are 1080 x 1920, 29.97 fps, and Surround.

> 00:00 total - 1080 x 1920 | 29.97 fps Surround

11 If your Audio meters are not visible, press Command-Shift-8 to display them.

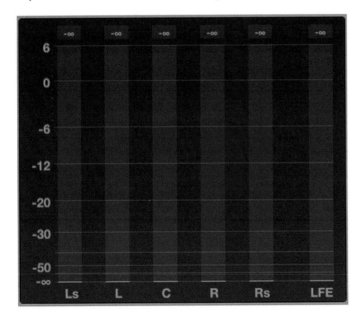

With the project set to Surround, the Audio meters update to display the project's 5.1 audio channels. The project is now set to edit video and graphics for a digital signage installation that utilizes HDTV sets in vertical or portrait orientation and with surround sound.

Sub-workflow 10.2
Synchronizing Dual System Recordings

When shooting film it is common to use separate devices (camera and audio recorder) to record image and sound. With the proliferation of small, relatively inexpensive DSLR video cameras, this *dual system recording* workflow has found its place in the video world. When video and audio are recorded separately, it falls to the editor to reassemble those separate recordings into a single, synchronized clip for editing. In this exercise, you'll discover that Final Cut Pro simplifies this task. Let's try it by first importing some media

1   From the FCPX Media folder, navigate to the LV3 folder, and import the Extras folder as a keyword collection into a new Lifted event, *Lesson 10*.

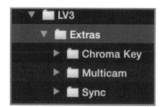

Select the Extras folder for import.

⦿ Create new event in:	"Lifted" library ⬍
Event name:	Lesson 10
Media Storage:	⦿ Copy files into: "Lifted" library ⬍
	◯ Leave files in place
Transcoding:	☐ Create optimized media
	☐ Create proxy media
Video:	☑ Import folders as Keyword Collections

Choose to import folders as Keyword Collections.

The Extras folder includes materials for use in this lesson's sub-workflows. The media you'll use here is in the Sync collection, which contains a video clip and an audio clip from Mitch's interview. Furthermore, the video clip comes with its own not-so-clean embedded audio that you'll need to synchronize with the separate audio clip.

2   To create one synchronized clip from the two clips, in the Sync keyword collection, select the two clips.

3   Control-click any one of the selected clips, and from the shortcut menu, choose Synchronize Clips.

Final Cut Pro analyzes the clip's audio for synchronization as well as timecode, if available, and generates a new clip with "Synchronized Clip" appended to the new clip's name. But where is that new clip?

4   In the Libraries pane, select the Lesson 10 event, not a collection, to locate the new synchronized clip.

The synchronized clip does not receive the Sync keyword that was applied during import; therefore, you must look for the clip in the event.

You have one more task. The synchronized clip is currently playing the camera's audio and the sync'd audio recorder's clips.

5   To view the dual audio playing simultaneously, Control-click the synchronized clip, and then choose "Open in Timeline" from the shortcut menu.

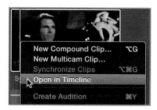

The Timeline opens the clip from the Lesson 10 event. You may verify this in the Timeline navigator.

Notice that the video clip and its embedded audio appear in the primary storyline.

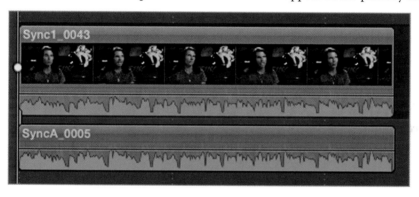

NOTE ▶ If the video thumbnails are not displayed, change the Clip Appearance setting.

6   The audio from the handheld recorder is connected to the camera clip. You need to disable the camera's audio so that only the audio recorder's clip is played. You can disable the camera's audio using one of two methods:

▶   Drag the volume control of the camera clip's audio down to −∞ to remove the camera's embedded audio from the mix.

▶   Disable the camera clip's audio using the Channel Configuration section of the Audio inspector.

Because you already have experience with the first method, let's use the second.

Configuring Audio Channels

The Channel Configuration section of the Audio inspector allows you to organize the clip's audio *components* as stereo, mono, or surround *channels* in addition to enabling or disabling the audio components.

1   In the Browser, select the synchronized clip.

2   In the Audio inspector, show the Channel Configuration section.

The Channel Configuration displays what you noticed in the Timeline: a storyline audio clip and a connected audio clip.

3   In the Channel Configuration, deselect the Storyline audio, which contains the camera's embedded audio.

In the Timeline, nothing changed. You are looking at the components that make up the synchronized clip. The change affects the synchronized clip container holding the clip. Let's append the synchronized clip into a new project and listen to the configuration difference.

1   In the Lesson 10 event, create a new project named *Syncd*, set to the automatic settings.

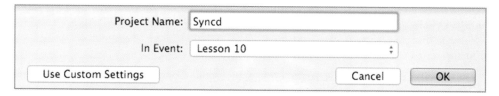

2   Append edit the synchronized clip into the Syncd project, and adjust the audio to an appropriate level.

3   In the Timeline, select the synchronized clip, and then look at the Channel Configuration

Now the interview video is synchronized with the higher-quality audio clip from the handheld recorder and the on-board camera audio is disabled.

Sub-workflow 10.3
Using Chroma Key

Until the recent increase of integrating LCD/LED displays everywhere on television news sets, the meteorologist presented the weather segment standing in front of a green or blue wall, commonly referred to as the "chroma wall." Still in use today, but for more than the weathercast, a chroma wall allows the editor to replace the wall color with a video clip or animation, transporting the person or object in the foreground to a different background location. A common use today (beyond weathercasts and movie visual effects) is to place talent or interview subjects on virtual sets or environments. And with portable chroma screens now available, formerly studio-bound chroma walls can now be used in the field. In this sub-workflow exercise, you'll start with a chroma key clip and superimpose the talent over a background graphic. You'll also use a mask to remove unwanted set items from the image.

1 In the Libraries pane, locate the Lesson 10 event's Chroma Key Keyword Collection.

Here you'll find **MVI_0013**, a short clip of an interview prep recorded in front of a chroma screen. This is your foreground clip. The workflow for chroma key is straightforward. You'll start by creating a project and placing the foreground clip into its primary storyline.

2 In the Lesson 10 event, create a new project named *Green Screen* and use the automatic settings to conform to the clip.

3 In the Browser, select **MVI_0013**, and then press E to append edit the clip into the primary storyline.

With the foreground clip in the project, let's apply the Keyer effect.

4 In the Effects browser, select the Keying category, and locate the Keyer effect.

5   With the the foreground clip selected in the Timeline, skim the Keyer effect to preview it.

The Keyer thumbnail and Viewer preview the Keyer effect as applied to the selected clip, similar to the effects you previewed in an earlier lesson. The green background disappears from view.

6   Double-click the Keyer effect to apply it to the selected foreground clip.

The green background is replaced with an alpha channel, which currently appears black because no video clip is beneath the foreground clip to represent the background. You'll fix that next.

7   In the Generators Browser, select a background such as Grunge.

You may have some concern here as to where the background clip will connect. Performing a connect edit by pressing Q will stack the background clip into a higher lane, thereby hiding the foreground clip. Although you could lift the foreground clip out of the primary storyline and replace the resulting gap clip with the background clip, another option is to connect the background clip to the lane beneath the foreground clip.

8   Drag the **Grunge** clip below the primary storyline, snap it to the start of the foreground clip, and then release the mouse button.

The background clip replaces the empty background behind the interview. With a
well-lit set, the Keyer effect does a great job of automatically keying out the chroma
screen. You'll next remove the extraneous set items from view.

> ### ▶ More Than Meets the Eye
>
> The generators within Final Cut Pro work much like the effects in that, only after you've applied one to your project do you get access to the generators' parameters. Grunge is not all there is for that particular generator. After adding Grunge to your project, select the clip, and then alter the available parameters to apply a different texture and/or color tint.

Masking Objects

Due to frame composition, lighting requirements, or location restrictions, some chroma key clips contain extraneous material that must be removed in editing. A simple way to crop these items from view is to use the Crop tool or a *mask* effect. You've already used the Crop tool, so let's explore the Mask effect.

1   With the foreground clip selected in the Timeline, cue the playhead over the clip so you may view the effect's results.

2   With the Effects Browser still set to the Keying category, double-click the Mask effect.

The image in the Viewer changed as four control handles appeared. These control handles allow you to define the mask's shape: everything inside the mask remains visible, while everything outside the mask is hidden.

3 Drag the control handles to create a shape that retains the interview but removes the extraneous equipment and set items from the image.

In addition to masks, you may use the Transform and Crop tools to further define the "keeper" parts of the image or the foreground's spatial relation to the background's contents.

Manually Selecting Color Key Samples

Sometimes location, time, and equipment—or a combination of all three—do not allow a well-lit chroma screen. In that scenario, you may need to use a manual keyer in which you define the chroma key color. In this exercise, you'll switch the current composite to manual controls to define the keyer's setup.

1   With the foreground clip selected in the Timeline and the playhead cued over the clip, in the clip's Video inspector, locate the Keyer effect.

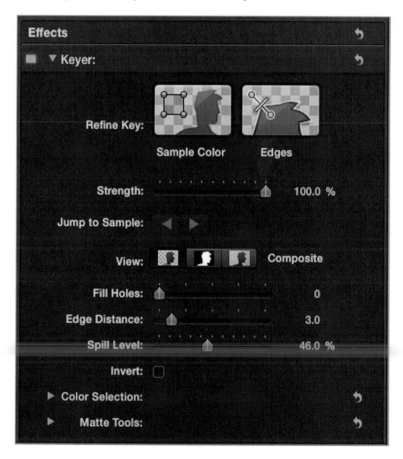

2 In the Keyer effect's parameters, change the Strength slider to a setting of 0%.

The Keyer is now in manual operation and the green background has reappeared. You will define which color from the foreground clip to replace.

3   In the Video inspector, locate the Refine Key's Sample Color button. This button activates a marquee-style selector to draw a selection rectangle around the color to be replaced.

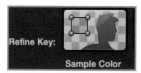

4   Click the Sample Color button, and then move the mouse pointer over the Viewer.

The pointer becomes a crosshair with a marquee box. You'll use this tool to identify the green color within the image.

5   Drag out a marquee selection in the green chroma screen area of the image, while being careful not to include the talent.

As you drag the selection, the green will begin to disappear.

NOTE ▶ You can select more than one color sample using the same tool.

6   Release the mouse pointer, and in the Video inspector, click the Sample Color button again. Drag the mouse pointer within the Viewer to select any remaining green areas of the chroma screen.

The residual selection rectangles are overlays that will not appear in your exports. And with a few clicks you've transported your talent to a new location.

NOTE ▶ Many additional parameters are available to fine-tune your chroma key composites. Refer to the *Final Cut Pro X User Guide* for additional information.

Sub-workflow 10.4
Working with Multicam

When more than one camera is simultaneously shooting a scene, you can use multicam as a powerful and efficient way to choose the best camera angle at any moment of the scene. Multicam effectively puts you in a live television director's chair, enabling you to monitor as many as 16 angles onscreen, and sync up to 48 different angles. Practically speaking, most single disk volume configurations function best with up to four streams of simultaneous video angles. With high-bandwidth volumes connected by Thunderbolt 2, however, Final Cut Pro easily handles 16 simultaneous streams of HD video.

Setting Up a Multicam Clip

As with other Final Cut Pro workflows, you begin by importing media files from your multiple camera setup. For this exercise, you'll work with an interview that was shot from two simultaneous camera angles.

1   With the Lesson 10 event selected, open the Media Import window.

The two-camera interview media was saved as two camera archives: **5D_MC1_CARD01** and **7D_MC2_CARD01**.

2   Navigate to the FCPX Media/LV3/Extras/Multicam folder, and click the disclosure triangles to reveal the contents of the two archives.

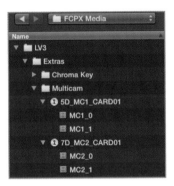

3   Command-click to select the two clips per archive, a total of four, and then click the Import Selected button.

The Media Import Options window opens.

4   In the options window, create a new *Interview Multicam* event in the Lifted library. Ensure that "Copy files into" is selected, and the pop-up menu set to "'Lifted' library." With the other analysis options deselected, click Import.

Four clips for the Interview Multicam event appear in the browser because each camera archive included two clips per camera angle. Final Cut Pro has already applied metadata to these four clips. Let's look at some of the metadata that is going to help you create a multicam clip. You'll first use metadata to reset the clips to their original file names.

5   Select all four clips in the Interview Multicam Keyword Collection, then select Modify > Apply Custom Name > Original Name from Camera.

Click in the Browser's grey area to update the clip names.

6   Select the first clip, and from the Metadata View pop-up menu, choose Extended.

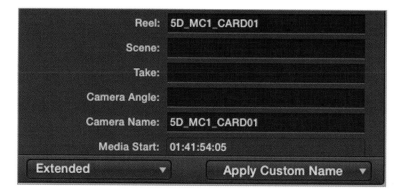

The Extended view reveals a considerable amount of metadata about the clip. In this case, notice that the first clip was automatically assigned a Reel and Camera Name.

7   Click each of the four clips, and note that each Reel and Camera Name displays two clips in the Info inspector.

Final Cut Pro will use this metadata to automatically assign clips from the same camera to the same multicam angle. Let's create the multicam clip.

8   In the Browser for the Interview Multicam event, select all four clips. Control-click any one of the selected clips, and from the shortcut menu, choose New Multicam Clip.

A multicam window appears, similar to the window you see when creating a new project.

9   In the window, enter *MC Interview* in the Name field, and ensure that the "Use audio for synchronization" checkbox is selected.

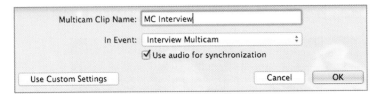

You'll be using the automatic settings for this multicam exercise. When clip metadata is less thorough, you can help Final Cut Pro create multicam clips in the custom settings by defining how clips are assigned to angles, the sequencing of those clips for each angle, and how to synchronize the angles with each other. Let's first try creating the multicam clip using the automatic settings and the current clip metadata.

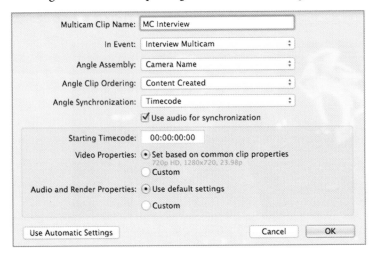

10   With the window set to use the automatic settings and audio for synchronization, click OK.

The multicam clip appears in the event represented by a special "four square" icon. To review and evaluate the synchronization that Final Cut Pro performed, you'll open the multicam clip into the Angle Editor.

11 In the Browser, double-click the multicam clip to open it into the Angle Editor.

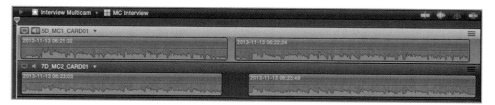

The Timeline displays the Angle Editor. To the left are monitoring angle controls with which you can specify which angle or angles to see and hear during playback in the editor.

12 Click the speaker icon of both angles to monitor them both, and start playback.

You'll hear both angles while viewing the select video angle.

13 Click the Video Monitor icon on each angle to switch between them.

You'll notice the 7D angle has quite a bit of echo. It is possible that with so much echo, the 5D angle and the 7D angle may be a frame out of sync. You may nudge the clips inside an angle to check for sync between angles.

14 Select the first clip in the 7D angle, and then start playback while monitoring the audio of both angles.

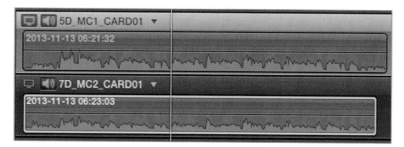

15 Press the , (comma) key once to nudge the clip left (earlier) by one frame.

Did the echo diminish or did you introduce a delay in the audio? You are listening for one voice to create the echo. When the clips are out of sync, there are two, very similar, voices speaking at once.

16 Press the , (comma) key once more to move the clip another frame to the left.

The audio should now be clearly out of sync.

17 Continue nudging the clip, this time pressing the . (period) key to nudge the clip to the right until the delayed, second voice (not the echo of the room) goes away. The second clip may not need any adjustment.

This multicam clip contains simultaneously shot clips from two different cameras. The source clips were created to simulate the cameras operated under a start/stop question-and-answer session. The pause between clips occurred when recording was paused. You will append this multicam clip into a new project and edit between the angles.

▶ **Set Your Camera's Date and Time**

The advanced multicam synchronization will sync multiple angles, even when camera operators stopped/started recordings at various times. When you're using clips in which the audio signal is degraded, the default audio synchronization process is augmented by accessing timecode information or the time/date stamp (content created). The multicam synchronization even aligns still images to video angles in the multicam based on the content-created date/time stamp.

Editing a Multicam Clip

The treat when editing with a multicam clip is the ability to make edit decisions in real time during playback. To do so, you'll use the Angle Viewer.

1 In the Libraries pane, Control-click the Interview Multicam event, and from the shortcut menu, choose New Project.

2 Name the project *Multicam Edit*, use the default automatic settings, and click OK.

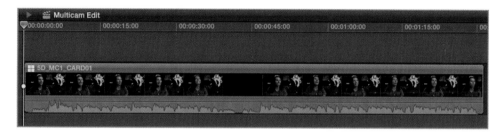

3 Append edit **MC Interview** into the project, and then recue the playhead to the beginning of the Timeline.

Most likely, the Viewer has gone to black to indicate the lack of synchronized video at the beginning of the multicam clip. Let's perform a quick ripple edit to trim this extra material from the beginning of the clip.

4 Because the lead time before the video appears is very short, it's most efficient to hold down the Right Arrow key, which slowly advances the playhead until video appears in the Viewer.

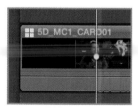

Cue the playhead to when
video appears.

5   When video appears, advance five additional frames to allow for black frames in the second angle, and press Option-[(left bracket) to trim the start point to the playhead.

Result of trimming
the start point to the
playhead

You have a little more preparation to finish before you can actually edit the multicam clip in the Angle Viewer. You'll need to open the Angle Viewer, which allows you to see several angles of the multicam clip at once. In the Settings pop-up menu, you can configure the viewer to display up to 16 of 48 angles at once (assuming your media storage volume can play back that many simultaneous streams).

6   Choose Window > Viewer Display > Show Angles to open the Angle Viewer.

The Angle Viewer may also be accessed in
the Viewer Display options.

7   To provide the Angle Viewer more screen real estate, hide the Libraries and Browser panes by choosing Window > Hide Browser.

By default, the Angle Viewer will cut and switch to the angle you click in the Angle Viewer. The cut will occur where the playhead is located at the time of the click. Furthermore, that cut and switch will change both the video and the audio of the multicam clip. While this technique is fast and convenient, it can also lend itself to error until you become skillful using it. To see what can happen when using the Angle Viewer, let's make an edit in error.

8   Cue the Timeline playhead over the first third of the multicam clip.

In the Angle Viewer, one of the two angles is outlined by a yellow border to identify the active angle visible and audible in the Viewer.

9 In the Angle Viewer, move your mouse pointer over the other angle, and notice that the pointer becomes the Blade tool.

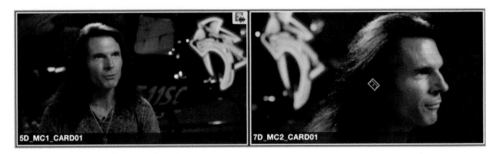

When used here, the Blade tool will cut the multicam clip in the Timeline into a new segment, and switch the active video and audio of the new segment to the other angle.

10 Click the Angle Viewer with the Blade tool while observing both the Angle Viewer and the Timeline.

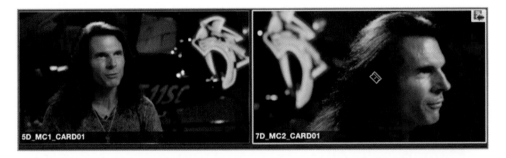

You cut the clip into two segments and switch to the other angle. This angle is now the active angle as indicated by the yellow outline in the Angle Viewer. The video and audio of this second angle are now active in the Viewer. This behavior suggests two facts:

▶ Clicking in the Angle Viewer without holding down a modifier key results in a cut and switch to the other angle at the playhead.

▶ A yellow outline indicates that the switch will include both audio and video of the new angle.

11 This edit was intended only to demonstrate one edit command of the Angle Viewer, so press Command-Z to undo the previous edit and cue the playhead to the start of the Timeline.

The 5D angle recorded the good production audio while the 7D angle has the not-so-great audio. The best strategy for using this multicam clip would be to cut between the video angles while playing the audio content of 5D throughout. This is a Video Only edit, which the Angle Viewer allows you to set up.

12 In the Angle Viewer, click the 5D angle.

A yellow border appears around the angle to show that it is active.

13 In the Angle Viewer, click the Video Only Switching button, and then click the 7D angle.

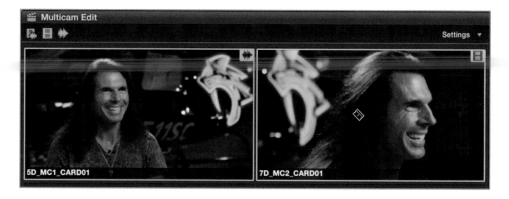

The 5D angle border turns green to indicate that its audio content only is the active audio angle, while the 7D border turns blue to identify its video content as the active

video angle. Also, in the Timeline, the new clip segment is labeled V: 7D_MC2_
CARD01 | A: 5D_MC1_CARD01.

14 Review the edit and notice that the audio of 5D remains active across the edit.

15 Press Command-Z to undo the edit.

You're just about ready to finally edit the multicam clip. To do so, you will play the
Timeline, and simply click the camera angle you want to cut to at any moment. The
Angle Viewer, Viewer, and the multicam clip will all reflect your edit. After you stop
playback, the Timeline clip's thumbnails will update to show your edit decisions.

16 With the playhead cued to the start of the Timeline, start playback, and then click an
angle in the Angle Viewer each time you want to cut to that angle.

17 If you make a mistake, stop playback, and press Command-Z to undo the most recent
cut. Recue the playhead, and then resume playback and cutting.

The multicam feature makes editing between multiple cameras a breeze and you'll feel
as if you're directing live TV. Seeing the multiple streams simultaneously allows you to
see the alternate angles, and therefore, make better editorial decisions. The ability to
use the Switch or Undo commands means switching to the wrong angle is a mistake
that is easily fixed. That's like directing live TV, but with a no-fault, do-over option.

Fine Tuning Within a Multicam Clip

The "live" playback and cutting between angles in a multicam clip is great for creating
an edit very quickly. However, you may have cut to the wrong angle (when there's more
than two), or more likely, cut a little later or earlier than you intended. These errors are
easy to correct.

1   In the multicam clip, find a specific cut point (the perforated line that divides the clip into multiple segments) that you want to move earlier or later in the clip.

2   With the mouse pointer located over the cut point, the Roll edit tool appears. Final Cut Pro assumes that you want to keep clips in sync, therefore, it enables the only Trim tool you can use here without causing sync problems.

NOTE ▶ If you need to perform another trim function, from the Tools pop-up menu, choose the Trim tool.

3   Drag the cut point to the left about 10 frames.

If you accidentally cut when you did not intend to cut, whether to the same angle or a different angle, you may remove the cut.

4   With the Select tool, click a cut point to select it, and then press Delete.

Before pressing Delete

After pressing Delete

The cut is removed and the angle on the left of the cut is extended to the next cut point. This is known as a *join through edit*.

NOTE ▶ Traditionally, a join through edit occurs when the content is the same on both sides of the cut point. Technically, that is true here because the content is the multicam clip container on both sides of the cut point.

▶ **Switching Angles**

When your multicam clip involves more than two angles, you may have cut to the wrong angle and just want to replace it. What you need to perform is a modified switch, as in a cut and switch without the cut. As with most functions in Final Cut Pro, if you need to perform an operation that is slightly (or radically) different, try combining it with the Option key.

With your playhead cued over a multicam clip segment in the Timeline, Option-click the other angle in the Angle Viewer. The mouse pointer changes from the Blade tool to the Hand tool in the Angle Viewer when the Option key is held down. The clicked angle replace edits the segment angle in the Timeline.

Configuring Audio Channels and Components

During a multicam edit, you may need to use audio from another angle. The first place to activate that channel for a multiclip segment is in the Audio inspector's Channel Configuration.

The Channel Configuration allows you to declare how Final Cut Pro will handle each audio component or component pair of a clip when it comes to enabling/disabling the desired audio channels and how the component is handled for output—as a stereo pair or dual mono for example.

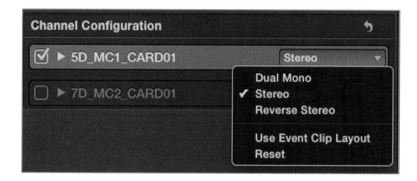

NOTE ▶ If you need to change the Channel Configuration for a multicam clip segment, in the Layout pop-up menu, deselect Use Event Clip Layout to override the preset.

After setting the configuration to enable the desired individual audio components within a multicam segment, choose the Show Audio Components shortcut menu item. Keyframing and audio fade handles are available per audio component in the Timeline when you choose to Expand Audio Components of a Timeline clip.

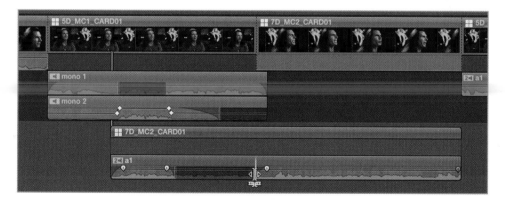

Revealing the individual components in the Timeline allows you to use and adjust the audio from any angle at anytime. This is further enhanced by the ability to make audio only edits from a multicam clip to a project. Additionally, multicam audio may be detached from a multicam clip for more edit flexibility.

Lesson Review

1. Which project Video Properties parameter must be selected to edit in a non-native video resolution?

2. Identify the default render format in Final Cut Pro.

3. What command creates a compound clip that synchronizes a video clip and an audio clip recorded on separate devices?

4. What command allows you to manually adjust the synchronization of audio and video within a clip?

5. In what vertical order should clips be placed for compositing?

6. In the Keyer effect, what parameter should you set to disable the auto-keyer and gain manual control over the settings?

7. Fill in the blank: Double-clicking a multicam clip opens the _____.

8. What button do you click to display a multicam clip's angles for monitoring and to choose the active angle during playback?

9. What do the three active angle colors indicate?

Answers

1. The Format parameter must be set to Custom using the manual settings.

2. Apple ProRes 422

3. Synchronize Clips

4. Open in Timeline

5. The foreground clip should be placed in a lane above the background clip.

6. Set the Strength slider to 0.

7. Angle Editor

8. Clicking Show Angles reveals the Angle Viewer.

9. Yellow indicates the active video and audio angle. Blue indicates the active video angle. Green indicates the active audio angle.

Appendix A
Keyboard Shortcuts

Although Final Cut Pro includes over 300 commands, the tables in this appendix focus on the most commonly used keyboard shortcuts. You also may create or reassign Final Cut Pro shortcuts to your liking.

Assigning Keyboard Shortcuts

Final Cut Pro allows you to create and modify keyboard shortcuts in the Command Editor.

1   From the menu bar, choose Final Cut Pro > Commands > Customize to open the
Command Editor.

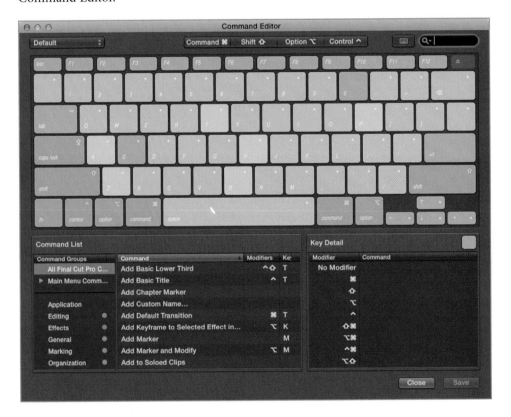

The Command Editor includes a keyboard, a search field, and a list of all available
commands. These three elements provide multiple methods for manipulating commands
and keyboard shortcuts.

NOTE ▸ When assigning new shortcuts, you will first duplicate the current command
set. If you forget to set up a duplicate keyboard command set, Final Cut Pro will
remind you.

2   From the Command Set pop-up menu, choose Duplicate.

3   Enter a name for the command set, and then click OK.

Using the Keyboard

Click a key on the Command Editor's keyboard. A list of that key's assignments appears in the lower-right of the Command Editor. You may use this list in conjunction with the other two interface elements to assign commands to the selected key.

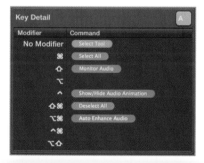

Using the Search Field

The search field allows you to search commands by name and description. For example, entering *cut* in the search field will return not only the Cut command, but also the Blade command because it "cuts" through clips.

The search field

Search results appear in the command list.

Using the Command List

Final Cut Pro completists may enjoy taking a scroll through the command list, which displays every one of the hundreds of assigned and assignable commands in Final Cut Pro. It's a great way to discover new commands.

Selecting a command list item displays a description at right.

Reviewing the Default Command Set

The following tables constitute a short list of default keyboard shortcuts.

Interface

Command	Shortcut	Description
Zoom to Fit	Shift-Z	Browser: Display one thumbnail per clip.
		Viewer: Adjust the Viewer's Zoom level to fit entire image.
		Timeline: Display the entire project within the Timeline.
Zoom In	Command-= (equals sign)	Browser: Display more thumbnails in a filmstrip.
		Viewer: Enlarge the image size within the Viewer.
		Timeline: Stretch the time scale of the Timeline.

Interface

Command	Shortcut	Description
Zoom Out	Command--- (minus sign)	Browser: Display fewer thumbnails in a filmstrip.
		Viewer: Reduce the image size within the Viewer.
		Timeline: Collapse the time scale of the Timeline.
Inspector	Command-4	Show/hide the details of one or more selected items.
Media Import	Command-I	Open the Media Import window.
Timeline Index	Command-Shift-2	Show/hide the Timeline Index.
Video Animation Editor	Control-V	Show/hide the Video Animation Editor.
Clip Appearance: Waveform Only	Control-Option-1	Display all Timeline clips only by their audio waveforms.
Clip Appearance: Increase Waveform	Control-Option- Up Arrow	Increase the waveform display size for Timeline clips.
Clip Appearance: Decrease Waveform	Control-Option- Down Arrow	Decrease the waveform display size for Timeline clips.
Show/Hide Video Scopes	Command-7	Show/hide the Video Scopes used for color correction.

Tool Palette

Command	Shortcut	Description
Select Tool	A	Select a clip.
Trim Tool	T	Ripple, Roll, Slip, and Slide Trimming functions
Blade Tool	B	Split a clip into two segments.

Navigation

Command	Shortcut	Description
Play	L	Play forward. Press up to four times for fast forward playback.
Pause	K	Pause playback.
Play in Reverse	J	Play reverse. Press up to four times for fast reverse playback.
Play Selection	/ (slash)	Start playback at range start point, and stop at range end point.
Go to Range Start	Shift-I	Cue the playhead to the start of the selected range.
Skimming	S	Enable/disable the skimmer.
Audio Skimming	Shift-S	Enable/disable the audio skimming (skimming must be enabled).
Position Playhead	Control-P	Position the playhead by entering a timecode value or relative time value in the Dashboard.

Event Metadata

Command	Shortcut	Description
Set Range Start	I	Start a range at the skimmer or playhead location.
Set Range End	O	End a range at the skimmer or playhead position.
Set Additional Range Start	Shift-Command-I	Mark a start point for additional ranges within a clip.
Set Additional Range End	Shift-Command-O	Mark an end point for additional ranges within a clip.
Clear Selected Ranges	Option-X	Clear one or more selected ranges (marked start and end points).
Favorite	F	Assign a selection a Favorite rating.
Delete	Command-Delete	Move the selected clip or event to the Trash.
		Collection: Delete the collection, removing the associated keyword from all clips within the event.

Audio

Command	Shortcut	Description
Expand Audio Components	Control-Option-S	Display the active, individual audio channels of a clip.
Create Audio Keyframe	Option-click	Create an audio keyframe using the Select tool.
Gain +1dB	Control-= (equals sign)	Boost the volume of the Timeline selection by 1 dB.

Audio

Command	Shortcut	Description
Gain −1dB	Command-– (minus sign)	Attenuate the volume of the Timeline selection by 1 dB.
Toggle Waveform Height	Control-Option-Up Arrow	Cycle through the six clip appearance options.
Solo	Option-S	Mute all nonselected audio items from playback.

Editing

Command	Shortcut	Description
Append Clip	E	Add the selected clip to the end of the primary or selected storyline.
Insert Clip	W	Insert the selected clip into the primary storyline within the marked range, or at the skimmer or playhead location.
Connect Clip	Q	Connect the selected clip to the primary storyline within the range, or at the skimmer or playhead location.
Overwrite Clip	D	Stamp the selected clip on top of any clips for the duration of and within the Timeline range, or within the duration of a selected clip at the skimmer or playhead location.
Backtimed Connect	Shift-Q	Perform a three-point connect edit in which the Timeline and Browser marked end points are used to start the edit. Content is backfilled from the end points the duration of the Timeline marked range.
Snapping	N	Turn on/off snapping in the Timeline.

Editing

Command	Shortcut	Description
Lift from Storyline	Command-Option-Up Arrow	Perform a lift edit, moving the selected clip vertically out of the containing storyline and leaving a gap.
Create Storyline	Command-G	Place the selected, connected clips into a storyline.
New Compound Clip	Option-G	Browser: Create an empty Timeline container for pre-edits/segments/composites. Timeline: Nest the selection into a compound clip.
Expand Audio/Video	Control-S, or double-click audio waveform	Display the embedded audio of a clip as a separate component allowing for independent adjustment of the start and end points of the audio or video.
Reveal in Browser	Shift-F	Display the Browser's selection for the current Timeline selection; Match frame.
Nudge Left	, (comma)	Timeline: Move the selection one unit to the left; trim a selected Timeline edge left one frame.
Nudge Right	. (period)	Timeline: Move the selection one unit to the right; trim a selected Timeline edge right one frame.
Trim Start	Option-[(left bracket)	Trim start point of clip to skimmer or playhead location.
Trim End	Option-] (right bracket)	Trim end point of clip to skimmer or playhead location.
Trim to Selection	Option-\ (slash)	Trim start and end points of a clip to the marked range within the clip.
Duration	Control-D	In the Dashboard, display and allow changes to the duration of the selected clip(s).

Editing

Command	Shortcut	Description
Blade	Command-B	Blade the primary storyline clip or one or more selected clips.
Extend Edit	Shift-X	Move the selected edge to the skimmer or play-head position.
Retime	Command-R	Display the Retime Editor for the Timeline selection.
Blade Speed	Shift-B	Create a speed segment at the playhead.
Insert Gap Clip	Option-W	Insert a three-second gap clip at the playhead or skimmer.
Undo	Command-Z	Delete the most recent edit.
Add Default Transition	Command-T	Apply the default transition to the selected edit or clip(s) (plus audio cross fade, when applicable).
Override Connections	` (accent)	Allow connected clips to lock to time while the anchoring primary storyline clip is manipulated.
Move Connection	Command-Option-Click	Click the connected clip to relocate the clip's connection point to the primary storyline.
Copy	Command-C	Copy the selected item(s) to the OS X clipboard.
Paste Attributes	Shift-Command-V	Allow a specific selection of attributes from a copied clip to be pasted to other clip(s).
Clip Disable/Enable	Shift-Command-V	Disable/enable a clip's visibility (or audibility).
Duplicate Project as Snapshot	Command-Shift-D	Duplicate the selected or active project as a snapshot.
Set Marker	M	Press once to set a marker. When cued to a marker, press once to edit the marker's settings.

Final Cut Pro

Command	Shortcut	Description
Hide Application	Command-H	Hide the application.
Continuous Selection	Shift-click	Select multiple contiguous items.
Non-Continuous Selection	Command-click	Select multiple noncontiguous items.
Select All	Command-A	Select all items in the active window, area, or container.
Deselect All	Command-Shift-A	Deselect all items in the active window, area, or container.
Preferences	Command-, (comma)	Open Final Cut Pro preferences.

Appendix **B**
Editing Native Formats

These tables list the native editing formats for Final Cut Pro. Native format editing means that no transcoding to another format is necessary. Final Cut Pro, OS X Mavericks, and the Macintosh hardware have more than enough power to push HD1080p. Whether you are using the MacBook Pro or the Mac Pro, the triumvirate of pro hardware, OS X, and professional applications is ready to tackle UltraHD, 5K, and future formats, all natively.

Native Video Formats

This table lists the SD, HD, and 1K+ formats.

SD	HD
DV, DVCAM, DVCPRO	DVCPRO HD, HDV
DVCPRO 50	H.264, AVCHD, AVCHD Lite, AVCCAM, NXCAM, AVC-Intra (50&100), XAVC
IMX (D-10)	XDCAM EX/HD/HD422, XF MPEG-2
iFrame, Motion JPEG (OpenDML only)	
Apple Intermediate	
Apple Animation	
Apple ProRes 4444, 422 HQ, 422, LT, Proxy, Log C	
REDCODE RAW (R3D)	
Uncompressed 10-bit and 8-bit 4:2:2	

Native Still-Image Formats

This table lists the native still-image formats used for photos and graphics, for example.

BMP

GIF

JPEG

PNG

PSD (static and layered)

RAW

TGA

TIFF

Native Audio Formats

This table lists the audio file formats natively supported in Final Cut Pro.

AAC
AIFF
BWF
CAF
MP3
MP4
WAV

Glossary

Codec Contraction of COmpressor/DECompressor; an algorithm used to convert video pixels into ones and zeros

Components The individual video or audio elements from a source media file within a clip. A typical clip with embedded audio has two or four audio components.

Contrast Amount of grayscale separation between the brightest and darkest pixels of an image

Create Archive Assemble a nonproprietary packaged clone of the source media files.

Destinations Share presets that export your project to platform-compatible formats suitable for iOS, YouTube, Tudou, and so on

Doppler Effect The perceived pitch rise of an approaching sound and the pitch lowering of a departing sound

Dual System Recording A recording workflow in which visuals are recorded on one device and production audio is recorded on a separate device

Duck Decrease in volume

External Media Source media files that are symlinked within the library as they actually exist at any accessible location on any available volume

Grouping A virtual channel assignment of audio or video clips

J-Cut A split edit scenario in which the audio leads the video edit

Join Through Edit Remove the selected edit point or cut between two Timeline segments.

Jump Cut When similar but nonsynchronized content appears to jump in space and time at an edit point

Keyframes Locks a parameter's value at a point in time. It takes a minimum of two keyframes to animate a parameter.

L-Cut A split edit scenario in which the audio lags the video edit

Lower Third A graphic located in the lower third of the Viewer that presents information to the audience. Typical information displayed includes the name of the on-camera person or the location or setting of the current video.

Luminance The brightness of a video pixel

Managed Media Source media files that physically exist in the event inside the library

Mask A shape used to designate areas of an image as visible or transparent

Media Empty A library utilizing external source media files referenced within the library file

Media Full A library utilizing source media files managed inside the library file

Media Handle Source media beyond a clip's marked range used for transitions and trimming

Media Management The process of collecting, storing, organizing, copying, and moving source media files

Nats Natural sound of a scene recorded by the camera's microphone

Ramps Quick fade-in or fade-out to ease in or ease out, respectively, a clip's audio, thereby avoiding a noticeable cut into or out of the audio

Rolling Shutter Process the video content to remove an artifact unique to CMOS sensors.

Stabilization Process the video content to remove camera shake.

Stems Discrete outputs of video audio or graphic content

Subclip A selected range within a larger clip treated as a separate clip

Swell Increase in volume

Through Edit A clip notation that contiguous content exists at the cut point

Traces The display of a signal's value on a video scope

Trimming Deleting or inserting frames from or to a clip

Video Scopes Three visual displays that represent the grayscale contrast and colors in an image

Index

Numbers

12-dB dynamic-range mix, 362, 366
36-dB dynamic-range mix, 362

A

Add Default Transition
(Command-T)
cross dissolve, 195–196, 302,
304, 307–309
defined, 474
montage or collage edits, 301
Page Curl, 312
Add Role (+) pop-up menu, 98–99
Add Rule (+) button
applying filters, 83–85, 87–90
creating Smart Collections,
91–93, 215
Add Subrole (+) button, 102
Aerials
editing with blade speed,
278–282
revised edit on, 246–247
speed transitions applied to,
284–285
Aerials, trimming
adding B-roll, 257–258
aligning bites and bits,
260–267
overview of, 253–257
removing transition and
moving clips, 258–260
AirPlay, 199–205
All Clips command, 78, 82, 87
Analysis keyword, 49
Analysis options, Media Import, 33
Analyze and Fix command, 94, 375
Analyzed state, Balance, 374, 376

Angle Editor, multicam clip, 453
Angle Viewer, 456–460, 462
Append button (E key), 113–114
Append edit
batch clips to primary
storyline, 115–118
chroma key workflow, 440
clips to connected storyline,
161–166
clips to primary storyline,
111–115
defined, 121
Apple ProRes 422 format, 401,
433–434
Apple TV, 203–205
Archives
creating, 22–24
creating library, 425–426
master file of final project for,
399–403
recovering original source
media files, 426
setting up multicam clip, 450
storage locations, 24
Aspect, defined, 21
Attributes
copying and pasting, 323–325
editing Info pane, in Share
inspector, 396–397
nesting compound clips, 325
Audio
adding sound to clip, 343–349
adjusting volume levels over
time, 358–372
analyzing and fixing, 34
clip-by-clip focus on, 342–343

editing clips below primary
storyline, 179–181
effects in Event Browser, 286
enhancement features,
372–373
investing in monitoring
equipment for, 189
keyboard shortcuts/command
set, 471–472
native formats for, 479
retiming borrowed, 349–352
slip trimming only, 182
source channel configuration
and, 34
splitting with another clip,
352–357
synchronizing dual system
recordings, 435–439
trimming at subframe
level, 337
volume levels. *see* volume
levels
Audio and Render properties, New
Project, 431–432
Audio channels
configuring, 34, 438–439,
462–464
manually setting number of,
432–433
switching from stereo to
mono, 364
Audio Enhancements, 372–373
Audio inspector, 363–364, 372–373,
438–439
Audio meters
adjusting clip volume levels,
187–189

dynamic range and, 362
reading, 361
setting volume levels by
role, 366
Audio Only Smart Collection
connecting music clips, 180
overview of, 91–93
replacing primary storyline, 220
roles, 99–100
Audio role, 97, 101–102
Audio Skimming button (Shift-S),
269, 470
Audio waveforms, 352–353,
366–369. *see also* volume
levels, adjusting over time
Audition window, 248–250
Auditions
aligning bites and bits,
261–267
avoiding ripple induced by, 250
building audition clip,
247–248
importing aerials, 246–247
overview of, 243–244
repositioning storylines/
deleting within, 244–246
spotlight badge identifying,
248–249
using Audition window,
248–250
Automatic setting, New Project
frame size/rate, 430

B

Background clip, chroma key
workflow, 440–443
Background Noise Removal
command, 373
Background Tasks, Dashboard,
95–96, 202, 395
Backspace key, as Delete key, 77
Backtimed connect (Shift-Q),
317, 472
Backup
automatic library, 426
camera archive, 22–24
master file of final project,
399–403

Balance feature, image color,
374–376
Batch edit, clips into storyline,
115–118, 164, 167
Batch renaming, of camera clips,
60–61
Blade command (Command-B),
137, 240, 474
Blade Speed (Shift-B), 280–282
Blade tool (B)
editing multicam clip, 458, 462
joining through edit, 139–140
splitting clip into two
segments, 132,
136–139, 474
Blend, previewing audio, 353–355
Brightness (luma), Waveform scope,
377, 379
B-roll clips
aligning bites and bits,
261–267
appending to connected
storyline, 163–166
clip volume levels, 187–189
connected clip sync, 152–155
connecting two additional,
189–192
converting into connected
storyline, 157–161
defined, 144
editing within connected
storyline, 178
realigning to music, 235–238
ripple trim, 183–185
in second edit pass, 257–258
slip trim, 185–186
trimming aerials, 253–257
trimming connected clips,
155–156
Browser
adding keyword to clips in,
52–53
assigning role to batches of
clips, 99
batch renaming camera clips,
60–61
creating compounds in, 327
displaying all ratings in, 78

dragging new clip to project
from, 110
new project displayed in, 108
sorting and organizing clips
in, 47
text searches in, 82–83
three-point edit for split
screen in, 317
viewing keywords in list
view, 64
Browser pane
defined, 20
enabling Connect button
when dimmed, 162
hiding, 456
how source files are displayed,
26
volume vs. camera import
in, 36
Bundle destination preset, 397–399

C

Camera
angle, editing multicam clip,
454–460
creating archive, 22–24
date and time settings, 454
disabling audio, 437
importing source media from,
24–25
navigating within filmstrip
preview, 26–28
preparing to import source
files, 18–19
SD card. *see* cloned
(simulated) SD card
synchronizing dual system
recordings, 435–439
"Catch a click," audio clips, 192–193
Centered Title, 336–340, 341–342
Channel Configuration
changing audio, 362–364
disabling camera audio, 437
multicam edit, 462–464
synchronizing dual system
recordings, 438–439
Chapter markers, 228

Chroma key
    manually selecting color key
        samples, 445–449
    masking objects, 443–444
    workflow for, 439–443
Chroma Key Keyword Collection,
    440–443
Circle Mask effect, 296
Clip Appearance
    Control-Option-1, 366, 469
    Control-Option-Down Arrow,
        367, 469
    Control-Option-Up Arrow,
        367, 469
    creating markers, 233–234
    duck/swell sound effects and
        music, 366
    keywording clip, 51
    viewing fade handles, 194
Clip container, 14
Clip skimming, 252, 263–264,
    356, 371
Clips
    deleting with Delete, 138
    deleting with gap clips. *see* gap
        edit (Option-W)
Clips, organizing
    adding notes, 65–69
    applying ratings. *see* ratings
    assigning roles, 96–103
    in Browser, 47–48
    customizing favorites, 80–81
    filtering event, 86–90
    Find People analysis, 93–96
    keywording. *see* keywords
    keywording ranges, 61–65
    in Libraries pane, 46–48
    overview of, 45
    review Q & A, 103–104
    search and filter, 83–85
    searching metadata, 82
    in Smart Collections, 85–86,
        91–93
    sorting, 82
    in Viewer, 47–48
Clips Index, 228–230, 363
Cloned (simulated) SD card

creating camera archive,
    22–24
importing camera source files,
    18–21
importing clips from, 28–30
leaving files in place, 36–37
navigating within filmstrip
    preview, 26–28
recovering original source
    media files, 426
Close Library command, 17
Codec (COmpressor/
    DECompressor), 21, 481
Collage edit, placing transitions, 301
Color
    balance, 33
    indicating active angle,
        457, 459
    manually selecting chroma
        key, 445–449
    matching clip, 384–386
    text font, 339–340
Color Adjustment pane, 376, 384
Color Board, 379–380, 382–384
Color Correction tools, 373–374
Command Editor window, 25,
    466–468
Command key, selecting multiple
    items, 28
Command list, Command
    Editor, 466
Command set, default, 468–475
Compatibility checker, Share
    window, 390
Completed markers, 228
Components, defined, 481
Composite of multiple clips,
    collapsing into compound clip,
    326–327
Compositing Opacity parameter,
    Video Animation Editor, 322
Compositing using spatial
    parameters
    creating two-up split screen,
        314–321
    overview of, 312–314
    using Video Animation Editor,
        321–325

Compounding clips, 325–327
Compressor
    adding setting to shared
        destinations, 404–405
    creating master file of final
        project, 399–403
    when to use, 406
Connect clip (Q)
    adding/trimming connected
        B-roll, 147, 149, 151
    appending clips to connected
        storyline, 162
    backtimed connect (Shift-Q),
        317, 472
    chroma key workflow, 441
    connect edits, 223
    editing within connected
        storyline, 178
    enabling when dimmed, 162
    music clips, 180
    retiming borrowed audio, 350
Connect edits
    connecting two B-roll clips,
        190–192
    creating time at 0:00, 222–223
    editing within connected
        storyline, 178–179
    performing, 144–152
Connected clips
    creating connected storyline,
        156–161
    overriding connection,
        154–155
    synchronization, 152–154
    trimming, 155–156
    when transition is applied, 195
Connected storyline
    appending clips to, 161–167
    converting connected clips
        into, 157–161
    creating, 156–157
    creating and editing third,
        176–179
    defined, 156
    editing within, 167–176
    relocating connection
        point, 251
Connection point, relocating, 251

Consolidate Find People results, 94–96

Consolidate Library Files command, 424–425

Context sensitivity, Final Cut Pro, 126

Continuous selection (Shift-click), 363, 475

Contrast
Balance maximizing image, 374
with color correction, 377
defined, 481

Copy Events to Library command, 426

"Copy files into"
importing media as external, 32, 35–36, 41–42
multicam clip setup, 450
redirecting imported media to external location, 416

Copying
attributes, 323–325
clips within library, 419–421
depth of field effect, 294
events between libraries, 426
events into library for portability, 421–425
inter-library, 90

Corrective effects, 291–293

Create Archive command, 22–24, 481

Create Smart Collections after analysis, Find People, 94–95

Create Storyline (Command-G), 157, 162, 179, 473

Create Transition button, 304

Credentials, sharing to online host, 394

Crop tool, 313, 320–321, 443–444

Cross dissolve transition
collapsing composite into compound clip, 327
customizing, 311–312
as default transition, 301–302
media handles for, 304, 307
refining edits, 194–197

Custom Speed window, 276–277, 351

Customizing
destinations for sharing project, 390, 398
favorites, 80–81
resolution/frame rate for new project, 430–434
transitions, 309–312

Cutaways. *see* B-roll clips

D

Dashboard, 233, 242, 311

Decorative effects, 291–293

Default command set, 468–475

Delete (Command-Delete), 54

Delete key
deleting clips, 138
deleting effect from clip, 293
fine-tuning within multicam clip, 461–462
rejecting clip, 77–80
removing transitions, 258

Delete Keyword Collection, 54

Deleted segments, 132–133

Delta (timing change), dragging clip to Timeline, 121

Depth of field effect, 293–299

Deselect All (Command-Shift-A), 391, 400, 475

Destinations (preset)
creating master file of final project, 400
creating viewable file for sharing media, 390
defined, 481
sharing to bundle, 397–398
sharing to online host, 391–397

Digital signage video, with non-native resolutions, 430

Distort tool, 313

Documents folder, 6, 23

Doppler effect, 360, 481

Downloading, source media files, 5

Downloads folder, 5, 7

Dragging
clips within library, 419–421
delta or timing change within Timeline when, 121

from Finder, 40–42, 418
sound from Sound Effects folder, 343–344
transitions, 258–260

Dual mono, switching clip from stereo to, 364

Dual system recording, 435–439, 481

Duck, 366–369, 481

Duplicate command, 466–467

Duplicate Project, 213

Duplicate Project as Snapshot, 213–214, 273

Duration (Control-D)
avoiding audition-induced ripple, 250
creating time at 0:00, 221–228
customizing transition, 310–311
defined, 473
editing blade speed, 280
inserting gap clip, 134–135
of lower third on screen, 340
roll trim vs. ripple trim and, 159
setting playback speed manually, 275–278
three-point edit for split screen, 314–321

Dynamic range, evaluating width, 362

E

Edit phase, workflow, 10

Edit points
applying transitions to, 301
defined, 125
media handles for transitions, 303–306
three-point edit for split screen, 316–317
using Transitions Browser, 308–309

Editing
default keyboard shortcuts for, 472–474
first. *see* first edit (rough cut)
multicam clips, 454–460
native formats, 477–479

Effects Browser, 286–288, 296, 440–444

End point

   aligning bites and bits, 263–264

   extend edits on title, 341–342

   refining, 142

   removing transitions, 258–260

   retiming borrowed audio, 349

   ripple trimming with keyboard, 129–131

   trimming aerials, 253–257

   video transitions. *see* edit points

Enhancement pass

   compositing. *see* compositing using spatial parameters

   compound clips, 325–327

   overview of, 271

   retiming clips, 272–285

   review Q & A, 328–331

   video effects. *see* video effects

   video transitions. *see* video transitions

Escape key, 337

Event container, 14–15

Event Manager, 4

Events

   combining library, 426

   copying to portable library, 422–425

   creating, 107–109

   defined, 106

   deleting extraneous, 426

   dragging items to, 41

   filtering, 86–90

   importing as managed clips, 415–417

   metadata command set for, 471

   moving or copying between libraries, 419–421, 426

   naming, 17

   upgrading existing, 3–4

   virtual storage and, 31

Exchangeable file, creating, 404

Expand Audio/Video (Control S), 355–357, 473

Exporting, 404–406. *see also* sharing project

Exposure, manually correcting clip, 376–381

Exposure pane, 378–379

Extend edits (Shift-X), 341–342, 345, 474

Extended view, Info inspector, 451

EXtensible Markup Language (XML), outputting to third-party apps, 404

External media

   as best practice for storage, 411

   copying source media files into, 37

   creating portable library, 421–425

   defined, 481

   importing as "Leave files in place" to, 412–414

   moving and copying clips within library, 419–421

   overview of, 32

   setting in Media Import options, 39

   symlinks created when using, 37, 411

Extras folder, 435

F

Face parameters, text font face, 338–339

Fade handles, 192–194, 322–323, 360, 368

Falloff parameter, Vignette effect, 289–290, 292

Favorite (F)

   adding camera archive to, 23

   appending batch edit to storyline, 117–118

   appending clips to storyline, 112–115

   customizing, 80–81

   as not always favorite, 76

   overview of, 69

   performing insert edits, 122–125

   rating clips as, 76

   setting marked ranges as, 73–75, 471

   unrating (U key), 76–77

FCPX Media folder, 7–8, 18–19

Filmstrip preview, 26–28

Filmstrip view

   appending batch edit to storyline, 115–118

   in Browser pane, 20

   expanding, 27–28

   keywording clip in, 50–51

   manually applied keywords in, 49

   navigating within, 26–28

Filter pop-up menu

   applying rules for searches, 83–85

   creating Smart Collections, 91–93

   filtering event, 86–90

   sorting clips, 82

Filters, 215

Final Cut Pro command set, keyboard shortcuts, 475

Find and Replace Title Text, 342

Find People, 33, 93–96

Finder

   dragging from, 40–42, 418

   harnessing metadata using keywords, 39

   locating camera archives in, 426

   managing external source media files, 32

   preparing source media files, 6, 8

Finessing, of first edit

   adjusting edits, 183–186

   clip volume levels, 187–189

   connecting additional B-roll clips, 189–192

   cross dissolves and fade handles, 192–197

   overview of, 181–182

Finishing edit

   adding and modifying lower third, 335–342

adding sound to clip, 343–349
audio, 342–343
audio enhancements, 372–374
neutralizing clips. *see*
    neutralizing clips
overview of, 333
retiming borrowed audio,
    349–352
review Q & A, 386–388
splitting audio with another
    clip, 352–357
titles, 334–335
volume levels. *see* volume
    levels, adjusting over time
First edit (rough cut)
    appending batch edit, 115–118
    appending primary storyline,
        111–115
    in connected storyline. *see*
        connected storyline
    creating project, 106–109
    defining primary storyline,
        109–111
    editing above primary
        storyline, 143
    editing below primary
        storyline, 179–181
    finessing. *see* finessing, of
        first edit
    modifying clips in primary
        storyline, 121–122
    overview of, 105
    performing connect edits,
        144–156
    performing insert edits,
        122–125
    playing project, 118–119
    rearranging clips in primary
        storyline, 119–121
    review Q & A, 206–210
    rippling primary storyline,
        126–131
    share project to media file,
        197–205
    timing. *see* timing primary
        storyline
    understanding project, 106

Folders
    creating for downloaded
        media, 6
    importing as Keyword
        Collections, 33
Foreground clip
    chroma key workflow,
        440–443
    manually selecting color key
        samples, 445–449
    masking chroma key clips,
        443–444
Formats
    available for this book, 4–5
    custom settings for new
        project, 430–434
    custom settings for non-native
        resolutions, 430
    editing native, 477–479
    master file of final project,
        400–401
Frame rate, 21, 430–434

G
Gap edit (Option-W)
    deleting clips with, 138
    first edit, 133–135
    lengthening connected
        storyline, 169
    Position tool replacing existing
        content, 235–238
    refining sound bite edits, 142
    replacing deleted clip, 246
    replacing deleted
        segments, 133
    replacing in primary storyline,
        219–221
    revising edit, 225–227
    Shift-Delete to replace
        selection with, 133
    timing primary storyline, 131
Gaussian Blur effect, 298–299
Generators Browser, 441, 443
Getting started
    downloading source media
        files, 5

introducing job and workflow,
    9–11
learned from a legacy, 2–3
overview of, 1
preparing source media files,
    5–8
review Q & A, 11
upgrading existing events and
    projects, 3–4
using this book, 4–5
Glossary, 4, 481–482
Graphics, 335
Grave key, overriding connected
    clips, 154–155
Grouping, 96, 481

H
H.264 format
    as native video format, 478
    preset destinations and, 198
    sharing master file, 399
    sharing to hosting service, 397
Hand tool, 462
Hardware, 3, 17
Help tag, adding notes to clip, 67
Hide application (Command-H),
    18, 475
Hide Rejected, Filter pop-up
    menu, 82
Hum Removal, Audio
    Enhancements, 373

I
iLife sound effects and musical
    clips, 343
Image Capture, 18
Image correction
    balancing color automatically,
        375–376
    Color Board, 381
    correcting clip color manually,
        382–384
    correcting clip exposure
        manually, 376–381
    finishing edit, 373–374
    matching color, 384–386
Image Mask effect, 296

Images
 native still-image formats, 478
 synchronizing dual system
  recordings, 435–439
Import All, clips from camera
 card, 28
Import Folders as Keyword
 Collections, 50
Import options
 creating Smart Collections, 93
 expanding filmstrip view,
  27–28
 importing camera source files,
  19, 24–25
 importing existing files from
  volume, 38
 importing files from
  volume, 36
 media management, 31
 using, 19–21
Importing
 camera source files, 18–19,
  24–25
 clip container, 14
 clips from camera card, 28–30
 creating camera archive,
  22–24
 creating library, 16–17
 by dragging from Finder,
  40–42, 418
 event container, 14–15
 existing files from volume,
  38–40
 files from volume, 36–37
 as "Leave files in place,"
  412–414
 library container, 15
 as managed clips, 415–417
 Media Import Options dialog,
  31–34
 Media Import window, 19–21
 navigating within filmstrip
  preview, 26–28
 options, 34–35
 recovering original source
  media files, 426
 review Q & A, 42–43

for revised edit, 246–247
setting up multicam clip,
 450–454
synchronizing dual system
 recordings, 435
Info inspector
 reassigning audio and video to
  correct roles, 365
 setting up multicam clip, 451
 verifying additional roles are
  added, 103
 verifying clip received
  assigned role, 99
 verifying events copied to
  portable library, 423
 viewing, 67–68
 viewing managed vs. external
  media in, 416–417
Info pane, Share window, 200,
 392–393
Insert edits (W), 122–125, 157,
 249, 257
Inspector button (Command-4), 99,
 288, 469
Inspector pane
 Exposure pane in, 377–381
 Info and Share inspectors in,
  396–397
 Text inspector in, 337
 Transition inspector in, 309
Intelligent Assistance, 4
Interface command set, keyboard
 shortcuts, 468–469
Inter-library copying, 90
Interviews, pre-editing process, 70
IOS-compatible file, sharing,
 198–203

J

J-cut, 353, 481
Job, workflow and, 9–11
Join through edit, 139–140, 462, 481
Jump cut, 139, 481

K

Keyboard, ripple trimming with,
 129–131

Keyboard shortcuts
 assigning, 466–467
 audio commands, 471–472
 Command-Z, 11
 customizable in Command
  Editor, 25
 editing commands, 472–474
 enhanced content for, 4
 event metadata
  commands, 471
 Final Cut Pro commands, 475
 interface commands, 468–469
 navigation commands, 470
 for playback, 27
 tool palette commands, 470
 using command list, 468
 using keyboard to assign, 467
 using search field, 467–468
Keyer effect
 chroma key workflow,
  440–443
 controlling with Strength
  slider, 446
 manually selecting chroma
  key color, 445–449
 masking chroma key clips,
  443–444
Keyframes
 adjusting volume levels over
  time, 358–361
 defined, 482
 ducking/swelling sound effects
  and music, 367–369
 Option key with Select tool
  creating, 358
 Range Selection for, 369–372
Keyword Collections
 adding keyword to, 52–53,
  54–56
 assigning keyword to clip
  range, 62
 import folders as, 33, 39
 keyword shortcuts and, 58–60
 organizing clips with
  keywords into, 49
 removing keyword, 54
 Smart Collections vs., 85–86

Keyword Editor (Command-K),
52–53, 56–60, 62
Keyword shortcuts, 56–60, 63
Keywords
adding clips to Keyword
Collection, 54–56
adding to one or more clips,
52–53
analysis, 49
applying to ranges, 61–65
batch renaming of camera
clips, 60–61
filtering event, 87–90
harnessing metadata in
Finder, 39
organizing clips using, 48–49
overview of, 50–51
ratings with, 69
removing, 54
search, sort and filter
metadata, 81
searching and filtering using,
83–85
using shortcuts, 56–60

L

Layering order, stacking effects,
291–293
Layout, viewing in Viewer, 47
L-cuts, 353, 356–357, 482
"Leave files in place," Media Import,
32–33, 37, 39, 412–414
Leave in place, Media Storage
option, 41–42
Libraries
applying Media Import
options, 35, 412–414
archiving, 425–426
closing existing, 17
creating, 16–17
importing as managed clips,
415–417
importing by dragging from
Finder, 418
media empty vs.media
full, 411
moving and copying clips,
419–421

no duplicate source media
files in, 418
other features of, 426
overview of, 409
portable, 421–425
relinking offline clips to
source media, 414–415
reverting, 426
review Q & A, 426–427
storing camera archives, 24
storing imported media,
410–411
upgrading existing events/
projects, 3–4
using clips between, 421
using inter-library copying, 90
Libraries pane
adding keyword to one or
more clips, 52–53
assigning role to batches of
clips, 99
editing multicam clip,
454–460
Keyword Collections stored
in, 49
keywording clip, 50–51
keywording range, 61–63
organizing clips, 46–48
toggling Hide/Show, 51
viewing keywords, 64
Library container, 15–16
Lift from storyline, 216–217, 221,
279
List view
in Browser pane, 20
customizing favorites, 80–81
manually applied keywords
in, 49
removing Rejected rating in,
78–79
viewing clip range keywords
in, 63–65
Locate option, upgrading existing
events/projects, 3–4
Login, sharing to online host, 394
Loop playback, 119
Loudness, Audio Enhancements,
372

Lower third
adding title, 335–336
defined, 482
identifying who's who in
project, 334
modifying title text, 336–340
performing extend edits on
title, 341–342
Luminance, 378–379, 482

M

Magnetic storyline, behaviors of,
109–111
Managed media
archiving library as, 426
copying source media files
into, 37
creating portable library,
421–425
defined, 482
importing media as, 415–417
moving and copying clips
within library, 419–421
overview of, 32
Marked clip, selected clip vs., 315
Markers (M)
adjusting edits with, 183–184
aligning bites and bits,
262–265
breaking up/adding new
sound bites with, 243
creating, 230–234
overview of, 228
previewing audio blend,
354–355
repositioning storylines/
deleting within, 245
using Timeline Index,
228–230
Marquee selection, manual chroma
key color, 447–449
Mask
compositing clip with,
298–299
creating depth of field,
295–298
defined, 482
Mask effect, 443–444

Master files, sharing, 399–403
Match color feature, 384–386
Maximize button, Video Animation
  Editor, 322
Media empty libraries, 411, 482
Media full libraries, 411, 482
Media handles, 302–307
Media Import (Command-I)
  applying Media Import
    options, 34–35
  choosing Media Import
    options, 31–34
  creating camera archives, 24
  creating Smart Collections,
    92–93
  defined, 469
  expanding filmstrip view,
    27–28
  importing aerials, 246–247
  importing as "Leave files in
    place," 413–414
  importing as managed clips,
    415–417
  importing existing files from
    volume, 38–40
  importing files from volume,
    36–37
  importing source media from
    camera, 24–25
  setting up multicam clip, 450
  using, 19–21
Media management. see also
  libraries
  beginning editorial process
    with, 13
  clip container, 14
  defined, 482
  event container, 14–15
  library container, 15
  using inter-library copying, 90
Media volume. see volume, media
Merge Events command, 426
Metadata
  adding keywords. see
    keywords
  adding notes, 66–68
  applying ratings, 71–75

automatic backups of
    library, 426
  camera archives, 24
  customizing, 81
  exchangeable file, 404
  Final Cut Pro creating, 46
  master file of final project, 400
  multicam clip, 451–452
  roles. see roles
  searching, 82–83
  sharing iOS-compatible
    file, 200
  sharing to online host,
    392–393
  viewing shared project in
    Inspector pane, 396–397
Motion, 335
Move Connection (Command-
  Option-click), 251, 474
Move Events to Library
  command, 426
Move tool, titles, 338
Moving
  clips within library, 419–421
  events between libraries, 426
Multicam
  configuring audio channels/
    components, 462–463
  editing clip, 454–460
  fine tuning within clip,
    460–462
  opening Angle Editor, 446
  overview of, 449
  setting camera date and
    time, 454
  setting up clip, 450–454
  switching angles, 462
Music and Sound Browser, 343–344,
  349, 356
Music clips
  adjusting clip volume levels,
    187–189
  adjusting edits, 183–186
  connecting, 180–181
  creating markers, 232–234
  ducking and swelling, 366–369
  finessing. see finessing, of
    first edit

lifting sound bites from
    storyline, 216–217
  replacing in primary storyline,
    219–221
  repositioning storylines/
    deleting within, 244–246
  using Range Selection for
    keyframing, 369–372
Music role, 100

N

Naming
  batch of camera clips, 60–61
  destinations (presets) for
    sharing media, 398
  markers, 228, 232, 262
  new role, 99
  preparing source media files, 7
  project, 107
  subroles, 102
Native formats, editing, 477–479
Nats
  adjusting volume levels over
    time, 358
  in B-roll content, 144
  defined, 482
  as natural sound audio, 98
  turning down volume of, 187
Navigation
  controls, 27–30, 113
  within filmstrip preview,
    26–28
  keyboard shortcuts, 470
Near-field loudspeakers, 189
Nesting compound clips, 325
Neutralizing clips
  balancing color automatically,
    375–376
  Color Board, 381
  correcting clip color manually,
    382–384
  correcting clip exposure
    manually, 376–381
New Compound Clip (Option-G),
  326–327
New Folder button, camera
  archive, 23
New Keyword Collection, 55

New Multicam Clip command, 451–454

New Project
creating, 106–109
editing multicam clip, 454–460
using manual settings for frame size/rate, 430–434

New Smart Collection, 91–93, 214–215

Non-native resolutions, custom settings for, 430

Nonvideo clips, custom settings for, 430

Not Analyzed state, Balance feature, 374, 376

Notes, 65–69, 81

Notification alert, sharing to online host, 395

Nudge Left (, [comma]), 454, 473

O

"On the Go" library, 421–425

Online host, sharing project to, 391–397

Opacity controls, Video Animation Editor, 322

Opacity tool, compositing, 313

Open in Timeline, 437

Optimized media, 33, 426

Option key
combining operation with, 462
with Select tool, 358

Overwrite edits, 235, 241

P

Page Curl transition, 308–312

Parameters, modifying video effect, 288–290

Paste Attributes, 323–325

Pasting (Command-V), 294, 323–325

Pause (K key), 27, 47–48, 470

Period (.) key, 130, 142

Physical storage, Media Import, 32–33

Play (L key), 27, 47–48, 470

Playback
keyboard shortcuts, 27
previewing video effect, 288
reverse, 223–224, 272
setting speed manually, 275–278

Playhead
applying ratings to clips, 71–75
editing multicam clip, 455
importing ranges from within camera file, 29–30
moving with Control-P, 222
playing project, 118–119
rearranging clips in primary storyline, 119–121
trimming start point to, 456

Portable library, creating, 421–425

Position playhead (Control-P), 222, 242, 470

Position tool
breaking up/adding new sound bites, 239–243
overwrite editing, 235
realigning sound bites/B-roll to music, 235–238
Select tool vs., 235–238

Preferences (Command-,), 40, 397–398

Preview (Spacebar), 26–27

Previewing audio blend, 353–355

Primary storyline
append batch edit to, 115–118
appending clips to, 111–115
connected. see connected storyline
editing above, 143–156
editing below, 179–181
lifting clips out of, 216–217
modifying clips in, 121–122
performing insert edits, 122–125
rearranging clips in, 119–121
replacing clip in, 219–221
rippling, 126–131
timing, 244–246
working with behaviors of, 109–111

Projects
creating, 106–109
understanding, 106
upgrading existing, 3–4

Properties, customizing for new project, 431

Proxy media, 33, 426

Puck values, clip exposure, 379

Q

QuickTime, sharing master files, 401–403

QuickTime Inspector window, 203

QuickTime Player
sharing iOS-compatible file, 201–203
using AirPlay with, 203–205

R

RAID (redundant array of independent disks), camera archives, 24

Ramps
adjusting volume levels over time, 358, 360
defined, 482
dragging fade handles for, 182
fading audio in or out with, 192–194, 197
previewing audio blend, 354
retiming borrowed audio, 352–353

Range End, additional (Command-Shift-O), 30, 471

Range End (O key), 29, 471

Range Selection tool (R), 252, 366, 369–372

Range Start, additional (Command-Shift-I), 30, 471

Range Start (I key), 29, 76–77, 222–223, 471

Ranges
adding notes to, 66, 69
applying keywords to, 61–63
deselecting when sharing, 198–199, 391
importing from within camera file, 29–30

performing insert edits,
        122–125
performing three-point edit
        for split screen, 315–317
setting as favorite, 71–75
viewing keywords in list view,
        63–65
Rate percentage field, Custom Speed
        window, 276–278
Ratings
    applying, 70–75
    customizing favorites, 80–81
    favorites as not always
        favorites, 76
    rejecting clips, 77–80
    search, sort and filter
        metadata, 81
    system of, 69
    unrating favorites, 76–77
Reading Audio meters, 361–362
Record button, pre-editing
        interviews in field, 70
Redundant array of independent
        disks (RAID), storing camera
        archives, 24
Refine Key's Sample Color
        button, 447
Reimport from Camera/Archive
        command, 426
Rejected rating, 69, 77–80
Relink Files, 414–415
Remove pulldown, transcode and
        analysis, 33
Render Format pop-up menu,
        433–434
Replace command, 218
Replace edits
    creating time at 0:00, 221–228
    performed by audition clip, 249
    replacing primary storyline,
        219–221
    using ripple trim to shorten
        clip for, 219
    versions of, 217–219
Replace from End command,
        218–219
Replace from Start command,
        218–219

Replace with gap edit (Shift-Delete),
        133, 138, 142, 209, 246
Reset button (X), 116, 290
Reset Speed, 275
Resolution, custom settings,
        430–434
Retime Editor (Command-R)
    associated with every clip, 274
    creating time at 0:00 and, 224
    defined, 474
    editing blade speed, 278–282
    setting constant speed
        change, 274
    setting playback speed
        manually, 275–278
    with speed transitions,
        282–285
Retime pop-up menu, 223–224
Retiming clips
    for borrowed audio, 349–352
    editing with blade speed,
        278–282
    overview of, 272–273
    setting constant speed change,
        273–274
    setting playback speed
        manually, 275–278
    with speed transitions,
        282–285
Reveal Project in Browser (Option-
        Shift-F), 395
Reverse playback (J key), 27, 47–48,
        223–224, 272, 470
Review Q & A
    advancing workflow, 464
    enhancement pass, 325–327
    finishing edit, 386–388
    first edit, 206–210
    getting started, 11
    importing media, 42–43
    libraries, 426–427
    organizing clips, 103–104
    revising edit, 267–269
    sharing project, 407–408
Revising edit (second pass)
    aligning bites and bits,
        260–267
    Auditions. see Auditions

continuing to add B-roll,
        257–258
creating time at 0:00, 221–228
importing aerials, 246–247
lifting from storyline, 216–217
overview of, 211–212
removing transition and
        moving clips, 258–260
replacing clip, 217–221
review Q & A, 267–269
snapshotting project, 213–215
trimming aerials, 253–257
trimming tops and tails,
        251–252
using Position tool, 235–243
versioning project, 212–213
working with markers,
        228–234
RGB Parade, 377–379
Ripple deletes, 132
Ripple field, Custom Speed window,
        277–278
Ripple trim
    added B-roll clips, 257–258
    adding sound to clip, 347
    adjusting music edits, 184–185
    aligning bites and bits, 260–261,
        266–267
    avoiding Audition-induced, 250
    breaking up/adding new
        sound bites, 240–241
    within connected storyline,
        167–168
    converting connected clips
        into connected storyline,
        158–161
    customizing transition,
        310–311
    defined, 122
    editing multicam clip, 455
    editing within connected
        storyline, 170–176
    in primary storyline, 126–131
    refining sound bite edits,
        141–142
    shortening clip for replace
        edit, 219
    tightening edit, 139

Roles
  assigning, 98–103, 269
  creating, 97–100
  delivering master file of final
    project, 401–403
  overview of, 96–97
  setting volume levels with,
    364–366
Roles as: Multitrack QuickTime
  Movie, 401–402
Roles Editor, 98–103
Roles Index, 229–230, 239, 242,
  364–366
Roll edit
  converting connected clips
    into connected storyline,
    160–161
  customizing transitions, 310
  ripple trim vs., 159
Roll edit tool, 461
Rolling shutter, 94, 482
Rules, searching using filter, 83–85

S

Sample Color button, chroma key,
  447–449
Sample rate, 348, 432–433
Saving
  libraries, 16
  master file of final project, 403
  portable library as On the
    Go, 422
  search collections as Smart
    Collections, 91–93
Search field, Command Editor,
  467–468
Searching
  marker names in Timeline
    Index, 228–230
  metadata, 82
  Sound Effects folder, 343–344
Second pass. *see* revising edit
  (second pass)
Select tool (A)
  adjusting volume levels over
    time, 358–359
  blading, 137–138

breaking up/adding new
    sound bites, 240
  fine-tuning within multicam
    clip, 461
  joining through edits, 140
  Position tool vs., 235–238
  removing transitions around
    start/end points, 258
  rippling primary storyline,
    127–129
  trimming audio clip, 345–347
  using Range Selection for
    keyframing, 371
Selected clip, marked clip vs., 315
Selection commands
  continuous selection
    (Shift-click), 363, 475
  selecting multiple items
    (Shift key), 28
  Trim to Selection (Option-\),
    252–257, 473
Send to Compressor command,
  405–406
Settings tab, Share window
  creating master file of final
    project, 400–401
  sharing iOS-compatible file, 201
  sharing to online host, 393
Share button, 199–203, 392, 400
Share inspector, 396
Share phase, workflow, 10–11
Sharing project
  to bundle, 397–399
  creating exchangeable file, 404
  creating viewable file, 390–391
  master file, 399–403
  with media empty library
    files, 411
  to online host, 391–397
  overview of, 389
  review Q & A, 407–408
  utilizing Compressor, 404–406
Sharing project to media file
  overview of, 197–198
  sharing iOS-compatible file,
    198–203
  using AirPlay with QuickTime
    Player, 203–205

Shortcuts, keyword, 56–60
Show Angles, Angle Viewer, 456
Show Video Animation, 321
Show Video Scopes
  (Command-7), 377
Sidebar, Media Import window, 20
Size parameter, Vignette effect,
  289–290
Skimming (S)
  aligning bites and bits,
    263–264
  breaking up/adding new
    sound bites, 240
  creating markers, 230–234
  filling project duration,
    221–222
  identifying/defining, 267, 269
  performing extend edits on
    title, 341–342
  performing insert edits, 125
  positioning for zooming in on
    edits, 260
  rearranging clips in primary
    storyline, 119–121
Slip edits, 181–182, 185–186,
  306–307
Smart Collections
  creating, 85–86
  creating after analysis, 34
  creating for compound
    clips, 327
  creating projects, 214–215
  saving search collections as,
    91–93
  working with, 91–93
Snapping (N)
  adding/trimming connected
    B-roll, 150
  disabling to lengthen gap
    clip, 169
  identifying/defining, 267, 269
  placing playhead between two
    clips with, 124
  tightening edit with Blade
    tool, 136–137
  toggling, 244
Snapshots, 213–215, 273

"Social Sites for Lifted bundle,"
    398–399
Software, not upgrading in midst
    of job, 3
Solo command (Option-S)
    adjusting edits, 184
    creating markers, 232, 234
    example of, 268–269
    identifying/defining, 267, 269
Sorting clips, 82
Sound, adding to clip, 343–349
Sound bites
    aligning, 260–267
    breaking up/adding new,
        239–243
    changing Channel
        Configuration, 362–364
    lifting from storyline, 216–217
    realigning to music, 235–238
    refining edits, 140–142
    selecting just, 363
Sound effects
    adding, borrowing, splitting
        audio, 355–357
    adding to clip, 343–349
    adjusting volume levels over
        time, 358–361
    changing Channel
        Configuration, 362–364
    ducking and swelling, 366–369
    previewing audio blend,
        353–355
    Range Selection for
        keyframing, 369–372
    reading Audio meters,
        361–362
    retiming borrowed audio,
        349–352
    setting volume level by role,
        364–366
    splitting audio with another
        clip, 352–353
    understanding audio
        enhancements, 372–374
    using range selection for
        keyframing, 369–372
Sound Effects folder, 343–344

Source frame editor, speed
    transitions, 283
Source media files
    clip container, 14
    copying to portable library,
        422–425
    creating camera archive,
        22–24
    downloading, 5
    event container, 14–15
    importing from camera, 24–25
    importing from volume,
        36–37
    importing to library by
        dragging from
        Finder, 418
    ingesting with Media Import
        window, 19–21
    no duplicate entries created in
        libraries, 418
    preparing, 5–8
    preparing to import camera
        source files, 18–19
    processed as clips during
        import phase, 10
    recovering, 426
    relinking offline clips to,
        414–415
    storage. see libraries
    using Media Import window
        to ingest, 19–21
Source Media pop-up menu, 350
Spacebar (preview), 26–27
Speed
    effects, 351. see also retiming
        clips
    transitions, 282–285
Speed pop-up menu, 276
Spell check, title text, 338
Split audio edits, 352–357
Spotlight badge, 248–249
Stabilization, 84, 94, 482
Stacking, video effects, 291–293
Stand-alone audio, 348
Standard markers, 228, 230–234
Stems, 401, 482
Stereo, 364, 403
Still images, native formats, 478

Stock footage, 421
Storage. see also libraries
    dragging items from Finder or
        other apps, 40–42
    external media, 32
    managed media, 32
    physical, 32–33
    preparing location for source
        media files, 6
    virtual, 31
Storyline
    primary. see primary storyline
    repositioning/deleting within,
        244–246
Strength slider, Keyer effect, 446
Studio headphones, 189
Subclips, 65, 482
Subframe level, trimming audio
    at, 337
Subroles, 97, 402–403
Swell, 366–369, 482
Symlinks, 37, 411–414
Sync keyword collection, 436
Synchronization
    of connected clips, 152–154
    dual system recording
        workflow, 435–439
    setting camera date and
        time, 454
    setting up multicam clip, 452
Synchronize Clips command, 436

T
Tags
    sharing iOS-compatible
        file, 200
    sharing to online host, 393
Tags Index
    creating markers, 232–234
    listing all markers in
        project, 229
    overview of, 229–230
    selecting just sound bites
        in, 363
    setting constant speed change,
        273–274
Takeoff storyline, 244–246
Templates, Motion, 335

Terms of Service, sharing to online host, 394

Text
adding notes to clip, 66–67
exiting entry with Escape key, 337
extending edit for title clip, 341–342
modifying title, 336–340
replacing title, 342
searches, 82–83
using titles, 334–335

Text inspector, 338–339

Third-party applications, outputting project in XML for, 404

Three-point edits, 314–321

Through edits, 132, 139–140, 482

Thumbnails, displaying in Timeline, 437

Timeline
adjusting audio in, 180–181
dragging video effect to, 288
fitting entire project within, 114, 220
opening project in, 108–109
retiming borrowed audio, 350
selecting just sound bites in, 363
synchronizing dual system recordings, 437
three-point edit in, 314–321
zoom into, 126

Timeline Index (Command-Shift-2)
editing blade speed, 279
setting constant speed change, 273–274
setting volume level by role, 364–366
using, 228–230
working with audio clips, 348

Timeline Navigator, 325

Timing
creating at 0:00, 221–228
retiming clips. see retiming clips

Timing primary storyline
blading and deleting, 136–139
inserting gap clip, 133–135

joining through edit, 139–140
overview of, 131–133
refining sound bite edits, 140–142

Titles
adding, 335–336
modifying, 336–342
performing extend edit, 341–342
replacing text, 342
using, 333–335

Titles Browser, 335–342

To-do markers
creating, 230–234
defined, 228
previewing audio blend, 354
retiming borrowed audio, 352
setting constant speed change, 273–274
working with audio clips, 348

Tool palette, keyboard shortcuts, 470

Traces, defined, 482

Transcode and analysis, Media Import options, 33–35

Transform tool, 313, 318–319, 444

Transition inspector, 309–312

Transitions
aligning bites and bits, 260–267
deleting for depth of field, 294
removing around start/end points, 258–260
speed, 282–285
video. see video transitions

Transitions Browser, 307–309

Trash can, emptying, 426

Trim edits, 130, 142, 155–156

Trim End (Option-]), 251–257, 283, 345, 473

Trim Start (Option-[), 251–257, 456, 473

Trim to Selection (Option-\), 252–257, 473

Trim tool (T)
ripple trims with, 170–176
roll trims with, 160
slip edits with, 185–186

slipping to create media handles, 306–307
three-point edits for split screen with, 316
trimming audio clips with, 347
between two clips, 225

Trimming
audio clips, 345
defined, 122, 482

Trimming tops and tails
continuing to add B-roll, 257–258
removing transition/moving clips, 258–260
revising edit, 251–252
trimming aerials, 253–257

Two-up display
converting connected clips into connected storyline, 159
editing within connected storyline, 170
slip edit for, 182, 186
three-point edit for, 314–321

U

Undo (Command-Z), 11, 236–237, 474

Unrated status, 69, 76

Unrating clip as (U key), 76

Update All option, events and projects, 3–4

Update Later, events and projects, 3–4

Upgrading, events and projects, 3–4

"Use audio for synchronization" checkbox, multicam clip, 452

Use Custom Settings button, new project, 430–434

V

Variable speed change, 278–282

Vectorscope, 379–380, 382–384

Versioning, 212–217

Video
adding cross dissolve, 194–197
angles. see multicam

customizing properties for
project, 431
native formats, 478
Video Animation Editor, 313–314,
321–325
Video effects
deleting, 293
depth of field, 293–299
locating in Event Browser, 286
modifying, 288–290
overview of, 285
previewing and applying,
287–288
stacking, 291–293
Video inspector, 288–293, 313,
375–377, 384–386
Video role, 97, 101–102
Video scopes, 377–381, 482
Video transitions
adding more cross
dissolves, 312
customizing, 309–312
experimenting with, 301–302
media handles, 302–307
overview of, 300–301
using Transitions Browser,
307–309
Viewer
defined, 20
Display options, 377
positioning images, 318–321
Transform, Crop and Distort
in, 313
working with clips, 47–48
Vignette effect, 288–293

Vignette Mask effect, 288, 296
Virtual storage, Media Import
option, 31
Visit button, sharing to online
host, 395
Volume, disabling camera's, 437
Volume, media
importing existing files from,
38–40
importing files from, 36–37
importing source media files
from, 32–33
storing camera archives on
separate, 24
Volume levels
adjusting, 187–189
adjusting in Timeline,
180–181
knowing controls, 189
previewing audio blend,
353–355
replacing music clip in
storyline, 220
Volume levels, adjusting over time
Channel Configuration,
362–364
ducking/swelling sound effects
and music, 366–369
keyframing using Range
Selection, 369–372
overview of, 358–361
reading Audio meters,
361–362
setting by role, 364–366

W
Waveform scope, 377–379
Wireframe, positioning images in
Viewer, 319–320
Workflow
manual settings for new
project, 430–434
overview of, 429
phases of, 10
review Q & A, 464
synchronizing dual system
recordings, 435–439
using chroma key, 439–449
working with multicam. *see*
multicam

X
XML (eXtensible Markup
Language), outputting to
third-party apps, 404
XSAN, 3–4

Z
Zoom In (Command-=), 126, 129,
244, 468
Zoom Out (Command--), 114,
166, 469
Zoom slider, 27–28, 51, 244
Zoom to Fit (Shift-Z), 114, 118,
220, 468

Differentiate yourself.
Get Apple Certified.

Stand out from the crowd. Get recognized for your Final Cut Pro X expertise by earning Apple Certified Pro status.

This book prepares you to pass the Apple Certified Pro – Final Cut Pro X exam and earn **Apple Certified Pro – Final Cut Pro X** status. The exam is available at Apple Authorized Training Centers (AATCs) worldwide. Earning this certification verifies your knowledge of Final Cut Pro X for video editing and finishing.

Three Steps to Certification

1   Choose your certification path. More info at training.apple.com/certification

2   Find a testing location. All Apple Authorized Training Centers (AATCs) offer all Apple certification exams, even if they don't offer the corresponding course. To find the closest AATC, please visit training.apple.com/locations

3   Register online and take your exam(s).

"Apple certification places you in a unique class of professionals. It not only shows that you care enough about what you do to go the extra mile and get certified, it also demonstrates that you really know your stuff."

— Brian Sheehan, Multimedia Studio Manager, MFS Investment Management

Why become and Apple Certified Pro?

- **Raise your earning potential.** Studies show that certified professionals can earn more than their non-certified peers.

- **Distinguish yourself from others in your industry.** Proven mastery of an application helps you stand out in a crowd.

- **Display your Apple Certification logo.** With each certification you get a logo to display on business cards, resumés, and websites.

- **Publicize your certifications.** Publish your certifications on the Apple Certified Professionals Registry (training.apple.com/certification/records) to connect with clients, schools, and employers.

Learning that matches your style.

- **Learn on your own** with this Apple Pro Training Series book from Peachpit Press. Advanced titles and video training are also available for select topics.

- **Learn in a classroom** at an Apple Authorized Training Center (AATC) from Apple Certified Trainers providing guidance.

Visit **training.apple.com** to view all your learning options

The Apple Pro Training Series

Apple offers comprehensive certification programs for creative and IT professionals. The Apple Pro Training Series is both a self-paced learning tool and the official curriculum of the Apple Training and Certification program, used by Apple Authorized Training Centers around the world.

To see a complete range of Apple Pro Training Series books, videos and apps visit: **www.peachpit.com/appleprotraining**